PSYCHOLOGICAL ASPECTS
OF LANGUAGE

PSYCHOLOGICAL ASPECTS OF LANGUAGE

The West Virginia Lectures

Edited by

PHILIP N. CHASE, Ph.D.

Department of Psychology
West Virginia University
Morgantown, West Virginia

and

LINDA J. PARROTT, Ph.D.

Department of Psychology
St. Mary's University
Halifax, Nova Scotia, Canada

CHARLES C THOMAS • PUBLISHER
Springfield • Illinois • U.S.A.

Published and Distributed Throughout the World by
CHARLES C THOMAS • PUBLISHER
2600 South First Street
Springfield, Illinois 62717

This book is protected by copyright. No part of it
may be reproduced in any manner without written
permission from the publisher.

© *1986 by* CHARLES C THOMAS • PUBLISHER
ISBN 0-398-05155-0
Library of Congress Catalog Card Number: 85-9960

With THOMAS BOOKS *careful attention is given to all details of manufacturing and design. It is the Publisher's desire to present books that are satisfactory as to their physical qualities and artistic possibilities and appropriate for their particular use.* THOMAS BOOKS *will be true to those laws of quality that assure a good name and good will.*

Printed in the United States of America
Q-R-3

Library of Congress Cataloging in Publication Data

Main entry under title:

Psychological aspects of language.

   Includes bibliographies and index.
    1. Psycholinguistics--Addresses, essays, lectures.
  2. Verbal behavior--Addresses, essays, lectures.
  3. Social interaction--Addresses, essays, lectures.
I. Chase Philip N.   II. Parrott, Linda J.   [DNLM:
1. Psycholinguistics.   2. Social Behavior.   3. Verbal
Behavior.   BF 455 P97445]
BF455.P785   1985   153.6   85-9960
ISBN 0-398-05155-0

To

B. F. Skinner

and

the memory of J. R. Kantor

CONTRIBUTORS

Daniel J. Bernstein, Ph.D. University of California, San Diego. Associate Professor of Psychology, University of Nebraska, Lincoln. Professor Bernstein's interests include: human operant behavior, models of reinforcement value and the interaction between language and learning.

A. Charles Catania, Ph.D. Harvard University. Professor of Psychology, University of Maryland, Baltimore County. Professor Catania's interests include: verbal behavior, rule-governed versus contingency shaped behavior, the evolution of language and the psychology of learning.

Philip N. Chase, Ph.D. University of Massachusetts, Amherst. Assistant Professor of Psychology, West Virginia University. Professor Chase's interests include: functional analyses of language, conceptual learning and the application of the principles of verbal learning to training and educational problems.

John W. Donahoe, Ph.D. University of Kentucky. Professor of Psychology, University of Massachusetts, Amherst. Professor Donahoe's interests include: reinforcement, stimulus control and complex human behavior.

Philip N. Hineline, Ph.D. Harvard University. Professor of Psychology, Temple University. Professor Hineline's interests include: resonance in behavior patterns, scales of behavior analysis, and relations between saying and doing.

James G. Holland, Ph.D. University of Virginia. Professor of Psychology, University of Pittsburgh. Professor Holland's interests have included: basic research in stimulus control, and applications in the area of educational technology. His current research interests are in verbal behavior.

Kent R. Johnson, Ph.D. University of Massachusetts, Amherst. Director, Morningside Learning Center, Seattle. Dr. Johnson's interests include: verbal behavior, behavior analyses of instruction, precision teaching and direct instruction.

Roy Moxley, Ph.D. University of Michigan. Professor of Education, West Virginia University. Professor Moxley's interests include: early childhood education and the development of language skills. Recently he has been writing microcomputer programs for developing the writing and reading skills of children at the West Virginia University Nursery School.

David C. Palmer, M.S. University of Massachusetts, Amherst. Doctoral candidate, University of Massachusetts, Amherst. Mr. Palmer's interests include: interresponse time analysis and response classes, verbal behavior and behavioral phenomena loosely grouped under the rubric of "memory."

Linda J. Parrott, Ph.D. Western Michigan University. Assistant Professor of Psychology, Saint Mary's University, Halifax. Professor Parrott's interests include: the philosophy of science and of the science of behavior in particular, and the psychology of language and other types of complex human behavior.

Ullin T. Place, D. Litt. University of Adelaide. Senior Fellow, Department of Philosophy, University of Leeds. Professor Place's interests include: the mind-body problem, intentionality and intensionality, the philosophy of language, the experimental analysis of emotional behavior and its clinical applications, verbal behavior, sociolinguistics, conversation analysis and narrative text analysis.

Hayne W. Reese, Ph.D. University of Iowa. Centennial Professor of Psychology, West Virginia University. Professor Reese's interests include: memory and learning in children as a function of cognitive processes, life-span research methodology, philosophical analysis of current systems of psychology.

Emilio Ribes, M.A. University of Toronto. Professor of Psychology, Universidad Nacional Autonoma de Mexico. Professor Ribes' interests include: the psychology of language and the design of behaviorally oriented educational programs. Also, as a result of the influence of J. R. Kantor's Interbehavioral Psychology, he has been elaborating on a field approach to behavior theory to include complex human activities in a framework stressing processes, ontogeny and phylogeny.

Roger Schnaitter, Ph.D. University of Minnesota. Professor of Psychology, Illinois Wesleyan University. Professor Schnaitter is the Department Chair and Director of the Division of Natural Sciences. His interests include: conceptual and philosophical issues in psychology and their relation to radical behaviorism.

PREFACE

DURING THE ACADEMIC YEAR of 1982-83 a number of scholars from various parts of the United States, Mexico and Great Britain visited the Psychology Department at West Virginia University. They were not a cohesive group, coming as they did from different philosophical backgrounds and working on different sorts of psychological problems. They came for different reasons, at different times, yet all spoke on the subject of language. Some attempted to extend and elaborate upon B. F. Skinner's analysis of verbal behavior, while others argued for substantial theoretical reform, basing their arguments on the work of J. R. Kantor and other language theorists. Still others dealt with the implications of language theory for basic research and application. But despite differences in focus and specific content, their message was the same: progress toward a natural science of psychology would depend upon a critical study of the relations among environmental events and behavior. The psychological aspects of language were being heralded as the new frontier for behavioral scientists.

This volume was an attempt to capture the spirit of these addresses. Most of the chapters and some of the commentaries were written by visitors to West Virginia University during 1982-83, hence the subtitle "The West Virginia Lectures." The remaining chapters and commentaries were invited to provide for the inclusion of other signficant positions on these issues which we felt would improve the collection. We hope the reader will find this collection illuminating and provocative.

Philip N. Chase
Linda J. Parrott

CONTENTS

Page

Contributors vii
Preface ix

SECTION ONE — THEORETICAL PERSPECTIVES AND CRITIQUES

Chapter One — Three Perspectives on Verbal Learning: Associative, Cognitive and Operant... 5
Philip N. Chase
Commentary — How Shall We Understand Complexity? 36
John W. Donahoe
Chapter Two — Chomsky's Nativism: A Critical Review 44
David C. Palmer
Commentary — An Alternative to the Sentence as a Basic Verbal Unit.......... 61
Philip N. Chase
Chapter Three — Is Operant Conditioning Sufficient to Cope with Human Behavior? 66
Emilio Ribes
Commentary — Comments on Ribes' paper 80
Hayne W. Reese

SECTION TWO — REFINEMENTS OF KEY LANGUAGE EVENTS

Chapter Four — On the Differences Between Verbal and Social Behavior........ 91
Linda J. Parrott
Commentary — Are They Really So Different? Comments on the Differences Between Verbal and Social Behavior........................ 118
Philip N. Chase
Commentary — Can Verbal Be Nonsocial? Can Nonsocial Be Verbal? 123
Philip N. Hineline

Chapter Five	— Intraverbal Behavior	128
	E. A. Vargas	
Commentary	— A Non-duplic Discussion of Intraverbal Behavior	152
	James G. Holland	
Chapter Six	— Ethics as a System of Behavior Modification	156
	Ullin T. Place	
Commentary	— The Role of Consequences in a Behavioral Theory of Ethics	179
	Roger Schnaitter	

SECTION THREE — AN EXAMPLE OF RESEARCH AND AN EXAMPLE OF APPLICATION

Chapter Seven	— Correspondence Between Verbal and Observed Estimates of Reinforcement Value	187
	Daniel J. Bernstein	
Commentary	— Verbal Interactions and Nonverbal Behavior	206
	A. Charles Catania	
Chapter Eight	— A Functional Analysis of Reading	209
	Roy Moxley	
Commentary	— A Behavioral Analysis of Moxley's Functional Analysis of Reading	233
	Kent R. Johnson	

Author Index 239
Subject Index 243

PSYCHOLOGICAL ASPECTS
OF LANGUAGE

Section One
THEORETICAL PERSPECTIVES AND CRITIQUES

Chapter One

THREE PERSPECTIVES ON VERBAL LEARNING: ASSOCIATIVE, COGNITIVE AND OPERANT

Philip N. Chase

WHENEVER I TELL someone in the academic community that I'm studying the problems of language it seems they have their own theories, methods and unique perspectives on the topic. Linguists describe their structures and taxonomies. Political scientists and communication theorists talk about persuasion, propaganda, and the media. Computer scientists argue the immediate gains of highly notated languages versus the long-term gains of friendly languages. Sociologists and philosophers discuss the relations between knowledge and language. In fact, it appears that every discipline that remotely considers human affairs has carved its own domain within the study of language. Accordingly, one of the classic ways psychologists have studied this subject matter has been to determine how verbal behavior is acquired and maintained over time. In other words, we have studied verbal learning.

The questions psychologists have asked about verbal learning have generated a vast literature. One supposes that this research has led to a better understanding of verbal behavior, yet except for a few simple relations, we are still at a loss to describe most of the verbal interactions that occur perpetually among humans. Writers still point out complex relations like metaphors, grammatical rules and the production of unique utterances for which we cannot account. Thus, we have not described the general rules for predicting and controlling verbal learning.

This conclusion suggests that there may be something fundamentally wrong with the ways in which we have studied verbal learning. Consequently, it seems useful to isolate the kinds of questions that have been unproductive and suggest alternate questions. Therefore, this paper attempts to trace the problems with previous studies of verbal learning to the two predominant models of learning: simple environmental perspectives, here labelled the associative model, and the cognitive perspective. Both of these models will be defined, critical assumptions will be specified, and some critical problems of each will be explicated. Then, I will present an alternative model, the operant model, and will discuss how it extends traditional environmental models and minimizes the problems related to both the associative and the cognitive models of verbal learning.

ASSOCIATIVE MODEL

Before proceeding with a critique of associative perspectives, I would like to make it clear that I distinguish associative models from other environmental or behavioral perspectives (e.g., radical behaviorism, interbehaviorism, modern reinforcement theory). The associative model I will discuss is a simple stimulus-response model. It will be contrasted later with modern reinforcement theory. The distinctions between associationism and reinforcement theory are not, however, pure. As argued by Hearst (1975) and others, the critical relations between antecedent events and behavior (associationism), and consequences and behavior (reinforcement theory) are probably similar. Nonethless, as many scientists equate behaviorism with simple associationism, I thought it important to reveal both some critical problems and some pseudoproblems with traditional associative theory so we can best see how to proceed with the investigation of verbal learning.

Associative Assumptions

The associative model states that verbal learning involves the formation of explicit relations among antecedent stimuli and response events. As this definition involves observable events, the associative model is an environmental model. However, the associative perspective has also described possible mental events, which mediate the relations among stimuli and responses. In this context, one would say that associative bonds are formed between representations of the stimuli and responses. Osgood (1980) has extended the representational associative model recently in his book *Lectures on Language Performance*. However, within this essay I will describe the associative relations in terms of observed stimuli and responses.

Psychologists' observations of the relations among stimuli and responses have led to the following eight rules for describing verbal learning:

1. Learning is strengthened with practice.
2. Learning is weakened with disuse.
3. Previous learning can influence current learning.
4. Current learning can influence the maintenance of previous learning.
5. If one stimulus-response (S-R) relation is formally similar to another S-R relation, learning is easier.
6. If one S-R relation is very different from another, learning is minimally effected.
7. If the stimuli in two sets of S-R relations are similar, but the responses are different, learning is difficult.
8. Complex learning is a hierarchy of simpler S-R relations.

—adapted from Ellis (1965), Osgood (1949), and Royer and Feldman (1983)

We can distill these rules further into three general principles: Learning is affected by:

1. the formal similarity between previous and current antecedent stimuli
2. the past frequency of occurrence of an S-R relation (practice), and
3. the hierarchial relation among S-R relations.

Thus, according to associative accounts, we should be able to predict the occurrence of a particular response if we can specify the stimuli which have been related to the response in the past.

Critiques of Associatism

The importance of formal similarity to verbal learning was perhaps best defined by Thorndike and Woodsworth (1901) in their theory of identical elements. They claimed that if two tasks share a set of stimulus elements, a response learned to one set of elements or features is likely to generalize to the other set of stimulus elements. For instance, a child is taught to say "four" when presented with the problem: "$2+2=$__." When given the problem, $2+2=$__, the child is likely to say "four" again because the two stimulus sets are very similar. They both have wavy line twos, plus signs, equal signs and the only discernible difference is the boldness of the typeface. If we were to increase the differences between the two sets of stimuli without providing any further training, then the child is less likely to make the same response. Thus, if we present the problem, two plus two equals ____, we are more likely to observe the wrong answer. This observation has been affirmed with many examples of stimulus sets and has been extended to account for some anomolies that were uncovered by verbal learning experiments (cf., Osgood, 1949).

However, many scientists have criticized associationists for investigating only simple relations (Chomsky, 1959)[1] and that the identical elements theory is impotent to deal with complex relations like generalization from school-like learning to real-world applications (far transfer) or for the production or interpretation of analogies and metaphors (Royer, 1979). For example, Royer (1979) argued that identical elements theory has little to say about the following situation:

> Assume that a child has learned to compute the area of a rectangle. After instruction, one might be able to predict with sufficient confidence that the child could successfully solve any problem involving the computation of the area of a rectangle. But now assume that the child is faced with the problem of determining the amount of carpet needed to cover a living room floor. Will she recognize that the mathematical skill learned in school is relevant to the solution of the real-world problem?
>
> —Royer, 1979, pg. 58

Royer's point is that identical elements theory can work only if one can specify, a priori, the relation between the stimuli involved in previous and current conditions. In the above example, it would be difficult to specify all the stimulus conditions that share formal properties with rectangle area problems. Is the rectangle of the living room floor similar to the rectangles in the child's arithmetic class? How about the area of a book jacket for designing book covers?

An example of an analogy might further this critique. We can describe an analogy as a problem of generalization if we see that in order to answer an analogy one must generalize from one relation between words to another relation. If I say, "an eraser is to chalk as correction fluid is to ____," not many readers would have trouble filling in the blank even if they have never seen this particular analogy before. However, there are few formal similarities between the two sets of stimuli. Therefore, the identification of common, formal characteristics does not seem necessary.

The criticism above is what I would call a pseudo problem of associa-

---

[1]Chomsky (1959) misclassified Skinner as an associationist. See MacCorquodale, K. On Chomsky's Review of Skinner's Verbal Behavior. *Journal of the Experimental Analysis of Behavior*, 1970, *13*, 83-89.

tive learning theory. The difficulty with this criticism is that it does not take into consideration the many levels of formal similarity suggested by Thorndike and Woodsworth (1901). Not only did they describe the identity of matter (i.e., identifying specific, static objects), but also the identity of procedures (i.e., identifying similar actions and relations). If the child has learned to identify a range of rectangles as well as situations that require the computation of areas, then we would predict her accurate calculation of the area of the carpet. If individuals have learned the operations of erasing and writing (in all their various forms), then we would predict that they would complete the analogy. One can identify the identical elements in many analogies, metaphors, and far transfer problems, but they are often elements of procedure.

The extension of identical elements theory to procedures, however, still may not account for certain kinds of verbal generalizations. A more critical problem may be the observation that similarity is relative to events in addition to the events of specific comparison. Two rectangles or two erasing operations may be similar to one person and not another or may be considered similar in one set of comparisons and different given an alternative set of comparisons. Can an associative model account for this relativity?

Similarity in most associative accounts is defined by the experimenter as an absolute relation among antecedent stimuli. In other words, the experimenter specifies the degree of point-to-point or procedural correspondence between stimulus sets in terms precise enough so that others can observe the relation and agree on their occurrence. These descriptions are based on the experimenter's previous observations and tend to be general, static summaries of what has been observed. For anyone who has tried to generate such precise definitions there is little wonder why experimenters have selected rather simple relations to study. Regardless, when we try to use these procedures with examples of real-world verbal learning we find ourselves asking some basic questions: (1) How do we define the boundaries between similar and different events, and (2) How do we account for individual differences in responding to "similar" events? The general problem that we must address is: if the similarity between two events is variable when we account only for the antecedent stimuli what other information do we need to predict the occurrence of a verbal relation.

Some associative theorists would agree that similarity is variable and would account for the boundaries of similarity and the individual differences in terms of different histories of practice. For example, Rudel (1958) found when training emphasized "absolute" properties of a discrimination, subjects generalized along "absolute" properties. Conversely, when training emphasized the "relational" properties of a discrimination (the same stimuli were used as were used for the "absolute" discrimination), subjects generalized along "relational" properties. However, iterating training or practice doesn't quite describe enough about the relations. We need to describe the practice conditions. Were subjects simply exposed repeatedly to the same stimulus? How was one kind of property emphasized as opposed to another? What kinds of practice lead to generalization?

Alternatively, some would claim that complex relations are hierarchical. Gagné (1962) described a method for determining a hierarchy for complex learning. Specifically, we identify a learning outcome and ask the question: what would an individual have to do in order to perform this task successfully? Then we write down the answers as sublearning tasks and ask the same question of each of these subtasks. We continue this analysis until we have identified a learning hierarchy or an outline of general to specific learning outcomes. Presumably, when we have written our hierarchy we will see that the most specific tasks are simple enough to rely on relatively static similarities in order to describe generalization.

This approach to developing a learning hierarchy has been used successfully with a number of complex mathematical and scientific relations (White, 1973), and it is especially useful for analyzing the relations a student might practice in school. Moreover, when one looks at the lower-level relations in these hierarchies, they indeed look as simple as the $2+2$ example we described earlier (cf., Gagné, 1962, pg. 359) for which stimulus similarity seemed adequate. However, can we apply this analysis to a seemingly more complex relation? Royer (1979) specified that associative models could not account for the kind of relation exemplified by unidirectional metaphors. For instance, we say "encyclopedias are goldmines" but not "goldmines are encyclopedias." Does a learning hierarchy help us to describe this phenomenon?

Our first step is to turn the metaphor into a learning outcome and then follow Gagné's procedures. One general learning outcome is to interpret the metaphor. Thus the first question is: what must individuals "know" to interpret the metaphor correctly? According to Claxton (1981) they must:

1. detect an inconsistency or discrepancy between the vehicle (gold mines) and the topic (encyclopedias).
2. change their conception of the topic based on the interaction with the vehicle.

3. possibly change their conception of the vehicle based on the interaction with the topic.

The second question asks: what must individuals be able to do to engage in these three subclasses of metaphoric behavior. It would appear that they need to be able to:

1. state at least some of the denotations and connotations of both the vehicle and the topic.
2. compare the denotations and connotations of the vehicle and the topic.
3. link the two based on similar connotations or denotations.

Thus, the denotations are:

A. Encyclopedias:
   1. sources
   2. of information
   3. on a large range
   4. of subjects
B. Goldmines:
   1. sources
   2. for extracting gold

Some connotations are:

A. Encyclopedias are sources of much information.
B. Goldmines are sources of much wealth.

The two terms can be compared on the basis of either denotations or connotations, but more likely the similarity is based on their common connotations.

Through such a process we can demonstrate the identical elements of the vehicle and the topic in a metaphor. Presumably we could produce such an interpretation by manipulating these common elements. However, we are still left with the question: why is the metaphor unidirectional? If we have behaved metaphorically in the past and can state the denotations and connotations of both encyclopedias and goldmines, then why are we more likely to say "encyclopedias are goldmines" than "goldmines are encyclopedias"? Simply evoking the processes of similarity between stimulus sets, practice and hierarchies does not seem sufficient. Again, we need more precise descriptions of the conditions that have existed when metaphors have occurred.

Thus, it appears that even if we can describe the formal similarities between two sets of stimuli, the hierarchical relations among events within these conditions and the particular responses that have been practiced in the presence of these conditions, we still may not be able to predict the occurrence of a particular response. We need some additional rules to account for the relations between previously learned verbalizations and current behavior.

COGNITIVE MODEL

The class of scientists who have most often critiqued associative theories are the cognitivists. They have suggested that we abandon environmental approaches to language problems and adopt a perspective that describes the processes that mediate environmental events and behavior. We need to examine this suggestion carefully to determine whether: (1) its assumptions are sound, and (2) it offers at least some logical hope for dealing with the kinds of problems that associative models have had. If the cognitive perspective is truly a paradigm shift, then it should account for the anomalies I have described.

The cognitive model defines both verbal learning and generalization in terms of three general processes: encoding, storage, and decoding (Simon, 1978). Thus, the cognitive model defines verbal learning in terms of the retrieval of relevant knowledge structures, and generalization as the likelihood of encountering the representation of a relevant bit of information or skill during a memory search process.

The critical assumptions of most cognitive models are:

1. internal mental activity exists and therefore can be determined.
2. mental activity is structurally connected to the perceptual systems (our senses).
3. mental activity is not described by the same rules as observable behavior.
4. mental activity can be inferred on the basis of environmental input and behavioral output.
5. mental activity controls observable behavior.

Let's examine these assumptions to determine how they differ from the assumptions of the associative model and to determine what logical problems we might find with these assumptions. Then, we will return to the problem of similarity to see how well it is circumvented by the cognitive model.

Comparisons of Cognitive and Associative Assumptions. Many critics of cognitive models agree with the first two assumptions. However, they find it necessary to qualify these assumptions by specifying that the mental activity is the same as neurological activity (cf., Skinner, 1969). In fact, if we make this qualification we see that the cognitive and associative models share these assumptions. The difference then would be methodological. Associationists would opt for direct observation of these internal events, whereas cognitivists opt for inferential studies based on direct observation of behavior. However, not all cognitive scientists agree that mental activity is synonymous with neural activity (Fodor, 1981). As Wessels (1981) stated, cognitive explanations are biologically-oriented, but are specified at a conceptual level. Therefore, they are not tied to specific neural or physiological structures or events. When such a strong idealist position is taken by cognitivists, then it is in direct conflict with environmental perspectives. As it is not within the scope of this paper to debate the relative merits of idealism and realism, I will simply critique these first two cognitive assumptions by saying that they mean different things to different theorists and therefore lead to inconsistent interpretations. It is difficult to support a position on verbal learning that covers such a vast range of philosophical assumptions. In fact, it is this inconsistency of assumptions that appears to cause so many of the other problems addressed below.

The third assumption of cognitivists departs from the associationist views. Associationists clearly expect the internal system to work in accordance with the principles that have been derived from the observations of behavior, cognitivists expect the studies of interval processes to expand and change these principles. Both assumptions need to be examined in relation to the results of on-going research. At this point in time it is impossible to say which is more accurate. Therefore, anyone with sufficient philosophic doubt should entertain both general hypotheses.

The fourth assumption also clearly distinguishes cognitive perspectives from associative. The distinction is methodological. Whereas associative theory makes passing reference to the organization of mental activity (again see Osgood, 1980 for an alternative associative view) cognitivists ask questions and make claims about the specific features of the mental system based on what stimulates the system and what the system produces. The cognitive approach is dependent on the deductive logic of hypothesizing a particular internal organization, describing a relation between stimuli and behavior that could exist only if the hypothesized internal state existed and testing this hypothesis on a group of subjects.

The first problem with this methodological assumption has been suggested by Anderson (1978). This paper described a debate that has centered on one question of cognitive science: what is the nature of representation in memory? Does representation consist of images or propositions? Anderson (1978) argues that there is no way to distingish between kinds of representation on the basis of a behavioral outcome: given the same input, different theories of representation produce the same behavior simply by postulating different process variables. Other criteria such as parsimony (e.g., fewest features needed to account for the most phenomena), plausibility (e.g., model does not contradict common experience), and efficiency (e.g., the latency between input and output takes the least amount of time), may limit hypotheses to certain kinds of representational systems, but without the basic knowledge of the physical dimensions of neurological activity these criteria are not sufficient for identifying any particular representational system. One example should suffice to describe why this is true. The laws of parsimony support a single-code theory of representation (either imaginal, verbal, or propositional). However, the criteria of efficiency suggests a tri-code theory. Some operations are more efficiently conducted if the representation is verbal, some, if the representation is propositional and others if it is imaginal (Anderson, 1978). The question remains as to how to tell the difference between representational systems. The conclusion is that one cannot determine whether representation is imaginal or propositional. Since all investigation of human learning uses behavior as its basic datum and since representation, a critical component of cognitive theory, cannot be determined by looking at behavior even when other criteria are used, cognitive models of verbal learning appear to be seriously limited.

This criticism of cognitive research is a specific example of a general critique of a mentalistic theory. Even though one can account for the input and output variables of a system, there are many different routes that might mediate these events (Law of equifinality) (Morris, Higgins & Bickel, 1982). Consider a geometric analogy. Two points in space may be connected by a line, but in order to determine exactly whether the points are connected by a straight line or some kind of curve, more than two points are needed. There are an infinite number of lines that connect two points. Likewise, there are an infinite number of possible ways that a stimulus and a behavior can be mediated. Since other criteria, such as parsimony and efficiency do not eliminate alternatives when applied to unknown qualities, such as the speed of electrochemical reactions to verbal stimuli, the methodology used in cognitive research is probably less than optimally efficient.

Ironically, the computer lends itself, by analogy, to another criticism of cognitive methodology. Palmer (1980) suggested that if one were to teach a college sophomore to use a computer it would be best not to concentrate on the internal mediating processes of the computer. Rather, one should concentrate on the operations the sophomore would perform and the feedback obtained from the computer. Furthermore, if one were to teach this sophomore the internal mechanisms of the computer, one would not suggest that the sophomore look at a series of inputs and outputs to try to deduce these mechanisms (as we have seen above this might take forever). Instead, it might be best to begin by either taking the computer apart piece by piece and putting it back together or by designing a schematic program that would demonstrate some of the critical features of the computer. Thus, both the function and the structure of the computer can be accounted for by direct, observational techniques.

If this analogy seems to be familiar, it is because it takes the same form as the age old story of first empiricist. A group of monks were sitting around a long table, discussing how they can determine the number of teeth in a horse's jaw. After days of such deliberation, a young upstart raised his hand and asked, "Why don't we find a horse and count his teeth?" Of course, the young monk was banished from the room and from all further investigations of natural phenomena (Johnston & Pennypacker, 1980). Certainly, determining the neurological activity that is part of the verbal process is a more difficult phenomenon to investigate than horses' teeth. However, the level of difficulty does not necessarily imply that a different methodology should be used. If neurological activity is to be described, then direct investigation of neural components of learning should be used.

This leads us to the fifth assumption of cognitive approaches: that mental events control behavior. If control implies that neurological structures limit an organism's interactions with certain environmental arrangements, then certainly no argument can be tendered. In these cases, the preceding argument for neurological study as opposed to cognitive study is germane. In addition, if the term, mental events, refers to a summary of a set of related empirical findings or observed relations, then it is merely a conceptual metaphor akin to concepts like reinforcement, or generalization (Morris et al., 1982). In these cases, one could argue against the strength of this particular metaphor, but no basic problem would exist. However, it is clear that some cognitive theorists claim that cognitive events produce behavior (Chomsky, 1965; Fodor, 1981). This position does pose specific problems. When someone insists that mental events produce behavior, the problem of infinite regression must be argued (Ryle, 1949). For example, when we say that someone has "acted intelligently" and then claim that this intelligence was controlled by corresponding mental activity, one might then inquire if this mental activity was done intelligently. If so, then we would have to postulate another mental activity to accompany the first. Then, one could ask the same question of this and all other mental events, indefinitely.

Wessells (1982) claims that the problem of infinite regression is solved when the processing mechanisms have been clearly specified. He asserts that in a successful computer model no homunculus is needed to interpret the internal representations. But this assertion needs to be documented. It seems to me that we would still find an infinite regression of sorts. For example, in order to say book in the presence of book, we see a book, the perception moves through our mental apparatus until it comes to a representation of a book and then the connection is made between the representation and the book. Supposedly, even for such a simple copy theory, when you specify how the mechanism works, the problems of infinite regression is solved (cf. Kosslyn & Shwartz, 1977; or Kosslyn, 1980). However, we would say that the regress occurs in the form of how the code and its specific operation got into the mental apparatus of the individual in the first place. In a successful computer program, we know how it got there, an electrical engineer built the mechanism and a computer programmer specified the code. In the information processing system of the mind, it is less clear. It could have been programmed by the ontogeny of the individual or the phylogeny of his/her ancestors. In either case, we return to the environment in order to describe some of the variables that account for the mechanism and its operations. However, if we are to say that the statement "book" is controlled by an internal process, and mean more than that the verbalization is in some way related to an internal mechanism, then we would have to look further *within* the system to describe how the code and the specific operation evolved. This is another example of infinite regression.

To summarize up to this point, I first contend that there is little disagreement between cognitivists and associationists on the first two assumptions. Internal activity probably does exist, can be determined and is structurally connected to our senses. However, this agreement exists only when cognitivists attempt to isolate neurological activity. Second, whether or not there are similar rules which govern neurological activity and behavior is an empirical question and therefore we need to collect more data on both sets of relations before answering this question. Third,

I suggested that serious methodological problems arise when one assumes that mental activity can be inferred from environmental input and behavior output. Finally, the assumption that mental activity controls observable behavior is overstated. Logical relations indicate that other variables, specifically environmental variables, have as much claim to causality as the internal processes discussed in cognitive theory. Thus, there appears to be some serious limitations to the cognitive model.

Cognitive Solutions to the Problem of Similarity. Whether one agrees or disagrees with the criticisms I have cited, one should concede that our next step is to examine how cognitivists approach the problem of similarity. The reader will recall that a previous section specified two difficulties with associative accounts of similarity. First, it is difficult, though not impossible, to specify a priori the similarity among events. Second, examples of figurative language, such as metaphors, point out a relation that exists for some verbalizations that cannot be ascribed to similarity among antecedent stimuli. If these problems can be handled by a cognitive model, then there is reason to pursue a cognitive approach to verbal learning.

As stated earlier, cognitivists have spent their time describing either the representational system and/or the encoding/decoding processes. For instance, they define generalization as encountering the representation of a relevant bit of information or skill during a memory search process. Therefore, I assume that the problem of similarity should be handled by the representational or search processes. Since Anderson (1978) fairly readily dispensed with the hope that we can describe a representational system by itself, it is necessary to look at the whole system to answer the questions concerning similarity.

The first question to address is: what does it mean to say that one encounters the representation of a relevant bit of information or skill? It seems to mean that our internal mechanisms must match incoming information with an existing representation within the internal system. First, the stimulus is encoded and the code activates a set of mechanisms related to it. If a complete set of mechanisms exists, then the stimulus is decoded and we behave in a manner consistent with what others would call verbal learning. The following is a simplified example adapted from Anderson (1978): Perceptual procedures encode and interpret an original stimulus into segmented picture units with each segment representing a meaningful subunit of a hierarchy of meaningful units. The picture units are interpreted as an x y array of dots where each dot can be specified according to frequency, amplitude, intensity, and light wave (i.e., sort of like a color

T.V.). If an array of dots exists for an encoded stimulus, then the stimulus is decoded and the individual behaves appropriately. An observer would call this an instance of generalization.

If we accept this as a representative example of a cognitive model, then we can examine how it would handle complex verbal relations like transfer of learning. Earlier, I suggested that in theory associative models could describe the procedures necessary to predict far transfer, problems like computing the area of a rug. But in practice it has been argued that we would find it difficult to arrange instruction for all the various examples of rectangles a child might encounter. In short, it is difficult to specify a priori the stimulus and procedural features that are shared by all of these situations. So, how does the cognitive model help solve this problem?

Cognitive models assume that in order to solve the problem of rug size the child has to have a representation of rugs and areas of rectangles, and the encoding and decoding processes necessary to access these representations. Thus, one would imagine the array of dots that makes up the rug representation has features representing a rectangle embedded in it. However, isn't this the same old problem? The representations for rugs and rectangles have to be compared for similar features. If one wants to relate rug size and rectangles, one has to be able to recogize or match the code for rectangles in the code for rugs. We are left with the problem of assuring that this will occur through procedures that emphasize identifying rectangles. We have not decreased the difficulty involved in determining the range of events that share these properties, we have simply removed ourselves from direct access to them.

The second problem that we need to address is whether cognitive models help us to understand the relativity of many verbal relations. In other words, we found that some verbal relations are unidirectional, relative to the individual and relative to the situation rather than simply the formal characteristics of S-R units. How can we account for this kind of relativity?

The cognitivists have addressed this problem through the concepts like representational variability (Royer & Feldman, 1983) and family resemblances (Rosch & Mervis, 1975). Representational variability refers to the unique memory or knowledge base of each individual; thus two individuals under the same conditions will react differently. Family resemblances refers to a family or set of features that define concept or concept membership. Not all of these features are necessary in any particular instance in order to include the instance as a member of a category. A critical component of family resemblances is their dynamic nature; they change from culture to culture and over time. A critical component of both representational variability and family resemblance is that they refer to internal or cognitive events and not environmental events.

The problem with these two concepts is the same as the problem specified for the cognitive description of far transfer. The terms do not specify anything more than what we know about the environment. Representational variability is simply a label for individual differences. It does not describe these differences or lead us to better predictions about individual performance. It simply suggests that we should expect some slop in our data. This is not news to associationists. Family resemblance is perhaps more useful as it deemphasizes a critical features analysis of verbal phenomena and suggests that though certain features control responding that these features can and do change. However, why it is necessary to place the family inside a person as opposed to placing it in direct relation between environmental events and behavior is not clear. What is clear is that we still have not accounted for relativity in verbal learning, we have simply ignored it. Our task is still to determine how individuals respond differently and how classification and "similarity" change from situation to situation.

Since we have found current cognitive perspectives unsatisfactory, let us turn to an alternative model of verbal learning to show how it deals with the problems of similarity. However, in keeping with the spirit of this paper, let us also examine the model's assumptions and its relations to the other models that we have discussed.

OPERANT MODEL

The term operant has been used here to denote the overwhelming influence of Skinner's attempts to describe an operant model of verbal behavior (Skinner, 1957; 1969). However, my use of the term is synonymous with modern reinforcement theory which attempts to unify both classical and operant procedures (Donahoe, Crowley, Millard & Stickney, 1982). Thus, the distinctions between the operant model and the associative model are *not* the distinctions that have been made between classical and operant conditioning. In a very general sense one could say that the operant model I will describe is a model of practice. It answers the question asked of the associative model: what kinds of practice lead to generalization of complex relations. The operant model is an environmental model that is directly related to the previously discussed associationist model. However, it analyzes more aspects of the environment than the associationist model. First, an operant account of learning does not attribute causality of learning solely to the relations among antecedent stimuli and behavior. In addition to these important relations, operant accounts look at the relations that exist among behaviors and consequences. The unit of interest is a three-term function unit: stimuli that precede a response, the response itself and the effect the response has on the environment. Second, an operant account does not necessarily require an immediate temporal relation between stimuli and behavior. Although immediacy determines to some extent the effectiveness of training procedures, events that are separated in time have been shown to be critically-related to each other (Wahler & Fox, 1981). Thus, given the operant model's relation to the associative model and these two extensions of the associative model, the assumptions of the operant perspective are:

1. Environmental events affect verbal learning and therefore need to be studied.
2. Phenomena are studied best by direct observation and measurement.
3. The organization of environmental events can be best conceptualized as functional relations among antecedents, behavior, and changes in the environment that result (i.e., the three-term contingency).
4. The three-term contingency is not limited to proximal events, but is rather a comparison of many sets of events that occur over time.
5. Prediction and control of verbal learning requires a historical analysis of individual behavior over time.

First, let me briefly address how assumptions one and two assist the investigation of verbal learning. I will state these points briefly because they are not as germane to the current discussion as points three, four, and five. Assumption one suggests that the study of verbal learning requires environmental analyses. This does not preclude physiological analyses; in fact, it is assumed that both sets of analysis are required for a detailed description of verbal learning. This assumption appears to be shared by associative models. Assumption two stresses the importance of direct observation and measurement. This assumption has been explicated clearly in a number of other publications (cf. Johnston & Pennypacker, 1981). I have also argued in a previous section that direct observation appears to be an effective strategy for determining the variables of interest to verbal learning. I will expand on this when discussing assumption five below. The operant emphasis on measurement and observation is also shared by associationists.

Assumption three begins to distinguish the operant model from the other models of verbal learning. It specifies that the effect of a response on the environment is included in an analysis of environmental-behavior relations. The change in the environment either leads to or makes it possible to engage in a similar behavior or it interferes with or makes it unlikely to engage in similar behavior. Thus, the operant model is concerned with extending the functional unit from an antecedent-behavior unit to an antecedent-behavior-consequence unit. Including the consequence in the unit of analysis might help us to resolve some of the anomolies that I have specified for the other models of verbal learning.

The first advantage of including consequences in our analysis is that it alleviates the mechanistic control implied by stimulus-response terminology. The operant model recognizes that stimuli have an effect on behavior, but also that behaviors have an effect on stimuli. Operant theorists maintain the temporal relation explicitly by discussing antecedent and consequential stimuli, yet the critical relations are bidirectional. This bidirectional control suggests that the individual is not simply buffeted by the environment, but that individual interacts with the environment.

Second, the concentration on how behavior affects the environment implies that response similarity can be defined in at least two ways: behaviors that are topographically similar and behaviors that are functionally similar. Associative accounts typically define similarity of the response topographically. Operant psychologists have found it useful to define the similarity of behavior functionally. Behaviors are similar or of the same class when they affect the environment in similar ways. This means that in order to use similarity as a factor when describing, predicting and controlling verbal learning, we have to describe the similarity of the effects of behavior as well as the similarity of antecedent stimuli.

This analysis of consequences leads us to look at one special kind of consequence. Operant analyses realize that an analysis of environmental change for human behavior would be incomplete if it did not account for the changes in the social environment as well as the physical environment. In fact, one of the features of verbal behavior that distinguishes it from other behavior is that its reoccurrence requires the mediation of another individual (Skinner, 1957). Thus, accounts of verbal learning from an operant perspective must include social consequences.

This emphasis on changes in the social environment suggests another set of variables that might be partially responsible for the dynamic nature of complex verbal relations. As stated above, verbal relations change over time and from individual to individual. Other models have not described how certain verbal relations are emphasized and how they are practiced. A concentration on social consequences describes one set of emphases: First, different individuals come into contact with different groups of people and each group reinforces a unique set of behaviors. Thus, to use a rather blatant example, Eskimos reinforce discriminating among different types of snow, while Mid-Atlantic Americans generalize across types of snow. Second, the individual histories of each of the people within a group are different. These differences also effect the kinds of behaviors that will be reinforced and the kinds of consequences that are likely to occur. For example, a dichotomy might exist between parents' consequation of an adolescent male's vocabulary. The mother may have a history of social reinforcement for vulgar speech, the father may have a history of social reinforcement for polite speech. The mother may, then, laugh at her son's use of vulgarity. The father may, in contrast, scold the son for vulgarity. Thus, in the father's presence the boy speaks politely regardless of other antecedent stimuli that might be similar to stimuli that have been present when vulgarity has occurred before. Given an analysis of the son's reinforcement history with both parents, this result is predictable. Give a history of the antecedent stimuli that are correlated with vulgarity, it is unlikely that we would make this prediction.

These situations demonstrate that in order to analyze a particular person's verbal behavior we need to describe the practices that occur frequently in the group of people with whom the individual interacts as well as the particular practices of the individuals who comprise this group. These histories will give us a more precise picture of the kinds of social consequences that are likely to occur. These social consequences help us to determine the emphases in a particular individual's training and answer the question of why the individual might have a history of practicing certain behaviors, but not others. Thus, the control exerted by social consequences adds to the general environmental processes of antecedent similarity, practice, and hierarchical relations that modern environmental models use to describe verbal relations.

Assumption four also distinguishes the operant model from the associative and cognitive models. It states that events other than the most proximal antecedents can exert control over verbal behavior. As discussed for assumption three, proximal consequences also exert control by selecting certain verbal relations. Moreover, implicit in this type of functional relation is the notion that events that occur some distance in time and space from a particular verbalization also control the verbalization. This suggestion requires some elaboration since it is not readily apparent from the animal experiments that one usually equates with the operant model.

In the typical description of an experiment, the temporal relations among antecedent, response and consequence are relatively short. The antecedent stimulus comes on, the response occurs, the consequence occurs and then the antecedent comes on again. This immediate temporal relation and some studies that have manipulated the immediacy of the consequence (Skinner, 1938) suggest that immediacy is a critical variable. However, both the logic of control by consequences and some subsequent studies demonstrate that control by distal events is also possible.

If proximal relations were required, then the operant model would succeed only in describing relations in which the same behavior occurred repeatedly within a short period of time without other classes of behavior mediating instances of the response. This is just not the case. Even in the simplest operant animal experiment a number of responses occur between the antecedent and the putative reinforcer. A light comes on, the animal orients itself to the light, pecks at the light, orients itself to the noise and movement of the food dispenser, bends to the dispenser, and pecks at the food. The behavior measured as an operant is pecking the light, but it and the consequence of ingesting food are mediated by a number of other behaviors. This relation has led to describing the immediate noise and movement of the food dispenser as being critical consequences (Ferster, 1979). This is an accurate description when removing these consequences results in a deterioration of the response of pecking the key. However, two other critical observations can be made: One, each instance of the antecedent-behavior-consequence relation is separated from other similar instances by other three-term relations. And two, other events are just as critical. If we take away the distally-related food ingestion, the key pecking will also deteriorate. Thus, if the consequence is critical, it is not because it changes the environment in such a way as to immediately set up the antecedent conditions for the same operant. Rather, it changes the environment so that another operant can occur. If the second operant in turn creates the conditions that promote the reoccurrence of the operant of interest, then a relation between two operants is established. In addition, what is established is the possibility that an event at time t can exert control over an event at time $t+n$. The length of time between t and $t+n$, though, is open to investigation.

A view that is consistent with this analysis was recently argued in Wahler and Fox (1981). These authors proposed an expansion of behavior analysis to include setting factors. Kantor (1959) described setting factors as the sum of circumstances that influence stimulus-response relations. Such examples as the presence or absence of a particular person, signs, verbal instructions, and deprivation conditions have been cited (Kantor, 1959; Bijou & Baer, 1961). Temporally, setting factors precede, but also may overlap with the presence of specific stimulus-response-consequence relations (Wahler & Fox, 1981). Bijou and Baer (1961) cite the example of an infant playing in its playpen. Following a nap the child played vigorously in its playpen. However, if other events prevented the child from sleeping, it cried and protested in its playpen. Events which keep the child awake are setting factors that affect the playpen-play or playpen-cry relations. Wahler and Fox (1981) also cite a small literature which supports the notion that setting events exert control over behavior (Krantz & Risley, 1977; Wahler, 1980; Wahler & Fox, 1980). For example, Krantz and Risley (1977) demonstrated that a rest period antecedent to a reading period increased children's attention during the reading period.

Michael (1982) constructed a description of the motivational conditions that are part of any discriminated event as another means of distinguishing between immediate and distal control. These conditions, called establishing operations and stimuli, are recognized by two characteristics of environmental change: "(1) if it alters the effectiveness of some event as a reinforcer, and (2) if it alters the momentary frequency of a behavior that is typically followed by that reinforcer" (Michael, 1982). A simple example is the operation of maintaining pigeons at 80% of their free feeding weight. This allows food to be a reinforcer and increases behaviors that are consequated by food. This operation is as much a controlling variable as the food itself, however, it occurs both temporally and spatially some distance from the behavior of interest, say key pecking.

A third set of literature which has addressed the apparent control by distal events is the delay of reinforcement literature. Although there are still relations to be tested, Williams (1975, 1978) concluded that delayed reinforcement maintained substantial levels of behavior when there was a definite response-reinforcer dependency. Thus, there is further empirical support that events separated in time can exert control over behavior.

This analysis certainly suggests a complexity often neglected in discussing environmental approaches, but how does it assist us in analyzing complex verbal relations? You will recall that the difficulty of many complex verbal episodes seems to be the mutability of the relations among events. Some of this variability may be due, in part, to the different setting factors and establishing stimuli that exist at different times. Quite simply, if we agree that distal factors have a controlling function, then we need to include these factors in our descriptions of behavior. We can not say that the conditions are similar to some preceding situation unless these distal events have also been observed again.

The importance of distal events has been recognized in lay terms as context. When we include distal factors in our descriptions, then we are describing the environmental context within which complex relations occur. Context has been shown to make apparent the similarities between conditions that exist in complex relations, like metaphors. For example, Claxton (1981) specified that the phrase "the waves beat relentlessly against the shore" is comprehended quickly as a metaphor for Franco, Spain's deceased dictator, when we provide the reader with descriptions of Franco's life. When provided with the background analysis we can "see" the similarity between conditions that lead to the metaphoric use of this phrase and the conditions such as the coast of Maine, Iceland, or Oregon that lead to its literal use. Another favorite example of the effects of context on verbal behavior is the interpretation of the phrase, "the notes were sour because the seam split." This seems nonsensical until we are provided with the contextual clue, bagpipes (Bransford & McCarrell, 1974). Thus, one way of accounting for the relativity of verbal relations is to analyze the context in which these relations occur. If we can describe the context, then we will be more likely to correctly predict the occurrence of a behavior.

Assumption four also specifies that we compare environmental relations over time. This suggests some additional relations that should be included in any modern analysis of verbal learning. We all recognize that given any specific environmental arrangement there is more than one class of responses that can be emitted. The rat can press the bar or groom itself, the man approaching a fork can take the high road or the low, a writer can compose a metaphor or write a concrete description. In all of these situations there are at least two responses that will have different effects on the environment. This seems to be the gist of behavioral science, to determine which of many responses an organism will perform given a range of choices. This notion has obviously occurred to many others in operant psychology as there is a large body of literature on behavioral choice (cf. deVilliers, 1977). This research has culminated in a set of related terms that operant psychologists now use to give a molar account of learning: matching, maximizing, and nonlinear analysis (Herrnstein, 1970; Rachlin, 1978; Goldiamond, 1984). These terms and their operational descriptions are used in an attempt to account for the complexity of environmental conditions that support concurrent behaviors. Such descriptions make explicit predictions about the effect of events other than the proximal antecedents and consequences of a particular response. Such descriptions also suggest that in order to predict the occurrence of behavior in complex environments it is necessary to compare the histories of reinforcement for concurrent behaviors.

Probably the least known of these terms is nonlinear analysis (Goldiamond, 1984). However, because nonlinear analysis was derived from both applied and basic invesigations it seems particularly general. Because it uses simple economic terminology it is perhaps the easiest for a wide range of readers to understand. Therefore, at the risk of obscuring the distinctions between these various molar analyses of behavior, I will attempt to describe a nonlinear analysis as presenting the critical similarities among these formulations.

Goldiamond (1984) juxtaposes nonlinear analysis with linear analysis.[2] Linear analysis refers to describing the contingencies operating in one behavior/environment relation, typically the proximal antecedents and consequences that exert control over one response class. Thus, many simple analyses are linear: John says "forest" in the presence of trees and his parents pay attention to him. If we observe this relation repeatedly we begin to predict that in the presence of trees and parents, John will say "forest." Nonlinear analysis, on the other hand, compares multiple responses that have or can occur under similar conditions. For example, in the presence of trees and parents, John can say "trees" or "forests" and secure attention from the parents. Individuals learn over time the costs and benefits of each of the various responses and engage in the behavior that is correlated with the least cost and the most benefits. Goldiamond (1984) stated that costs and benefits are observable, relative and empirically derived from the reinforcement history of the individual. That is, we have to measure the individuals' behaviors and consequences over time. Thus, with our simple verbal example, John learns over time that talking about forests in the presence of trees and his parents is more often attended to than talking about trees (we could say that John does not lose the forest for the trees). We would predict, therefore, that he is more likely to talk about forests when these conditions arise in the future. The additional

---

[2] A number of reviewers of this chapter took exception with the words linear and nonlinear analysis. However, I attempted to use them as Goldiamond (1984) has. Linear suggests observing a simple sequence of behaviors and environmental events, thus concentrating on one set of relations. Nonlinear suggests a multiplicity of behaviors that occur or could occur in the same environment. It should not be confused with curvilinear. Nonlinear simply denotes an analysis of multiple relations.

historical relations included in a nonlinear analysis make it more likely that our predictions will be correct.

The particular example presented above was simple and therefore does not fully illustrate the additional power accrued by a nonlinear analysis. If we add the complexity that typically exists in any verbal episode, we will see the benefits derived from a nonlinear analysis. We can also add some additional power to the analysis by combining a nonlinear analysis with an analysis of contextual factors.

One example of how an operant analysis operates with respect to complex verbal episodes can be seen from examining our previous example of an unidirectional metaphor. Let us presume that the metaphor, "encyclopedias are goldmines" arose with a conversation between two people, Maria and Jerry. The situation is as follows: Jerry notices Maria reading an encyclopedia, he approaches her and Maria looks up, sees that he is staring at her encyclopedia, and she blurts out, "You know, encyclopedias are goldmines." Jerry ponders, 'Hmm, I suppose there is an awful lot of stuff in 'em," and Maria says, "Yeah, that's why I like to read them, to know a lot of stuff." Jerry concludes, "I guess I don't have to ask you why you read 'em." Given this complex verbal episode, our job is to determine at least two things:

1. What information do we need in order to predict the occurrence of this metaphor?
2. How were the conditions that lead to the use of this metaphor different from the conditions that lead to saying the opposite: "goldmines are encyclopedias"?

In simple operant terms one is more likely to state a metaphor when in the past a metaphor has changed the social environment in a particular way. Figure 1-1 presents a diagram of how the verbal exchange described above fits into an operant framework of a three-term relation. I have assumed by the labelling of the episode in the figure that similar episodes will occur in the future. Of course, we don't know this, but in its simple form, the operant model assumes that the more often we observe a relation among antecedent conditions, behavior and consequences, the more likely we will be correct in predicting the reoccurrence of the relation or that changes in the conditions will effect the reoccurrence of the episode. However, we can be more accurate in our prediction if we add some information. We need to describe the histories of the two individuals involved in this and subsequent conversations. In an ideal situation we would know the groups with whom they have interacted and some particulars about the individuals involved in these groups. Finally, we ought to account for other responses and their effects that have occurred under similar circumstances. If metaphors lead to certain changes in the social environment more often than other responses, then we would predict metaphoric behavior. This type of analysis can be applied to both the metaphor in question and the reversed metaphor.

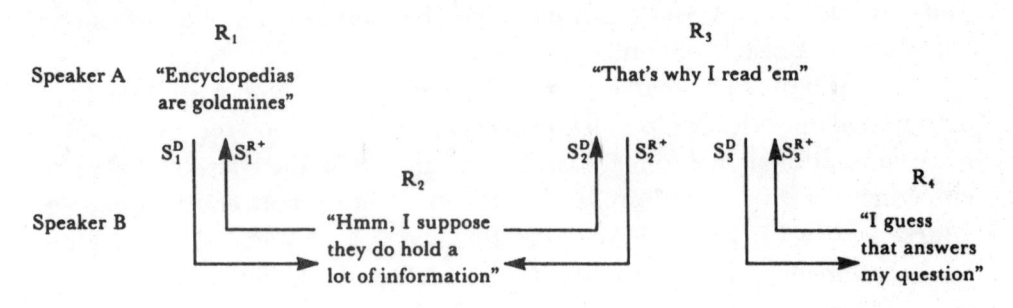

```
                    R₁                                    R₃
Speaker A    "Encyclopedias                        "That's why I read 'em"
             are goldmines"

             S₁ᴰ │ ↑S₁ᴿ⁺              S₂ᴰ↑│ S₂ᴿ⁺    S₃ᴰ│ ↑S₃ᴿ⁺
                           R₂                                    R₄
Speaker B            "Hmm, I suppose                     "I guess
                     they do hold a                      that answers
                     lot of information"                 my question"
```

S^D — discriminative stimulus if it is reliably followed by a particular response.
R — response.
S^{R+} — reinforcer if the consequated response occurs again under similar conditions.

Figure 1-1: A conversation segment that illustrates the three-term relations of an operant unit of analysis and the reciprocity of two speakers.

Let me compose a possible history for Maria, the encyclopedia reader. Like many adolescents, approval from her peers is an extremely powerful reinforcer. In other words, we have observed that she will engage in behavior in the presence of her peers that gains their attention. In addition, Maria has a history of attention from adults (teachers and parents) for being able to state facts. Therefore, her history of reinforcement includes peer approval and adult approval.

If life were simply divided between adults and peers, we might rely on a simple discrimination analysis to account for Maria's actions: in the presence of peers, Maria engages in behavior that brings about peer approval, whereas in the presence of adults she engages in behavior which evokes adult approval. However, life isn't so discrete. In our example, a peer "catches" Maria engaging in a behavior that leads to adult reinforcers. Many of the events in the situation are critical: the encyclopedia, the peer, being "caught," and so forth. We could describe these events as setting factors or contextual factors for engaging in a behavior which will bridge the gap between Maria's "adult" behavior and the presence of a peer. The presence of a peer may be discriminative for engaging in a behavior which will gain peer approval, but the particular behavior is equally governed by the setting events.

If we delve further into Maria's history we find that situations like this have occurred before. When Maria has told peers that she likes to engage in fact-finding behavior she has had to spend countless hours explaining herself. This often does not lead to approval from the peers. At other times, though, she has found that most of her peers respond positively to various statements made about money, especially relations between objects or events and "lots of money." Thus, of these two possible classes of behavior, the latter is reinforced more often than the former, therefore we would predict that Maria is more likely to engage in the latter. If we had a more precise quantitative history we could make predictions about the relative frequencies of these behaviors.

Given these three sets of related historical information, the relation between the audience and approval, the extension of antecedent conditions to contextual factors and the relative reinforcement history of potential responses, we can now specify the contingency: if Maria states a metaphor that uses money as a vehicle for describing the topic of encyclopedias, then her audience, Jerry, will give her attention and not ask her to explain her behavior of reading encyclopedias. Although the exact form of the metaphor might require even more precise historical information, the general prediction can be made. Thus, we have answered our first question, what information do we need to predict the occurrence of metaphoric behavior.

The description of Maria's hypothetical history also helps us resolve the issue of unidirectionality. There is no absolute reason why one does not say "goldmines are encyclopedias." In fact, one could create a situation similar to the one produced above to illustrate how it might arise. However, the situation would have different setting factors, discriminative factors and relative reinforcement factors than the example I have described. For instance, in a highly literate, socialist culture in which money is denigrated, a person "caught" counting her pieces of eight might be expected to state a metaphor that uses literature as vehicle for describing the topic of money. It does not occur in our culture because there are few, if any, situations in which we have to establish the value of money. Situations just do not occur where the relation between an audience, approval, contextual events, and the relative likelihood of reinforcement depend on relating money to some vehicle like encyclopedias. It seems unfortunate, but we often have to establish the value of learning and thus it is necessary to relate topics like encyclopedias to already established reinforcers like money.

To summarize up to this point, operant analysis claims that the consequences of behavior are important to consider when analyzing the environmental impact on verbal learning. This concentration on consequences has led operant investigators away from strict contiguity notions to look at the relation of the environmental relations that are temporarily and spacially separated from the response of interest. Thus, setting factors, motivational factors as well as the relation over time among alternative, concurrent behaviors and their consequences have been discussed. The operant model accounts for the relativity of responding in the presence of similar stimuli by investigating the differences in setting factors, establishing operations and the patterns of reinforcement related to potentially concurrent behaviors. The difficulty in predicting a particular response does not stem from inadequacies of the model, but rather from incomplete information regarding these critical environmental relations.

This brings us to the final features of the operant model that distinguishes it from the other models I have discussed. The operant model has developed a set of experimental methodologies that help us to keep track of many of the critical environmental events which I have described. A thorough exposition of these methodologies is not within the scope of this paper, nor need it be. Very thorough analyses of behavioral or intrasubject methodologies exist elsewhere (cf. Johnston & Pennypacker, 1981). However, a brief overview of operant methodologies and the relation to the critical problems that I have outlined for verbal learning might help.

Assumption five states that the prediction and control of verbal behavior requires an historical analysis of individual behavior over time. This historical analysis of the individual is accomplished by systematically manipulating environmental variables and observing the changes in the patterns of behavior that occur over time. In the best experiments this systematic manipulation and observation includes a precise definition of variables, calibration of the observing and recording equipment (including the behavior of people who observe), frequent data collection, manipulation of variables when an agreed upon level of stability has been reached and within-subject replication. When multiple variables are to be evaluated, they are either manipulated as a package, in which case, they are grouped together as a single variable, or they are taken in and out of the environment one at a time and cumulatively added together. When the particular order of variables is important to describe, then between subject comparisons are made. A typical strategy is to use a Latin square design or a counter balanced design to compare the different sequences of conditions or variables.

Assumption five fits well with the conclusions I have drawn in each section of this paper. All three models include concepts that refer to the effect of individual history on the prediction and control of verbal learning. Associationists talk about practice, cognitivists discuss representational variability, and operant scientists describe individual differences. However, only the operant model explicitly uses individual histories to determine its general rules. My assumption is that by continuing to use and refine these experimental methods, operant psychologists will continue to make discoveries with respect to the general rules that describe verbal learning.

My conclusion about intrasubject methodologies does not eliminate all of the problems related to understanding verbal learning. For example, these methods work best when one starts with a precise description of the history of the subject. Thus, many operant investigations begin with naive organisms, reared under controlled conditions. The extent to which the experimenter cannot describe the history of the organism is a limiting factor in the level of prediction and control that can be obtained. It is often difficult to describe the history of the individual subjects in verbal learning experiments. However, this is not a philosophical problem, but rather a technical problem. Many refinements of intrasubject methodologies are related to developing equipment and techniques which allow experimenters to gain access to more historical information. In the past, technological advances have led to the kinds of expansions of the environmental perspective that I have discussed in this paper. The ability to observe concurrent operants developed when the technology for scheduling different reinforcement schedules on two or more keys in an operant chamber was developed. Similar developments in verbal learning experiments hold much promise. For example, sensitive pretesting conditions allow the experimenter access to information about the subject's general verbal skills, study habits, and verbal relations that are prerequisites to the relations being evaluated in the experiment (Chase, 1982). Or graphing procedures that allow experimenters to compare large quantities of data on many different behaviors across large segments of time (White & Haring, 1982) help analyze intensive historical studies. Also, the use of computers in verbal learning experiments makes it more likely that the experimenter can analyze the increased data that such refinements provide. The possibilities of combining computer technology with video technology for gathering and analyzing data have only begun to be tapped (cf. Pear, 1983). The possibilities seem endless if scientists continue to look for methods of gathering historical information about the individuals being investigated.

SUMMARY AND CONCLUSION

This essay has attempted to describe in general terms the state of psychologists' understanding of verbal learning. As promised in the introduction, I have compared three models of verbal learning. I argued that two predominant models, the associative and the cognitive, have led to some important findings, but both lack certain features to help us expand our understanding. It was suggested that modern reinforcement theory, here called the operant model, helps to minimize the problems of the other models while being consistent with productive features of these other models. These points are summarized below.

The associative model leads to incorrect predictions because it relies on antecedent stimulus similarity and does not concentrate on the many relations among environmental events that effect the occurrence of verbal behavior. Since these events are different for different individuals and change across time for each individual, the associative model lacks the ability to account for the dynamic properties of verbal behavior. It is hoped that the example of unidirectional metaphors was sufficient to demonstrate this point. Other criticisms of the associative perspective appear to specify additional examples of this phenomenon (e.g., the "ed" past tense use by children, Rickard & Denner, 1978), and therefore could be dealt within similar fashion.

The cognitive perspective was criticized because it also failed to account for variability in verbal learning. Cognitivists push the investigation of similar events inside the organism rather than looking for variability in the history of the organism's interaction with the environment. This would be worthwhile if it eliminated the need to gather historical information (i.e., if there really was a storage component or processing mechanism that could be accessed to determine what the history of the individual was). However, I argued that this internal search is unlikely to produce satisfactory results because the methodology used by cognitivists is too indirect. A preferred methodology for describing the internal variables that undoubtedly effect verbal learning might be an integration of environmental and neurological investigations. I also argue that some cognitive assumptions seem dangerously close to the age old logical problems of mentalism. Revitalizing mentalism because of a new metaphor, the computer, does not eliminate the problems of infinite regression and equifinality. Thus, it is concluded that cognitive models will not lead to better predictions, control, and understanding of verbal learning than associative models.

Finally, I argued that operant theory has specified some additional variables that help us predict the changes that occur in verbal learning. First, the operant perspective includes an analysis of consequences. Studying the effects of behavior minimizes the mechanistic implications of more traditional environmental perspectives because the investigator recognizes that behavior has an effect on stimuli as well as stimuli having an effect on behavior. More importantly, however, studying the consequences allows the investigator to determine what verbal relations were emphasized by the verbal community. Second, the operant pespective analyzes distal and molar events that effect the occurrence of a verbal relation. It is insufficient in most complex cases to simply specify the proximal antecedents and consequences of behavior. One must also specify contextual and motivating factors such as setting events and establishing operations as well as compare the history of alternative behaviors that have occurred under similar conditions. Finally, the operant perspective has developed methodologies which allow one to compare the effects of the above variables on an individual's verbal learning. It is argued that such individual analyses are necessary in order to describe the dynamic relations that account for verbal behavior.

It is rather easy to draw some specific conclusions about the future of verbal learning investigations because I am convinced that given certain assumptions, one model of investigation promises to bear more fruit than other models. The key word of my conviction is, however, promises. The operant model promises to be more fruitful, although I cannot say that it has answered more questions concerning complex verbal relations. Verbal learning in particular has been, at best, an intermittent concern for behavior analysts. The problems of verbal learning will be solved only when it becomes a more important phenomenon for operant psychologists to study. This book is one indication that the phenomenon is becoming an important concern. Hopefully, this essay will clear the air of unproductive conceptions of verbal learning and direct more investigators back to an environmental study of verbal learning. Obviously, I conclude that it is the variables and assumptions that are described by the operant model that should direct the next wave of environmental investigations of verbal behavior.

REFERENCES

Anderson, J. R. (1978). Arguments concerning representations for mental imagery. *Psychological Review, 85*, 249-277.

Bijou, S. W., & Baer, D. M. (1961). *Child Development I: A Systematic and Empirical Theory.* Englewood Cliffs, NJ: Prentice-Hall.

Bransford, J. D., & McCarrell, N. S. (1974). A sketch of a cognitive approach to comprehension. In W. B. Weimer & D. Palermo (Eds.), *Cognition and Symbolic Processes*. Hillsdale, NJ: Lawrence Erlbaum Associates.

Chase, P. N. (1982). *Transfer, Study Behavior and the Pursuit of Conceptual Learning*. Ann Arbor, MI: University Microfilms International.

Chomsky, N. (1959). A review of B. F. Skinner's Verbal Behavior. *Language, 35*, 26-58.

Chomsky, N. (1965). *Aspects of a Theory of Syntax*. Cambridge, MA: MIT Press.

Claxton, G. (1981). *Cognitive Psychology: New Directions*. Boston: Routledge Kegan Paul, Inc.

de Villiers, P. (1977). Choice in concurrent schedules and a quantitative formulation of the law of effect. In W. K. Honig & J. E. R. Staddon (Eds.), *Handbook of Operant Behavior*. Englewood Cliffs, NJ: Prentice-Hall.

Donahoe, J. W., Crowley, M. A., Millard, W. J., & Stickney, K. A. (1982). A unified principle of reinforcement: Some implications for matching. In M. Commons, R. Herrnstein & H. Rachlin (Eds.). *Quantitative Analysis of Behavior: Vol. II. Matching and Maximizing Accounts*. Cambridge, MA: Ballinger.

Ellis, H. (1965). *The Transfer of Learning*. New York: The MacMillan Co.

Ferster, C. B. (1979). A laboratory model of psychotherapy: The boundary between clinical practice and experimental psychology. In P. O. Sjödén, S. Bates, & W. D. Dockens (Eds.), *Trends in Behavior Therapy*. New York: Academic Press, Inc.

Fodor, J. A. (1981). The mind-body problem. *Scientific American, 244*, 114-123.

Gagné, R. M. (1962). The acquisition of knowledge. *Psychological Review, 69*, 355-365.

Goldiamond, I. (1984). Training Parents, Trainers and Ethicists in Nonlinear Analysis of Behavior. In R. F. Dangel & R. A. Polster (Eds.), *Parent Training: Foundations of Research and Practice*. New York: Guilford Press.

Hearst, E. (1975). The classical-instrumental distinction: Reflexes, voluntary behavior, and categories of associative learning. In W. K. Estes (Ed.), *Handbook of Learning and Cognitive Processes: Conditioning and Behavior Theory. Vol. 2*. Hillsdale, NJ: Lawrence Erlbaum Associates.

Herrnstein, R. S. (1970). On the law of effect. *Journal of the Experimental Analysis of Behavior, 13*, 243-266.

Johnston, J.M., & Pennypacker, H. S. (1980). *Strategies and Tactics of Human Behavioral Research*. Hillsdale, NJ: Lawrence Erlbaum Associates.

Kantor, J. R. (1959). *Interbehavioral Psychology*. Granville, OH: Principia Press.

Kosslyn, S. M. (1980). *Image and Mind*. Cambridge, MA: Harvard University Press.

Kosslyn, S. M., & Shwartz, S. P. (1977). A data-driven simulation of visual imagery. *Cognitive Science, 1*, 265-296.

Krantz, P. J., & Risley, T. R. (1977). Behavioral ecology in the classroom. In S. G. O'Leary & K. D. O'Leary (Eds.), *Classroom Management: The Success-Use of Behavior Modification*. New York: Pergamon Press, Inc.

Michael, J. (1982). Distinguishing between discriminative and motivational functions of stimuli. *Journal of the Experimental Analysis of Behavior, 37*, 149-155.

Morris, E. K., Higgins, S. T., & Bickel, W. K. Comments on cognitive science in the experimental analysis of behavior. *The Behavior Analyst, 5*, 109-125.

Osgood, C. E. (1949). The similarity paradox in human learning: A resolution. *Psychological Review, 56*, 132-143.

Osgood, C. E. (1980). *Lectures on Language Performance*. New York: Springer-Velag.

Palmer, D. (1980). *Notes from a Course on Cognition.* Unpublished manuscript, University of Massachusetts/Amherst.

Pear, J. L. (1983). *Relations between operants and respondents.* Presented at a conference on the Future Directions in the Experimental Analysis of Behavior, West Virginia University, Morgantown, WV.

Rachlin, H. (1978). A molar theory of reinforcement schedules. *Journal of the Experimental Analysis of Behavior, 30,* 345-360.

Rickard, J. P., & Denner, P. R. (1978). Inserted questions as aids to reading text. *Instructional Science, 7,* 313-346.

Rosch, E., & Mervis, C. (1975). Family resemblances: Studies in the internal structures of categories. *Cognitive Psychology, 7,* 573-605.

Royer, J. M. (1979). Theories of transfer of learning. *Educational Psychologist, 14,* 53-69.

Royer, J. M., & Feldman, R. S. (1983). *Educational Psychology.* New York: Random House, Inc.

Rudel, R. G. (1958). Transposition of response to size in children. *Journal of Comparative Physiological Psychology, 51,* 386-390.

Ryle, G. (1949). *The Concept of Mind.* London: Hutchinson, Ltd.

Simon, H. A. (1978). Information processing theory of human problem-solving. In W. K. Estes (Ed.), *Handbook of Learning and Cognitive Processing: Vol. 5.* Hillsdale, NJ: Lawrence Erlbaum Associates.

Skinner, B. F. (1938). *The Behavior of Organisms.* Englewood Cliffs, NJ: Prentice-Hall, Inc.

Skinner, B. F. (1957). *Verbal Behavior.* Englewood Cliffs, NJ: Prentice-Hall, Inc.

Skinner, B. F. (1969). *Contingencies of Reinforcement: A Theoretical Analysis.* Englewood Cliffs, NJ: Prentice-Hall, Inc.

Thorndike, E. L., & Woodworth, R. S. (1901). The influence of improvement in one mental function upon the efficiency of other functions: I, II, III. *Psychology Review, 8,* 247-261, 389-395, and 553-564.

Wahler, R. G. (1980). The insular mother: Her problems in parent-child treatment. *Journal of Applied Behavior Analysis, 13,* 207-219.

Wahler, R. G., & Fox, J. J. (1980). Solitary toy play and time-out: A family treatment package for aggressive and oppositional children. *Journal of Applied Behavior Analysis, 13,* 23-29.

Wahler, R. G., & Fox, J. J. (1981). Setting events in applied behavior analysis: Toward a conceptual and methodological expansion. *Journal of Applied Behavior Analysis, 14,* 327-338.

Wessels, M. G. (1981). A critique of Skinner's views on the explanatory inadequacy of cognitive theories. *Behaviorism, 9,* 153-170.

White, R. T. (1973). Research into learning hierarchies. *Review of Educational Research, 43,* 361-375.

White, O. R, & Haring, N. G. (1976). *Exceptional Teaching.* Columbus, OH: Charles E. Merrill Co.

Williams, B. A. (1975). The blocking of reinforcement control. *Journal of the Experimental Analysis of Behavior, 24,* 215-225.

Williams, B. A. (1978). Information effects on the response-reinforcer association. *Animal Learning and Behavior, 6,* 371-379.

Commentary

HOW SHALL WE UNDERSTAND COMPLEXITY?

John W. Donahoe

THE ASSOCIATIONIST, cognitive, and behavioral approaches to language represent three specific efforts to solve the most pressing problem confronting psychology: What is a fruitful approach to the study of complex human behavior? Investigators of all theoretical persuasions agree that the phenomena grouped under such conventional headings as perception, language, and memory are complexly determined. The disagreement lies in the choice of the conceptual and experimental means by which to achieve the common goal of understanding that complexity.

In seeking to discern the characteristics of a fruitful approach, it is instructive to examine the means whereby other natural sciences have sought to understand complex phenomena in their respective fields. This examination—although of necessity a cursory one in the present forum—reveals a coherent theme across diverse disciplines: Complexity results from the action of a selective mechanism operating upon a substrate whose variations are random with respect to the quantities subject to selection. Two examples, one from the physical and the other from the biological sciences, must suffice.

Consider first the formation of the solar system as described by astronomy. The phenomenon to be explained is the movement of the planets about a central star, our sun. The paths described by the planets are grossly circular and in approximately the same plane. How is this complex, yet orderly set of observations to be understood? The prescientific analysis invoked primary organizing principles that were essential to the phenomena and that directly imposed the observed order. Thus circular orbits were held to be an expression of the general perfection of the universe, the circle being an inherently optimal form. Indeed, such order was taken to be the hallmark of a guiding intelligence. Scientific analysis has shown, however, that these characteristics of our solar system arise indirectly as a byproduct of the operation of the principles of Newtonian mechanics. When Newtonian principles are applied to randomly moving particles, computer simulations indicate that planetary motions having the characteristics of our own solar system are a common outcome.

Consider next the development of species described by evolutionary biology. The phenomenon to be explained is the diversity of species, yet with each species seemingly perfectly suited to the environment in which it lives. Again, the problem is one of order in the context of complexity. The prescientific explanation called upon an order-giving principle—here, special creation—that yielded the desired complex order as a direct consequence of that principle: Each species was suited for its environment because each species was expressly made for that particular environment. Once more, scientific analysis has shown that the observations may be understood as the indirect byproduct of the action of a lower order principle. When the Darwinian principle of natural selection operates on randomly varying hereditary material, population genetics shows that species develop that are adapted to their environments. Order amidst complexity is the result of selection from random variation and not the consequence of an order-producing principle per se.

Both the development of planetary systems and of species are now seen as the outcome of selection from variation, and not as the direct expression of an inherent guiding principle that constitutes the essence of these phenomena. The notion that complexity results from selective processes, hereafter called the *selectionist approach*, is such a pervasive theme that Schroedinger has characterized modern scientific theory as a tale of how order may emerge from chaos. One by one, accounts that have postulated an inherent ordering principle have been replaced. These superseded theories exemplify an *essentialist approach*, and are variants of philosophical idealism in that they conceive of ordered complexity as the direct consequence of an intrinsic property of the events being observed rather than as the indirect result of extrinsic agents. (See Campbell, 1974a, b for a general discussion of selectionist epistemology and Mayr, 1982 for its ascendance in biology.)

ASSOCIATIONISM

Keeping in mind the distinction between the selectionist and essentialist approaches to the explanation of complex phenomena, let us examine the associationist, cognitive, and behavioral accounts of language. At first glance, the associationist account has the appearance of the more modern theoretical stance. That is, associationism attempts to understand linguistic and memorial phenomena as the product of more elementary processes, namely associations. However, the resemblance to a selectionist approach is only superficial because the experimental procedures whereby the putative associations are studied minimize the sensitivity of behavior to the influence of the selecting effect of the environment. Through the use of nonsense syllables and procedures that severely constrain the presentation of stimuli and the occurrence of responses, the associationistic approach seeks to prevent or to obscure the influence of prior experience. Thus, in the guise of controlling individual differences, associationism eliminates the complex experience upon which complex behavior depends. To suppose that "memory" and "language" can be studied apart from complex experience is to accept tacitly the assumption that "memory" and "language" are things having essential characteristics that transcend experience. For the associationist, what is of concern is average performances on tasks in which the effects of experience are minimized. For the selectionist, such averages are meaningless abstractions; it is only individual differences reflecting individual experience that are real.

COGNITIVISM

As an approach to understanding complexity, associationism has been largely replaced by cognitivism over the past twenty-five years (Broadbent, 1958; Lachman, Lachman, & Butterfield, 1978; Neisser, 1967). The dominance of the cognitive approach is so complete and the content and method of cognitive psychology are so intimately intertwined that, for many psychologists, the study of complex behavior is inconceivable from any other perspective.

Whereas a commitment to essentialism is only implicit in the associationistic approach, it is explicit in cognitivism. The goal of research from the cognitive perspective is to infer from behavioral data the underlying nature of the processes responsible for "perception," "language," and "memory." Cognitivism is essentialist because to seek the *nature* of the complex behaviors to which these terms refer is to assume that they indeed *have* a nature, i.e., enduring essential qualities that are invariant over different procedures.

The commitment to essentialism is most apparent in the work of

Chomsky (1966, 1980) and his colleagues, who view their efforts as a triumph of rationalism over empiricism, but it permeates much of the cognitive enterprise. As an example, some short-term memory procedures indicated that visually presented verbal stimuli were retained for less than 18 seconds (Peterson & Peterson, 1959) and that errors in such procedures were apt to be based on phonological rather than visual similarity (Conrad, 1964). From these findings, an enduring memory structure was inferred—short-term memory—in which memories were said to be stored for no more than 18 seconds and in a phonological code (Atkinson & Shiffrin, 1968). Note the basic strategy of the cognitive approach, particularly in its original realizations: Make experimental observations, postulate underlying hypothetical structures and processes to which are attributed those characteristics that are thought to be required by the observations, and then "explain" the observations by the postulated characteristics. These "explanations" deny the very theory they purport to support since they are adequate only for those who have no short-term memory for the origins of the theory! As noted by Lord Russell in another context, such "explanations," as compared to genuine explanations, have "all the virtues of theft over honest toil."

The cognitive approach has slowly begun to change, however, under the impetus of the self-corrective process of science. In the study of "memory," for example, the rigid structural models that deified the computer metaphor have been increasingly displaced by more flexible formulations as illustrated by the transitions to level-of-processing (Craik & Lockhart, 1972) and depth-of-processing (Craik & Tulving, 1975) models. Still more recently, these liberalizations of cognitive theory have themselves been seen as too constrained to capture the richness of memorial phenomena (e.g., Baddeley, 1982; Neisser, 1976). Even the usefulness of such a formerly fundamental assumption as short-term memory is now denied (Crowder, 1983). The older structural models of memory are increasingly being replaced by ones which indicate that experience simply changes the organism so that present stimulation has a different behavioral effect than would the same stimulation given at an earlier point in the organism's conditioning history (e.g., Murdock, 1982). This latter view is, of course, congruent with Skinner's conception of memory (Skinner, 1974).

The current self-criticisms of cognitivists go beyond specific reservations about theories of restricted domains, such as memory, and extend to the fruitfulness of the general approach itself (e.g., Estes, 1975; Jenkins, 1980; Newell, 1973). A prime example of the questioning of basic assumptions, one mentioned in Chase's review, is the denial of the ability to draw inferences about underlying structures and processes (i.e., "representations") from behavioral data (Anderson, 1978). The claim that representations are not identifiable from behavioral observations alone is hotly debated because it strikes at the very heart of the cognitive enterprise. In light of the present theoretical turmoil in cognitive psychology, it would seem prudent for those who are belatedly considering participation in what has been called "the cognitive revolution" to proceed with caution. Cognitive animal learners and cognitive social psychologists may be climbing aboard a bandwagon pulled by dying horses.

BEHAVIORISM

Unlike the implicit essentialism of associationism and the explicit essentialism of cognitivism, the behavioral approach is avowedly selectionist. From the behavioral perspective, complexity is the product of the selecting effect of the environment—both the ancestral environment of the species as summarized by the principle of natural selection and the contemporary enviroment of the individual as summarized by the principle of reinforcement (Skinner, 1965, 1981; cf. Donahoe & Wessells, 1980; Donahoe, Crowley, Millard, & Stickney, 1982). Complex human behavior is the cumulative result of selection by complex environments. In fact, on *a priori* grounds, it would seem at least as plausible that complex behavioral processes such as "language" and "memory," could arise *via* reinforcement as that the human species arose from unicellular organisms *via* natural selection.

From a behavioral perspective, the analysis of complex behavior is functionally equivalent to the task which confronts the evolutionist seeking the origins of complex structures. Both tasks are facilitated by the fact that the search is guided by principles that have been uncovered through work with simplified experimental preparations. Thus complexity is approached from a position of strength relative to those approaches whose principles are generated by the very observations that they seek to explain. It is also the case, however, that the tasks of both the behaviorist and the evolutionist are complicated by imperfect knowledge of the prior selecting environments and the absence of at least some of the intervening products of selection. To secure information about the products of past selection, the evolutionist draws upon the fossil record and the behaviorist has available the nervous system.

The relevance of neuropsychology to a behavioral analysis has long been recognized, as in Skinner's discussions of aphasia (Skinner, 1957), but such information has been insufficiently exploited by behaviorists. The following is but one example of many that might be given. A stroke patient was presented with a line drawing of a pistol and asked to name the object depicted. He was unable to do so. However, as he continued to look at the drawing, his "trigger finger" began moving back and forth and then he said, "Oh, it's a gun, no, a pistol." Even without knowledge of the specific brain structures damaged by the stroke, these behavioral observations are richly illuminating. First, since the trigger finger moved appropriately *before* naming (i.e., tacting) occurred, at least some instances of complex behavior may occur without verbal mediation. Second, since naming occurred only *after* the trigger finger moved, these movements provided stimuli sufficient to control naming. Third, since both "gun" and "pistol" were emitted, the common behavior (trigger-pulling) occasioned by both guns and pistols may provide the basis for functional similarity—an important feature of Chase's survey of the behavioral position. Finally, since naming was controlled by movement of the trigger finger but not by visual stimuli, this is an instance of differential stimulus control—a phenomenon readily understood from a behavioral perspective but problematic from commonly-held alternative approaches in which naming is used to infer a structure such as a "concept." To summarize, prior environments change the organism, the locus of these changes is the organism's physiology, and behavioral observations of the consequences of perturbing that physiology provide valuable insights into the behavioral processes selected by those prior environments.

The foregoing interpretations of behavioral observations following damage to the nervous system are, of course, neither uniquely determined by these observations nor sufficiently compelling without additional information. What they do provide is some glimmer of the covert processes that intervene between the presentation of a stimulus and the emission of a verbal response in a highly experienced human organism. Changes in the nervous system are the legacy of that experience. It is in this context—how to understand what intervenes between remote environmetal antecedents and present behavior—that one aspect of Chase's characterization of behaviorism is potentially troubling. Assumption 4 states that "the three-term contingency is not limited to proximal events, but is rather a comparison of many sets of events that occur over time." If by this it is meant that temporally remote events change the organism so that the response to subsequent environments is altered, then no difficulty is presented. If, on the other hand, assumption 4 attributes to the organism an inherent capacity for "comparison" whereby some environmental events are aggregated in a molar fashion, then problems are foreseen. Fromwhence does this capacity arise? How does the organism "know" which types of events to aggregate and how many of those events are to be aggregated?

While it is true that organisms may sometimes behave *as if* molar aggregates were the controlling variables, to assume that such is the case is to endow the organism with the very capacities that we seek to explain. This is the error to which cognitive theory fell victim. Behavioral analysis has consistently indicated that putative molar controlling variables are the product of more molecular variables. The molar variable is the product of selection, and not its antecedent. To mention but two recent examples, contingency theory (Rescorla, 1967) in classical conditioning has been replaced by discrepancy theory (Rescorla & Wagner, 1972) and matching (Herrnstein, 1970) in operant conditioning is increasingly seen as the product of moment-to-moment interactions between behavior and its consequences (Staddon, Hinson, & Kram, 1981). A similar abandonment of molar principles has occurred in other sciences as they matured—for example, the replacement in physics of the law of least effort by the Hamiltonian equations of motion (Yourgrau & Mandelstam, 1968).

Chase's overall conclusion that the behavioral approach offers the best hope of understanding "language" and other complex behaviors seems well substantiated, however. Some of the more accomplished investigators of basic operant conditioning phenomena are now turning their experimental and theoretical attention to complex human behavior, and a burgeoning literature is in the making. This book and Chase's chapter are valuable contributions to that effort—the effort to account for complex behavior as the product of selection by reinforcement.

REFERENCES

Anderson, J. R. Arguments concerning representations for mental imagery. *Psychological Review*, 1978, *85*, 249-277.

Atkinson, R. C. and Shiffrin, R. M. Human memory: A proposed system and its control processes. in K. W. Spence and J. T. Spence (Eds.), *The psychology of learning and motivation*. Vol. 2. New York: Academic Press, 1968.

Baddeley, A. D. Domains of recollection. *Psychological Review*, 1982, *89*, 708-729.

Broadbent, D. E. *Perception and communication*. London: Pergamon Press, 1958.

Campbell, D. T. Unjustified variation and selective retention in scientific discovery. In F. J. Ayala and T. Dobzhansky (Eds.), *Studies in the philosophy of biology*. New York: Macmillan, 1974. (a)

Campbell, D. T. Evolutionary epistemology. In P. A. Schilpp (Ed.), *The philosophy of Karl Popper.* Vol. 14. LaSalle, Ill.: Open Court Publishing, 1974. (b)

Chomsky, N *Cartesian linguistics.* New York: Harper & Row, 1966.

Chomsky, N. Rules and representations. *The Behavioral and Brain Sciences,* 1980, *3,* 1-61.

Conrad, R. Acoustic confusion in immediate memory. *British Journal of Psychology,* 1964, *55,* 75-84.

Craik, F. I. M. and Lockhart, R. S. Levels of processing: A framework for memory research. *Journal of Verbal Learning and Verbal Behavior,* 1972, *11,* 671-684.

Craik, F. I. M. and Tulving, E. Depth of processing and the retention of words in episodic memory. *Journal of Experimental Psychology: General,* 1975, *104,* 268-294.

Crowder, R. G. The demise of short-term memory. Paper presented at the meeting of the American Psychological Association. Anaheim, California, August, 1983.

Donahoe, J. W., Crowley, M. A., Millard, W. J. & Stickney, K. A. A unified principle of reinforcement. In M. L. Commons, R. J. Herrnstein, and H. Rachlin (Eds.), *Quantitative analyses of behavior (Vol. 2): Matching and maximizing accounts.* Cambridge, Mass.: Balinger, 1982.

Donahoe, J. W. & Wessels, M. G. *Learning, language, and memory.* New York: Harper & Row, 1980.

Estes, W. K. Some targets for mathematical psychology. *Journal of Mathematical Psychology,* 1975, *12,* 263-282.

Jenkins, J. Can we have a fruitful cognitive psychology? *Nebraska symposium on motivation.* Lincoln, Neb.: University of Nebraska Press, 1980.

Lachman, R., Lachman, J. L. & Butterfield, E. C. *Cognitive psychology and information processing: An introduction.* Hillsdale, N.J.: Lawrence Erlbaum, 1978.

Mayr, E. *The growth of biological thought: Diversity, evolution, and inheritance.* Cambridge, Mass.: Harvard University Press, 1982.

Murdock, B. B., Jr. A theory for the storage and retrieval of item and associative information. *Psychological Review,* 1982, *89,* 609-626.

Neisser, U. *Cognitive psychology.* Englewood Cliffs, N.J.: Prentice-Hall, 1967.

Neisser, U. *Cognition and reality.* San Francisco: Freeman, 1976.

Newell, A. You can't play 20 questions with nature and win. in W. G. Chase (Ed.), *Visual information processing.* New York: Academic Press, 1973.

Peterson, L. R. & Peterson, M. J. Short-term retention of individual verbal items. *Journal of Experimental Psychology,* 1959, *58,* 193-198.

Skinner, B. F. *Verbal behavior.* New York: Prentice-Hall, 1957.

Skinner, B. F. The phylogeny and ontogeny of behavior. *Science,* 1966, *153,* 1205-1213.

Skinner, B. F. *About behaviorism.* New York: Random House, 1974.

Skinner, B. F. Selection by consequences. *Science,* 1981, *213,* 501-504.

Staddon, J. E R., Hinson, J. M., & Kram, R. Optimal choice. *Journal of the Experimental Analysis of Behavior,* 1981, *35,* 397-412.

Yourgrau, W. & Mandelstam, S. *Variational principles in dynamics and quantum theory.* Philadelphia: Saunders, 1968.

Chapter Two

CHOMSKY'S NATIVISM: A CRITICAL REVIEW

David C. Palmer[1]

IS GRAMMAR largely innate? Noam Chomsky holds that it is, or, more accurately, that the hypothesis that it is innate is the only coherent and plausible one that has yet been proposed to account for the acquisition of language. Extrapolating to broader issues, he has championed a retreat from behaviorism and empiricism to cognitivism and rationalism, from approaches that seek to determine the relationship between an organism's behavior and the environment to those that wish to discover the organism's "essential nature," of which behavior is an incomplete expression. His arguments, which are detailed, polemical, and persuasive, are evidently inspiring to a thriving school of linguists and to many laymen with an interest in language and philosophy. It is important to assess his position carefully, not only because he concludes that little is to be gained by pursuing the analysis of verbal behavior with the assumptions and methodology of radical behaviorism but because he claims to have achieved considerable success with very different assumptions and methodology. Success in explaining complex behavior deserves our attention whatever the approach.

When we examine Chomsky's position, however, we find that, not only are his objections to other approaches weak, but that the success of which he speaks has been achieved by rendering other problems more difficult, if not completely insoluble. This paper outlines Chomsky's position, emphasizing his argument that the brain of the newborn infant must

---

[1] I am indebted to John Donahoe for his conversations about these issues and for his many indirect contributions to the present paper. For a more exhaustive critical analysis of Chomsky's position I refer the reader to Pere Julia's excellent book *Explanatory Models in Linguistics: A Behavioral Perspective*, Princeton University Press, 1983.

be organized to extract rules of grammar from samples of speech. This position is criticized on two grounds. First, it places too heavy a burden on evolutionary principles. Second, the putative innate mechanisms must respond to stimuli, to actual physical events, but it appears to be impossible in Chomsky's system to characterize these events. Finally, Chomsky's sophistical arguments against behavioral accounts of language are rejected on grounds that he has confused properties of his formal system with properties of human beings. The notion that language consists of an infinite number of sentences must be abandoned when we move from the rarefied atmosphere of formal analysis to the world of stimulus and response classes.

CHOMSKY'S ASSUMPTIONS

Chomsky shares a number of fundamental assumptions with behaviorists and most other experimental psychologists. He believes that organisms are a joint product of their genetic endowment and individual experience and that the experimental approach of the natural sciences is appropriate for the study of language. He is tentatively monistic; while he freely uses mentalistic terminology, he does so for the sake of convenience, believing these terms to be abstractions of physical structures or processes in the body, presumably the brain. (See Chomsky, [1980a] for a recent review of his position). His goals, however, are different from those of behaviorists. He is not particularly interested in verbal behavior itself, influenced as it is by the idiosyncratic history and circumstances of the speaker; rather, he is interested in the "essential nature" of human beings that enable us to acquire a language. Specifically, Chomsky wishes to discover those elements of our nervous systems implicated in language that are genetically coded, hence "universal." Chomsky calls these elements "universal grammar," a name that suggests his view of the task accomplished by these innate mechanisms: providing a set of rules to be used in speech production and comprehension.

Chomsky is not dogmatic about the nature of universal grammar, so defined. He concedes that it may prove to be some general-purpose reinforcement mechanism, but this strikes him as implausible. Just as cells in the visual cortex are organized in special ways apparently not characteristic of cells controlling, say, digestion, those elements of the nervous system responsible for our ability to acquire language should not be expected to be organized in the same way as those implicated in learning to ride a bicycle. The language system, the visual system, and no doubt other systems, he asserts, may be modular.

Chomsky's interests in species differences are not what make his views controversial. Species differences, of course, are of as much interest to behaviorists as to linguists. A child learns to speak, and the family dog does not. No one doubts that this is due to genetic differences, and any illumination of these differences will contribute to our understanding of the behavior of organisms. Direct evidence of the genetic contribution to human behavior is hard to acquire, however. Programs of genetic engineering, surgical intrusions of the nervous system, and well-controlled behavioral experiments are, for ethical reasons, seldom possible. We must usually make do with speculation and extrapolation from indirect evidence. It is Chomsky's particular speculations and his rejection of alternative speculations that are controversial.

A TERMINOLOGICAL QUIBBLE

To begin with, we may object to Chomsky's terminology, particularly his use of the term "universal grammar" to refer to unspecified innate properties of the nervous system. A writer is free to define his terms as he chooses, but as Winograd (1977) has pointed out, the reader who has agreed to Chomsky's definition finds, in subsequent discussion, that he has agreed to some kind of innate grammar in the traditional sense of the term, i.e., a simple set of rules. This lends a spurious cogency to Chomsky's argument. Additionally, Chomsky freely uses mentalistic terms such as intention, belief, purpose, will, and mind without defining them. Occasionally he indicates that he is merely talking about properties of the nervous system, but he does not tell us where in the nervous system we will find the mind with its intentions, beliefs, and will. As a consequence, his discussions remain abstract and metaphorical apparently awaiting the day that someone can operationalize his terms without endangering the formal system that has been erected on this terminological quicksand.

Even within the formal system itself, Chomsky's terms are not always clearly defined. A language, we are told, is "a set (finite or infinite) of sentences, each finite in length and constructed out of a finite set of elements" (Chomsky, 1957, p. 13). Subsequently, we learn that human languages are infinite sets of sentences. But what is a sentence? Chomsky uses two definitions of "sentence," a formal, precise one and an informal one, and he does not consistently use either one. The informal definition is simply that which native speakers agree to be a sentence when they are not encumbered by "irrelevant" problems of memory, motivation, time, or patience. This is a relatively small set owing, apparently, to the ubiquity of these encumbrances. By the formal definition, a sentence is any string of symbols characterized by the grammatical rules devised by the linguist. At the very least, these grammatical rules must be consistent with the set of sentences defined by consensus. Thus, the formal definition is derived from data provided by using the informal definition, and both definitions depend ultimately upon the grammatical intuitions of native speakers. However, Chomsky does not provide us with criteria for deciding when a judgment of grammaticality is to be considered valid, an important omission considering that these judgments are notoriously variable.

ARGUMENTS FOR A GENETICALLY-DETERMINED GRAMMAR

One could argue that these terminological issues are irrelevant to evaluate the substance of Chomsky's position, particularly his argument that there is an innate language module. So let us turn to this critical argument. As noted above, his unit of analysis is the sentence, and his data are his judgments, and presumably the judgments of others, that particular sentences are or are not "well-formed." (He is not concerned with prescriptive rules of grammar, such as proper use of the objective case, but with regularities in language that are respected by native speakers without formal training.) Thus, (1) is a well-formed sentence, while (2) is not.

(1) Is the man who is hungry here?
(2) Is the man who hungry is here?

Similarly, (3), (4), and (5) are well-formed, while (6) is not, though its meaning is reasonably clear:

(3) Each of the men likes the others.
(4) The men like each other.
(5) Each of the men expects John to like the others.
(6) The men expect John to like each other.

What is it, Chomsky asks, that prevents people from uttering sentences such as (6)? Surely no one has been taught such things in grammar school.

. . . it can hardly be maintained that children learning English receive specific instruction about these matters, or even that they are provided with relevant experience that informs them that they should not make the obvious inductive generalization, say, that "each other" takes some plural antecedent that precedes it. Children make many errors in language learning, but they do not assume, until corrected, that "The candidates wanted me to vote for each other" is a well-informed sentence meaning that each candidate wanted me to vote for the other. Relevant evidence is never presented for most speakers of English, just as no pedagogic or traditional grammar, however compendious, would point out these facts. Somehow this is information that children themselves bring to the process of language acquisition as part of their mode of cognition (Chomsky, 1980a), pp. 43-44).

A similar problem is raised by "question formation":

> We select some noun phrase in a sentence, replace it by an appropriate question word, place the latter at the beginning of the sentence, and with other mechanical operations, form a question. Thus on the model of the sentence, "John saw a man," we can form "Whom did John see?" Or, to take a more complex case, on the model of the sentence, "The teacher thought that his assistant had told the class to study the lesson," we can question "the class" and ask: "Which class did the teacher think that his assistant had told to study the lesson?" But consider the following example of roughly comparable complexity: "The lesson was harder than the teacher had told the class it would be." Here, if we question "the class," we derive: "Which class was the lesson harder than the teacher had told that it would be?" Evidently, this is not a well-formed question, though its intended sense is clear enough and perfectly intelligible, with a little thought. It is difficult to imagine that people capable of these judgments have all had relevant training or experience to block the obvious inductive generalization. Rather it seems that some specific property of the human language faculty—hence a general property of language—leads to these consequences, a property that derives from our modes of cognition (Chomsky, 1980a, p. 42).

When we analyze the structure of language at a certain level of abstraction, according to Chomsky, we discover that there are general principles of grammar that are violated in sentences such as (6), for example, the principle that a reciprocal expression such as "each other" may not refer to an antecedent outside of the clause in which "each other" occurs unless the latter happens to be the subject of an infinitive (Chomsky, 1980a, p. 174), as in (7). Note that (8) is ungrammatical according to this principle:

(7) The candidates expect each other to win.
(8) The candidates expect each other will win.

Because children quickly learn to respect such distinctions with little, if any, formal instruction, and because no one has proposed a satisfactory explanation of these facts in terms of a theory of learning, Chomsky assumes that fundamental elements of the grammar of human languages must be expressed somehow in the genetic code. He suggests that universal grammar, triggered by relatively brief exposure to a particular language, is able to extract or construct a grammar for that language. Universal grammar presumably contains those fundamental principles that are common to all human languages and constrains the particular grammars that can be acquired.

Grammar is seen as fundamental; "language" is an epiphenomenon influenced by motivational variables, memory, nonlinguistic concept learning and other things. The task of the linguist is to characterize abstractly grammars of various languages as they would be spoken by ideal speakers in a homogeneous verbal community in an attempt to discover principles of grammar of wide generality, if not universality. Work of this sort has been in progress for several decades and, according to Chomsky, has met with considerable success. He concedes that conclusions are tentative and will undoubtedly be refined or replaced, a state of affairs to be expected in any empirical inquiry. Nonetheless, linguists are becoming increasingly able to characterize universal grammar and hence to offer hypotheses about the capacities that newborn infants bring into the world as a product of their genetic endowments.

In the current form of Chomsky's theory, a given sentence is presumed to be represented in the "mind" at several levels. It begins as a declarative sentence, with expressed (as opposed to "understood") subjects, verbs, direct objects, and so on. Elements of the sentence may then be deleted or rearranged subject to various constraints such as those governing reciprocal expressions like "each other." At this level the sentence includes "traces" of deleted and rearranged elements in their original positions as well as the rearranged elements in their new positions. Finally, the surface structure, the sentence as it appears at the behavioral level, is generated by representing phonetically all elements except trace elements. This scheme accounts for intuitions about relatedness among sentences, ambiguities, and many fine distinctions about what is grammatical and what is not.

This picture is incomplete, of course, but Chomsky asserts that it stands in sharp contrast to alternative theories which do not even attempt to explain the kinds of grammatical judgments people are capable of, judgments which have served as grist for the theories of linguists. Chomsky writes:

> The critic's task is to show some fundamental flaw in principle or defect in execution or to provide a different and preferable account of how it is that what speakers do is in accordance with certain rules or is described by these rules, an account that does not attribute to them mental representation of a system of rules (rules which in fact appear to be beyond the level of consciousness). If

someone can offer such an account of how it is that we know what we do know, e.g., about reciprocals, or judge as we do judge, etc., there will be something to discuss. Since no such account has been forthcoming, even in the most primitive or rudimentary form, there really is nothing to discuss (1980a, p. 130).

CHOMSKY'S CHALLENGE

One need not be disconcerted by this challenge. Chomsky is charging his critics to provide an alternative explanation for hypothetical behavior, the behavior of judging particular sentences grammatical or ungrammatical. He evidently believes that everyone will respond in the same way and for the same reason, that is, that there is an independent variable called "grammaticality" that controls the behavior of anyone asked to judge utterances. Since judgments of grammaticality are in fact highly variable, he insists that we consider only the behavior of an ideal speaker in a homogeneous verbal community.

Chomsky's reasons for doing this are similar to the use of ideals in other sciences. When many variables interact it is common practice to consider each in isolation. Hence the physicist assumes point masses, frictionless surfaces, and perfectly elastic collisions. However, these idealizations are useful only if the variables being omitted are unimportant for an understanding of the phenomenon under study. If one's verbal behavior and judgments about utterances are in fact a function of the individual's particular experience within a specific community, then consideration of the intuitions of an ideal speaker in a hypothetical community will tell us nothing. Faced with disorderly data, Chomsky removes to a hypothetical world where order emerges. It is not surprising that no one has proposed an alternative account, for this is a world of Chomsky's own making. Order has not been demonstrated; it has been assumed.

However, even if we satisfactorily demonstrate that instances like those provided by Chomsky are not universal the task remains of explaining why certain novel expressions "sound right" to someone while others do not. From a behavioral point of view the task is formidable, requiring that we know a great deal about the individual's reinforcement history—more than it is usually possible to know. We would have to determine appropriate units of behavior and the individual's history with respect to these units. We might find, for example, that "each other," though two words, is a single operant or that the frame "X . . Y . . each other" is a single operant, where

X and Y have certain prosodic, temporal, functional, and perhaps formal features but are otherwise free to vary. (We would resist the temptation to call X "a plural noun phrase" and Y "a verb," for that merely raises the question of what the formal, functional, prosodic, and temporal characteristics are of plural noun phrases and verbs.) We might find that "each other" is a component of half a dozen larger units or that it is under intraverbal control of a number of stimuli. In the latter case a number of different operants would be formally identical.

Once relevant units of behavior and their controlling variables were identified it would be possible to speculate whether a particular utterance would sound natural or strange to an individual. Since the value of such a prediction by no means justifies the effort necessary to gather the relevant data, it is unlikely that anyone will answer Chomsky's challenge. (We can, of course, invent contingencies to explain any given example, but he would regard this as empty.) Nonetheless, there are alternatives to Chomsky's account that depend, not on internal representations or underlying competence, but on the individual's long history with relevant verbal operants. It is hard to see how it could be otherwise, for we have no intuitions about strings of grammatical symbols by themselves or about sentence tree diagrams. Despite Chomsky's suggestion that intuitions about a full range of uses of the term "each other" follow from learning that it is a reciprocal expression and not the name of a tree, surely we have no intuitions about strings of nonsense syllables drawn from bins labelled "noun," "verb," "reciprocal expression," and so on. Knowing grammatical categories of words is no help in judging utterances "by ear."

As for a "flaw in principle" that Chomsky exhorts his critics to cite, there appears to be none. There are no objections in principle to the notion, however vague, that the nervous system is innately designed to extract a grammar from a sample of speech, but we can question the extent to which this serves as a parsimonious explanation of verbal behavior. Rather than shedding light on the problem, it renders it more mysterious.

Chomsky begins by characterizing grammar in formal terms. Having achieved some success at this he then simply imputes the formal apparatus to the speaker as an innate mechanism. This is a tidy solution to a complex problem, and it might even be true, but note that, as it stands, it is a homunculus theory, and as such it is unsatisfactory until the homunculus has in turn been explained. The genetic endowment is a convenient source of homunculi for every behavioral phenomenon we don't understand. If we ask nothing further of such an explanation then it is a universal solution. There are no limits to our invoking it. Two questions immediately arise to which Chomsky has provided no satisfactory answer. First, how did universal grammar get selected, and second, how does universal grammar get "triggered" by a verbal environment?

UNIVERSAL GRAMMAR AND EVOLUTION

Certain grammatical conventions serve a communicative function and might be learned because they do so. Other principles are arbitrary and seem to have little point, such as that concerning reciprocal expressions. Of this principle Chomsky (1975, p. 175) writes, ". . . it is often a difficult problem even to discover examples that bear on the hypothesis in question." It is principles such as this that Chomsky argues must be innate: the examples are few and the grammatical rules are arbitrary and unnecessary. This is an argument that cuts both ways; the same evidence that he adduces to support his position can be used in a parallel argument against it. If a grammatical principle is an arbitrary restriction without practical consequences in the ontogenic environment and hence cannot be accounted for in terms of communicative contingencies (Chomsky, 1980c, p. 41), then it clearly cannot confer a selective advantage to an organism endowed with it. Chomsky acknowledges this problem but points out that a child has only a few years to construct a grammar while the principle of natural selection has had many thousands of years (Chomsky, 1980b, p. 44). This will not suffice, however. If the rules are arbitrary it doesn't make any difference how long selective forces have been at work. Natural selection is simply not an appropriate mechanism to explain universal grammar.

This conclusion does not trouble Chomsky. He writes:

> . . . it is, in fact, perfectly possible that the innate structure of mind is determined by principles of organization, by physical conditions, even by physical laws that are now quite unknown, and that such notions as "random mutation" and "natural selection" are as much a cover for ignorance as the somewhat analogous notions of "trial and error," "conditioning," "reinforcement," and "association" (Chomsky, 1969, p. 262).

Again, Chomsky might be right that there are additional principles involved, but this hardly offers support for his position. Rather, it adds a further burden of proof. In addition to explaining the origins of grammar, he must now formulate and explain the workings of new evolutionary principles or "physical laws now quite unknown."

Perhaps not wanting to depend on unknown principles, Chomsky has suggested another solution, namely, that universal grammar:

> . . . may well have arisen as a concomitant of structural properties of the brain that developed for other reasons. Suppose that there was selection for bigger brains, more cortical surface, hemispheric specialization for analytic processing, or many other structural properties that can be imagined. The brain that evolved might have all sorts of special properties that are not individually selected; there would be no miracle in this, but only the normal workings of evolution. We have no idea, at present, how physical laws apply when 10 neurons are placed in an object the size of a basketball, under the special conditions that arose during human evolution (Chomsky, 1980c, p. 321).

It is certainly true that not everything coded by the genes must be adaptive. Hair color, eyecolor, and blood type are all genetically determined and are not obviously adaptive, but neither are they universal. When a trait is not actively selected for we expect variability, not universality. Moreover, to the extent that arbitrary structures require energy and resources, we would expect them to be selected *against*.

The chances that a universal grammar was an accidental by-product of other properties of the nervous system, an unexpected bonus when the human nervous system exploded in size, seem remote indeed given how abstract and complex the putative innate rules are. Moreover, in the absence of suggestions about the structure of which grammar is a by-product, and what the relationship between them is, Chomsky's answer is no answer at all. We might just as plausibly assert that language is an accidental by-product of other behavior acquired in the first few years of life.

Chomsky (1980a, 1980c) repeatedly asserts that the problem of explaining the genetic basis of universal grammar is no different from the problem of explaining the origin of any physical organ, say, the liver. No one ever asserts that we learn to have arms rather than wings, or that we learn to have a heart, he argues. No doubt there are many things that we don't know about the origin and development of the physical organs, but to be confident that the genetic endowment exerts considerable control, surely it is sufficient to note that such structures are adaptive and that they are, in fact, physical structures.

A hypothesis about behavior need not specify physiological correlates or evolutionary origins to be useful, but a complex structure with no adaptive significance is anomalous. In contrast, functional analyses of verbal behavior (e.g., Skinner, 1957) require few, if any, principles in addition to those already known to apply to nonverbal behavior; moreover, these principles are clearly adaptive (Skinner, 1966), and apply with appropriate qualification down the evolutionary ladder. Humans have the necessary vocal musculature and are particularly sensitive to secondary reinforcement, social contingencies, and, apparently, private stimuli generated by other behavior. These are quantitative differences from other organisms that are both adaptive and easily accommodated by evolutionary principles. These differences alone may be sufficient to account for verbal behavior in humans.[2] Chomsky, in attributing grammatical competence to the newborn infant, has not solved the problems of language acquisition; he has simply transferred them to the shoulders of the evolutionary biologist where they remain as intractable as before.

THE STIMULUS CONTROL OF INNATE BEHAVIOR

An additional difficulty facing Chomsky's position is perhaps more fundamental. Let us assume that he is correct, that humans are innately equipped with a neurological module that extracts an acceptable grammar from a small and degenerate sample of speech, triggered perhaps by critical experiences and with parameters set by developments in "other cognitive domains." Subsequent performance is a hodgepodge of behavior, an epiphenomenon, determined in part by the grammatical module and in part by many other factors. The problem that now arises is the relationship between "degenerate speech" and the device that extracts a grammar from this speech. The putative mechanism is an input-output device. In go samples of speech, and out comes the grammar, or perhaps a set of candidate grammars, most of which will be winnowed out later. Setting aside the improbability that such a device is an accidental by-product of, say, increased cortical surface, we must determine the functional relationship between this input and output. This can be considered a kind of problem in stimulus control since each verbal stimulus controls a particular response of the device as in a reflex. However, unlike the reflex, the relationship between stimuli and the grammar is arbitrary. Languages vary from culture to culture and within a language there is no relationship between the sound of an utterance and its grammatical structure. Clearly there is no physical property of the stimulus that suffices to

---

[2]The development of vocal musculature sensitive to reinforcement contingencies may be especially significant. First, it is a response system that is free from the demands of locomotion, orientation, and the manipulation of objects. Primates usually have plenty to do with their hands other than sign with them. Second, and perhaps more importantly, when we speak we stimulate ourselves exactly as we stimulate others, and we do so essentially instantaneously. This immediate and faithful stimulation, which is not characteristic of, say, sign language, is no doubt important both in maintaining somewhat uniform contingencies throughout the community and in facilitating the acquisition of verbal operants. Under some conditions reinforcement will be "automatic."

identify its part of speech. Nothing about the word "house" enables us to conclude that it is a noun, or that it might be a "subject."

The input to this device, then, must be the product of a grammatical analysis rather than raw stimuli. At the very least, words must be classified into their parts of speech. But parts of speech have formal definitions; they do not have operational ones, nor does it seem possible to provide operational ones. Nouns are often uttered in the presence of "things" and verbs in the presence of activity, but many nouns are not "things" and many verbs are not perceptible actions. Perhaps when a child utters a particular word in the presence of a particular class of objects (or state of affairs) and is reliably reinforced for doing so, that acoustic signal is represented and tagged with an "N". Thus every grammatical distinction might be traced to a particular set of reinforcement contingencies. This is unsatisfactory since we still do not end up with a class of symbols that coincides with the concept "noun." We do, however, end up with a repertoire of behavior that coincides precisely with Skinner's concept of "tact." Once grammatical distinctions are traced to contingencies of reinforcement the innate grammar is no longer doing any work. On the other hand, if they cannot be traced to reinforcement contingencies then the child (or the innate mechanism) has no way of generating a grammar.

Chomsky's allusions to imprinting and fixed-action patterns as examples of complex innate behavior (1959, pp. 41, 43) suggest that he fails to appreciate that these behaviors do not occur spontaneously but are elicited by specific stimuli. Herring gull chicks do not "peck at their mothers' bills to get food;" they peck at red spots. Ducklings do not "follow their mothers;" they are reinforced by proximity to objects similar to the particular object that was bustling around when they hatched. If we wish to say that a particular behavior is genetically determined or "wired in" it must be possible to specify the environmental events that elicit, release, or trigger it. Not only has Chomsky failed to do this for his hypothetical grammar-generating device, he apparently thinks it cannot be done:

> ... although one might propose various operational tests for acceptability, it is unlikely that a necessary and sufficient operational criterion might be invented for the much more abstract and far more important notion of grammaticalness. (Chomsky, 1965, p. 11)
> Furthermore, there is no reason to expect that reliable operational criteria for the deeper and more important theoretical notions of linguistics (such as "grammaticalness" and "paraphrase") will ever be forthcoming (Chomsky, 1965, p. 19).

If there are no stimuli, objective criteria, or even a set of operations by which we (or our innate language acquisition devices) can identify such theoretical entities as "grammatical sentence," "subject," "noun phrase," and so on, then it is a mystery how we can reflexively generate rules characterizing permissible relationships among these entities. Chomsky has been able to formulate precisely his theoretical ideas because they have remained abstract, but useful theories cannot remain abstract forever. If there is no way to use them to predict, control, or describe actual events, then they are empty.

THE UNIT OF ANALYSIS AND THE NOTION OF INFINITY

The choice of a unit of analysis in behavior is critical. The orderly relationship between behavior and its controlling variables deteriorates if we consider units that are too broad, too long, or too narrowly specified (Skinner, 1935). If one defines one's units *a priori* rather than empirically it is possible that behavior will appear to be infinitely variable and to bear little relationship to environmental events. Chomsky commits this error by choosing the sentence as a unit of analysis. He does not defend this choice; he appears to regard it as self-evident, despite the fact that people often do not speak in sentences and in appropriate contexts regard single words or phrases as "well-formed." As noted above, the sentence is a formal unit, not a behavioral one, though Chomsky pays little heed to this distinction. Since the speaking of sentences, however defined, typically does not display the same dynamic properties as, say, keypecking in pigeons, he concludes, not that he has erred in his choice of units, but that principles formulated in the experimental analysis of behavior are of only peripheral interest in the study of language.

Of special significance to Chomsky is the notion that humans have the capacity to speak and understand an infinite number of grammatical sentences, though actual performance is limited by motivation, memory, time, and other resources. There is no limit to the number of adjectives we can insert before a noun or the number of times we can repeat the word "very" for emphasis; nor is there any limit to the number of sentences or clauses that we can add or insert in other sentences, as in (9) and (10).:

(9) The rat the cat the dog chased killed ate the malt.
(10) Anyone who feels that if so many more students whom we haven't actually admitted are sitting in on the course than ones we have that the room had to be changed, then probably auditors will have

to be excluded, is likely to agree that the curriculum needs revision (From Chomsky & Miller, 1963, p. 286).

Although native speakers gape in dismay when asked if 10 is a grammatical sentence, the authors assure us that this "is a perfectly well-formed sentence with a clear and unambiguous meaning, and a grammar must be able to account for it if the grammar is to have any psychological relevance." It is obvious that such sentences are not behavioral units but are strings carefully constructed to be consistent with grammatical rules. It is true that there are an infinite number of such strings, but their relevance to verbal behavior is doubtful. Nevertheless, Chomsky uses the notion that there are an infinite number of grammatical sentences to dismiss the use of the term probability in discussions of language and particularly to criticize Skinner's analysis of language as a repertoire of verbal operants:

> It is unclear what sense there would be to the assertion that a person has "learned" a sentence that takes twice as long to say as his entire lifetime. . . . On empirical grounds, the probability of my producing some given sentence of English—say, this sentence or the sentence "Birds fly" or "Tuesday follows Monday" or whatever—is indistinguishable from the probability of my producing a given sentence of Japanese. Introduction of the notion of "probability relative to a situation" changes nothing, at least if "situations" are characterized on any known objective grounds. . . (Chomsky, 1969, p. 267).
> But what does it mean to say that some sentence of English that I have never heard or produced belongs to my "repertoire," but not any sentence of Chinese (so that the former has a higher "probability") (Chomsky, 1971, p.20).

According to Chomsky, this follows from the fact that most sentences are unique and hence have a probability near zero.

Chomsky is making an extraordinary leap from asserting that a grammar can generate an infinite number of sentences to asserting that humans have the competence to generate and understand an infinite number of sentences. This is clearly not an empirical fact. It is not even a valid generalization from the empirical fact that behavior is variable. Let us suppose that we have arrived at a definition of "sentence" that allows us to determine when a sentence has been uttered. We have no justification for predicting future variability until we analyze the variables of which a sentence is a function. If we can show that these are infinitely variable and that human behavior tracks the full range of this variability then we are perhaps justified in predicting the infinite variability of sentences. However, behavior and its controlling variables are not divisible into an infinite number of orderly pairs, a point made by Skinner as early as 1935. We can illustrate the point by considering the "language" of honey bees.

As is well-known, a bee, having returned from successful foraging, fly in a pattern with a distinctive orientation, depending on the position of the sun and the location of the food source. Other bees, observing this pattern will successfully locate the food source. As a circle has an infinite number of diameters, so there are an infinite number of orientations of a pattern of flight. Undoubtedly no two bee "sentences" have ever been identical. However, this variability is irrelevant if it is not functionally related to the location of the food. Clearly, no honey bee can discriminate an infinite number of patterns either as a "speaker" or as a "listener." While an abstract characterization of bee communication could generate an infinite number of "sentences," it is unlikely that bees generate or respond appropriately to more than a hundred or so. (Note that since bees have other ways of locating flowers, this number would be more than sufficient to satisfy the contingencies of natural selection.) To argue that the bees have the "competence" to interpret an infinite number of patterns is to confuse a property of our formulation with a property of the organism.

We can make a similar argument with respect to human language. Sentence (11) is indiscriminable from (10) in normal discourse.

(11) Anyone who feels that if so many more students whom we haven't actually admitted are sitting in on the course than ones we have that the room had to be changed, that probably auditors will have to be excluded, is likely to agree that the curriculum needs revision.

If the two sentences are in print we can detect a physical difference in them given a pencil and enough time, but we do so in a purely mechanical way, analogous to comparing signatures in a forgery case. We clearly do not do so on the basis of grammar. Once again, talk of competence is mere invention. There is no behavioral justification for calling these strings different stimuli, or, if emitted, different responses. Nonetheless, they are different *sentences* as defined by Chomsky. Evidently the sentence is an inappropriate unit of analysis of verbal behavior. Dropping it in favor of an empirically defined unit not only avoids the problem that only an infinitesimal fraction of all sentences are discriminable, it accommodates the awkward fact that people seldom speak in sentences at all. Moreover, it obviates the need to find a translation between the formal apparatus and actual data. That is, we no longer need to find an operational definition of "sentence" to match the formal one.

But when we have abandoned the sentence as a unit of analysis and the notion that language consists of an infinite number of sentences, the argument against an analysis of language as a repertoire of verbal operants breaks down. It now makes sense to say of a string of phonemes that would take twice as long to say as one's lifetime that it simply is not a unit of behavior, and it now makes sense to ask whether a particular unit is in one's repertoire.

BACK TO THE VERBAL OPERANT

By choosing the sentence as his unit of analysis Chomsky has been led to maintain that grammar is central to language and that grammar must be genetically determined, since extracting a completely adequate grammar from samples of speech is an achievement that has eluded many years of effort by linguists; surely it could not be accomplished by every three-year-old unless the job were, in important respects, genetically coded.

As we have seen, this offers only the illusion of an explanation since we must now explain the origin of the code in the genes, a task for which evolutionary principles are ill-suited. Moreover, any innate device must respond to actual physical events, not metaphors or abstractions; unless grammatical terms can be defined physically or operationally there is little reason to believe that such a device is possible. Chomsky and his colleagues have analyzed formal properties of language in commendable detail and have found a wealth of curious regularities that deserve explanation. However, they have not advanced the functional analysis of verbal behavior at all.

When we turn from the sentence to the verbal operant as a unit of analysis we avoid many of the problems faced by a formal analysis. Our terms are empirically defined, and the principles invoked are clearly adaptive. Chomsky's arguments notwithstanding, novelty and diversity are not problems for a functional analysis. The tremendous diversity in language, like the tremendous diversity of living organisms, is a function of selecting contingencies in a diverse environment.

Methodological problems remain. Owing to ethical constraints, it may never be possible to account for verbal behavior to the satisfaction of the most cautious critic. At the moment perhaps the best we can do is to continue the work that Skinner and others have begun; analyze complex verbal contingencies informally while attacking experimentally the more tractable problems in verbal behavior.

REFERENCES

Chomsky, N. (1957). *Syntactic structures*. The Hague: Mouton.
Chomsky, N. (1959). Review of *Verbal Behavior* by B. F. Skinner. *Language, 35*, 26-58.

Chomsky, N. (1965). *Aspects of a theory of syntax*. Cambridge: MIT Press.
Chomsky, N. (1969). Some empirical assumptions in modern philosophy of language. In S. Morgenbesser, P. Suppes, & M. White (Eds.), *Philosophy, Science and Method* (Essays in honor of Ernest Nagel). New York: St. Martin's Press.
Chomsky, N. (1971). Review of *Beyond Freedom and Dignity* by B. F. Skinner. *The New York Review*, 18-24.
Chomsky, N. (1975). *Reflections on language*. New York: Pantheon.
Chomsky, N. (1980a). *Rules and representations*. New York: Columbia University Press.
Chomsky, N. (1980b). Rules and representations (author's response). *The Behavioral and Brain Sciences, 3*, 1-61.
Chomsky, N. (1980c). On cognitive structures and their development: a reply to Piaget. In M. Piattelli-Palmarini (Ed.), *Language and Learning: the Debate between Jean Piaget and Noam Chomsky*. Cambridge: Harvard University Press.
Chomsky, N., & Miller, G. A. (1963). Introduction to the formal analysis of natural languages. in R. D. Luce, R. R. Bush, & E. Galanter (Eds.). *Handbook of Mathematical Philosophy Vol. II*. New York: Wiley.
Skinner, B. F. (1935). The generic nature of the stimulus and response, *Journal of General Psychology*.
Skinner, B. F. (1957). *Verbal behavior*. New York: Appleton-Century-Crofts.
Skinner, B. F. (1966). The phylogeny and ontogeny of behavior. *Science, 153*, 1205-1213.
Winograd, T. (1977). On some contested suppositions of generative linguistics about the scientific study of language. *Cognition, 5*, 151-179.

Commentary

AN ALTERNATIVE TO THE SENTENCE AS A BASIC VERBAL UNIT

PHILIP N. CHASE

THERE ARE A NUMBER of stimulating aspects of David Palmer's chapter on Chomsky that warrant comment. However, I will limit my discussion to one critical criticism of Palmer's. I would like to elaborate on the problems of using the sentence as a basic unit in the analysis of language and suggest that the units defined and used by operant investigators are more appropriate for answering questions concerning language use and development.

Contrary to Palmer's presentation, my first reading of the chapter suggested that Chomsky's informal and formal definitions of the sentence were reasonable for answering questions concerning language use. Chomsky claims that the sentence as a unit of language can be defined informally by some functional, community-based criteria but that the formal definition, though bound by what society loosely defines as a sentence, is more tightly, arbitrarily and structurally defined in terms of the rules that linguists apply to sentences. These definitions seem akin to the relations among most informally defined phenomena and corresponding scientific definitions. After all, pecking is a different operant for the casual bird watcher than it is for the pigeon experimenter.

A second look at Chomsky's definitions of a sentence, particularly his insistence on studying ideal behavior in a homogeneous community, however, revealed such obvious problems with the formal definition as a scientific unit that I could not help but think that I had misunderstood. Can it be that linguists such as Chomsky have defined one of the basic units of language so that it corresponds with only one form of language, written language, while ignoring the other two basic forms, spoken and gestural language? Can linguists such as Chomsky actually ask questions about universal principles of language that are true for examples of language used only by linguists and a few other scholars? Affirmative answers to these questions seem preposterous, but nonetheless true.

As Palmer pointed out, judgments by lay people on what constitutes a sentence are variable; people often fail to discriminate grammatically correct sentences from incorrect sentences. This is particularly true with spoken sequences. In my day-to-day work as a teacher, I hear people uttering many kinds of grammatically incorrect sequences of words. In fact, upon listening to tape recorded conversations among highly verbal humans, I categorized more grammatically incorrect sentences than correct. However, this was a difficult task because determining where one sentence ended and another began was often impossible. The people I had tape recorded did not seem to talk in complete sentences. As psychologists and others have known for years, spoken language is not analyzed easily in terms of sentences defined by grammatical rules.

Even if one concentrates solely on written language, there are still difficulties with the notion of a sentence as a scientific unit. I assume that many lay people would not be able to discriminate between some of the written sentences and nonsentences that have been used as examples by Chomsky. For example, Palmer presents one example from Chomsky:

1. Each of the men expect John to like the others.
2. The men expect John to like each other.

Frankly, I thought both sentences were odd and if someone offered me money to say whether each was grammatically correct without access to a grammar text, I would say neither. It is, perhaps, only a small portion of society who would distinguish between these sentences. If this hypothesis is true and still the linguist argues that the grammar that separates (1.) and (2.) is innate or conforms to some universal principle, then serious problems arise. Is it universal simply for linguists? Or is it universal and lay people are not aware of it? If the populace is not aware of this particular grammar, then how do we determine if it is universal? If we cannot test the proposed universal principles with sentences as units of analysis, then the sentence is not a scientific unit.

It seems that the grammatically defined sentence can not be used to answer questions concerning language use because the sentence so defined is such a small, possibly insignificant component of language use. Perhaps, such structural units can help answer questions concerning precision in communication, for example, questions that trace the problems of communication to ambiguities in sentence structure. However, to answer questions regarding the development, acquisition and/or maintenance of language requires units that reflect the examples of language that people generate. The sentence is just not up to the task.

This critique of the sentence as the basic unit in the analysis of language begs the question: how have or will operant investigators improve upon this unit? Is an operant definition of the basic verbal unit(s) any more fruitful? My position and bias on this question are clearly specified in Chapter One. There, I argued for continued studies of environmental/behavioral relations with a particular emphasis on molar changes in response patterns and stimulus changes. From this point of view, a different definition of verbal units emerges.

First, an operant analysis begins at the most general level by distinguishing between verbal events and nonverbal events. A defining feature of verbal events is that they require the mediation of another individual (Skinner, 1957). Though this feature does not distinguish verbal from social events (see Chapter Four for a description of this problem), it may be sufficient for our purposes. For example, given this defining feature, it is clear that leaves rustling, birds pecking, pieces of cake, and a hike in the woods are nonverbal events, whereas talking on the phone, singing an opera, arguing politics, and whispering sweet nothings are verbal events. Furthermore, there may be no reason to distinguish between social and verbal events. Examples of conventionally defined verbal events (e.g., speaking, writing, and gesturing) may be kinds of social behavior that are particularly effective and that allow for a range of specific effects on the social environment. In fact, there seem to be four features of these conventional forms of verbal behavior that facilitate their effectiveness as methods for producing specific effects on other people. First, as Palmer indicated, these response modes stimulate the behaver at the same time and in essentially the same way as they stimulate the observer. The letters formed when writing, the words uttered when speaking, and the gestures made when signing can be observed by the person behaving as readily as by society. This feature allows for specific orderly correspondence between members of a social group. Second, verbal response modes are exceedingly portable. Speaking and gesturing require no tools or environmental props and writing requires few. This portability allows us to use verbal responses in a variety of social settings and under a variety of conditions. Third, conventional verbal behavior can mediate distances among people. An observer does not have to be in contact with the same environment as the behaver in order to be affected by that environment if the behaver responds verbally. This is particularly true of writing. Fourth, the response modes of speaking, writing, and gesturing provide the behaver with an almost infinite number and variety of specific behaviors each of which may have a specific effect on the observer. This feature allows for a fine-grained level of specificity which should facilitate social interaction. In sum, verbal events are particularly effective social events and social events are distinguished from other events by requiring the mediation of another person.

An operant analysis of language units does not stop at distinguishing between verbal and nonverbal events, it also distinguishes among different kinds of verbal events. There are events defined by the relation between nonverbal stimuli and verbal behavior, verbal stimuli and verbal behavior and motivational operations and verbal behavior. Skinner (1957) used these distinctions to describe his typology of verbal operants, the tact, the intraverbal, the mand, and so forth. These distinctions describe smaller, more unique classes of environment/behavior relations that allow for more precise prediction and control, yet these distinctions retain the functional or relational character of operant analysis.

Currently, the most precise level of analysis from an operant view is to distinguish between the different kinds of nonverbal stimuli, verbal stimuli and motivational operations that affect verbal behavior. Skinner (1957) began this work with the distinctions he drew among generic, metaphoric and metonymic tacts, echoics, transcriptives and intraverbals and various forms of the mand. Vargas' chapter in this book attempts to further classify verbal behaviors that are stimulated by verbal stimuli. Elsewhere, Johnson and Chase (1981) and Chase, Sulzer-Azaroff and Johnson (in press) have distinguished between types of intraverbals that are relevant to instruction. The purpose of the fine-grain distinctions is to define repeatable, measurable units of behavior/environment relations that will help us to describe language precisely enough to be able to predict and control it. At a general conceptual level it may be sufficient to distinguish among mands, tacts, and intraverbals. However, at the experimental and practical levels our analysis must consist of particular kinds of mands, tacts, and intraverbals. For instance, we might distinguish between manding information and manding objects. Investigations, then, could observe the conditions that lead to these various forms of mands. If these conditions can be reproduced reliably and the effect predicted, then we have added substantially to our knowledge about language use.

Though the basic units of operant analysis are not without their critics (see Ribes' chapter in this book), these units are useful. Each of the units can be applied equally well to different verbal response modes, each of these units is consistent with examples of observed language, and the different levels of specificity facilitate answering different levels of questions. These features suggest that the problems facing the use of the grammatical sentence as a unit of analysis are avoided or at least minimized when the verbal operant is used. If this logic holds up and if future research using these units adds to our understanding of language development, acquisition and maintenance, then the operant units of verbal behavior will be a true alternative to traditional and current linguistic units.

REFERENCES

Chase, P. N., Sulzer-Azaroff, B. and Johnson, K. R. (in press). Vebal relations within instruction: Are there sub-classes of the intraverbal? *Journal of the Experimental Analysis of Behavior*.

Johnson, K. R. and Chase, P. N. (1981). Behavior analysis in instructional design. *The Behavior Analyst, 4*, 103-122.

Skinner, B. F. (1957). *Verbal Behavior*. Englewood Cliffs, NJ: Prentice-Hall, Inc.

Chapter Three

IS OPERANT CONDITIONING SUFFICIENT TO COPE WITH HUMAN BEHAVIOR?[1]

EMILIO RIBES

OPERANT CONDITIONING PRINCIPLES have become the most influential set of concepts in behavior theory. Derived originally from observations of animal behavior under the restricted conditions of the laboratory, these principles have come to be assumed relevant to the explanation of human behavior as well. Skinner's works, *Science and Human Behavior* (1953) and *Verbal Behavior* (1957), are well known attempts to extend the applicability of these principles to human behavior, as are later developments in the area known as behavior modification or applied behavior analysis. These applications are defended on the grounds that they constitute a logical and empirical extension of principles identified in the animal behavior laboratory.

Whether or not operant conditioning principles are sufficient to cope with human behavior depends on more than the success with which these principles have been applied to human behavior, however. It also depends on the adequacy of the broader philosophical system under the influence of which these principles were constructed. The philosophical system upon which operant conditioning principles were developed is Cartesian Mechanics, and it is the opinion of this author that an adequate theory of human behavior cannot be expected to arise under these auspices. The purpose of this paper, then, is to examine the influence of Cartesian Mechanics on operant conditioning theory and to show how this influence has resulted in a set of principles which are ill-suited to the analysis of

---

[1]Read as an invited address at the Eighth Annual Convention of the Association for Behavior Analysis, Milwaukee, May, 1982.

human behavior.

CARTESIAN MECHANICS

Cartesian science is a contradictory enterprise. On the one hand, the Augustinian and Thomistic doctrines about the ultimate divine nature of knowledge, and its necessary reliance on revelation and rational elaboration of sensible experience, established the primacy of the Spirit, the Reason, in the very process of knowledge. The paradigm of genuine scientific knowledge would become, in this way, that representation of reality in which no material or sensible elements would be needed, that is, it would consist exclusively of concepts based in pure forms, i.e., geometry. On the other hand, science could not neglect a study of the sensible and extensional world, the material reality, and therefore, a boundary between extentional, and nonextentional knowledge had to be drawn. Science would cope with the extensional world, while trying to put aside its contingential elements through geometrical descriptions of its being. The only science at the time was Physics, and more accurately said, Mechanics. All the extensional properties of the world would be the subject matter of Mechanics, including the behavior of animals and the animal aspects of human beings, in other words, human nonrational responsibility of accounting for the nonextensional aspects of the world, and since these aspects were basically accessible only through reasoning and "nonoptical" self-observation, psychology became the specific form adopted by metaphysics for the purpose of building up a science-like conceptual system.

An analysis of body behavior in mechanistic terms can be found in Descartes' general writings (*Discourse of the Method, Metaphysical Mediations*, and in *The Principles of Philosophy*.) In these writings, movements are always regarded as having been produced by forces, or other movements, occurring within the body, external to the body, or in the soul's interaction with the body. The dichotomy of mechanics and metaphysics, however, made it necessary for objectivists to discard vitalistic or mentalistic references to the soul's interaction with the body. Hence, from the standpoint of objectivists, the concept of the reflex arising out of Cartesian Theory was interpreted as the mechanical relation between an external impulse or force, the stimulus, and the movement of the body, the reaction. More broadly stated, any objective study of matter and material bodies, including living organisms, was thought to require a mechanistic conception of their being, along with its companion, a deterministic mode of explanation. In short, Mechanics became the official philosophy of science, the omnipresent paradigm of any description of objective reality.

Objective psychology didn't escape from this design. In the late 19th and 20th centuries, formal attempts to develop a systematic psychology based on the reflex concept are to be found in the works of Sechenov (1978, trans.) and Bechterew (1913). In their work, all processes, including imagination and thinking, were treated as special cases of voluntary reflexes occurring on the basis of neural mechanisms such as inhibition, stimulus trace, etc. Although, as Skinner (1931) points out, Descartes' concept of the stimulus as an external impulse provoking the movements of the biological machine did not influence historical formulations of the reflex concept in neurophysiology, the paradigm itself, of body or organism as machine moved by another body or substance, became the conceptual matrix of both the biological and psychological sciences.

THE INFLUENCE OF CARTESIAN MECHANICS ON OPERANT CONDITIONING THEORY

Theoretical efforts in the scientific enterprise are always founded on an accepted paradigm as a conceptual representation of the subject matter under research (Kuhn, 1971). While this conceptual representation is not necessarily explicit in the language data and categories of a given theoretical approach, its conceptual and empirical boundaries are in a sense still prescribed by the paradigmatic assumptions underlying them. Consequently, analytical and experimental procedures may reflect a conceptual system of which investigators are not fully aware. This has been the case in the development of operant conditioning theory. As Shimp (1982) remarks referring to Skinner:

" . . . he in fact had tacit knowledge of a 19th century theory, and this tacit knowledge wound up being embedded in his experimental procedures. By virtue of the fact that he was, and is, unaware of his own knowledge, that is, unaware of his theoretical committment, the theory continues to lie hidden to this day in the methods of many applied and laboratory researchers in behavior analysis."

The theory embedded in his experimental procedures is that of Cartesian Mechanics and the concept of the reflex derived from it.

The reflex paradigm as a conceptual scheme, is not indigenous to behavior, however. It is a third-hand paradigm, originally formulated in the context of Mechanics, borrowed initially by Biology, and from this discipline finally transferred to Psychology. As such, psychological theory within the reflex tradition has been developed on the basis of conceptual premises derived from the study of a different subject matter. For this reason, even in those cases where dualism, as the official doctrine in psychology, is explicitly repudiated, the adoption of the reflex paradigm, irrespective of whether the word "reflex" is used or not, brings into theoretical accounts the dualistic assumptions of Cartesian dogma, and with them, a reductionistic conceptualization of behavior.

Three general characteristics of operant conditioning theory, shared in many ways with other conceptual approaches, are traceable to the mechanistic reflex tradition. Those are the materialistic definition of Psychology's subject matter, explanation as a cause-effect or functional relationship, and associationism as a logical framework for empirical relations.

DEFINITION OF SUBJECT MATTER. Mechanistic conceptions have always identified matter, as a general category by which to describe reality, with the physical category of matter. Physical matter, thus conceived, is framed in the Cartesian Physics tradition of matter as body or substance within or between bodies. No place is given to a nonspiritualistic entity different from a corporeus substance. Interactions different from the bodies or substances interacting are always reduced to a body movement or to an inferred physicalistic substance. Consequently, materialistic definitions of the subject matter for psychology have always stressed movements or brain workings. Skinner's (1938) definition although pointing to particular features that movements as behavior have to fulfill, has this same character. In other words, through the influence of Cartesian Mechanics, the subject matter of psychology has been formulated in organo-centric terms.

EXPLANATION AS CAUSE AND EFFECT. Descartes, in his *Principles of Philosophy* sees causality in physical bodies in terms of the movements of bodies contacting each other. Things remain in the same state in nature until something else changes them. For most bodies, this something is the movement of another body (solid or fluid). In the case of man, the soul is regarded as capable of producing bodily movement. Proximity, immediate or mediated through a succession of similar bodies' contacts, in time and place, is necessary to explain any movement as caused by another body's action. Thus causality is interpreted, in the mechanistic formulation, as requiring contiguity of body action, and is described as a linear, unidirectional process. Hume's causality principle is the subjectivistic culmination of dualistic tradition. In present operant theory, the search for functional relationships between an independent and a dependent variable, is just an operational substitution of the causal scheme inherited from Mechanics.

ASSOCIATIONISM AS A FRAMEWORK FOR EMPIRICAL RELATIONS. Associationism is a necessary partner of the cause-and-effect principle. In his book, *On Understanding in the Treatise of Human Nature*, Hume articulates his view of causality in terms of two basic formulae: contiguity in time and space, and the link between the cause and the effect (Section XV). Now, since the necessity of the connection is not in the objects, but in their reflection on our impressions, necessity exists only in the spirit. That is, causality exists in the mind to the extent that ideas about objects are associated: Association is the mental mechanism that provides for causal connections among objects in the outer world. Without idea-association, cause-effect relations between objects could not be appreciated.

Undoubtedly, associative mechanisms have played an important role in behavior theory, either as a Humean-type principle to explain how organisms internally establish relations among stimulus events and their behavior, or as the principle defining the necessary conditions for events to become functionally related.

CONTRIBUTIONS TO OPERANT THEORY FROM THE BIOLOGICAL CONCEPTION OF THE REFLEX

As previously indicated, the reflex paradigm was originally borrowed from Mechanics by Biology, after which it was transferred to Psychology. Given this sequence, we may expect to see an influence in the psychological formulation of the reflex coming from Biology as well as Mechanics. Five aspects of this influence are indicated below.

DISCONTINUOUS NATURE OF THE REFLEX. The reflex as a unit of behavior came to be described as a discrete, discontinuous relation between stimulus and response. This all-or-none characteristic of the reflex has its origins in the rest-motion distinction of Cartesian Mechanics. As a behavioral unit, the reflex was defined as a covariation or correlation between a stimulus and a response, wherein the "strength" of a reflex, a mechanistic metaphor, referred to the state of such a correlation.

Skinner's (1931) early writings suggest that this conception of the reflex was sufficient to account for variations in behavior. In his words:

> "the study of the reflex, then leads to the formulation of two kinds of law. The first are laws describing correlations of stimulus and response. . . . Secondly, there are laws describing changes in any aspect of these primary relationships as functions of third variables. . . . It is difficult to discover any aspects of behavior or organisms which may not be described with a law of one or the other

from these forms. From the point of view of scientific method, at least, — the description of behavior is adequately embraced by the principle of the reflex? (1931, pp. 456-457).

Later, of course, Skinner (1938) adopted the view that reflexes, as here described, were only a part of behavior, called respondent behavior, nonetheless he continued to use the term to refer to operant behavior as a separate class of reflexes. The final abandonment of the reflex as a useful concept didn't change the general conceptual premise upon which it was developed as a unit of behavior. That premise is succinctly stated in the following passage:

"The essence of the description of behavior is held to be the determination of functional laws describing the relationship between the *forces* acting upon, and a *movement* of, a given system. The reflex is, by definition the precise instrument for this description" (Skinner, 1931, p. 458).

PUNCTUATE NATURE OF RESPONSES AND STIMULI. Closely linked to the discontinuous nature of the reflex as a unit of behavior is the punctuate nature of responses and stimuli. The reflex, as an all-or-none relation, implies a correlation between atomistic events. In Skinner's words:

". . . in the description of behavior it is usually assumed that both behavior and environment may be broken into parts, which may be referred to by name, and that these parts will retain their identity from experiment to experiment. . . . Thus, a stimulus or a response is an *event*, that is to say, not a property; and we must turn, therefore, to a definition on the principle of classes" (1935, pp. 40-42).

As Schoenfeld (1976) has already pointed out, it was the reproducibility principle of events in scientific knowledge that forced Skinner to group punctuate events as instances of functionally-defined classes. Nonetheless, it is important to note that the concept of class, operant or respondent, is a logical consequence of having adopted the reflex as a conceptual paradigm in the analysis of behavior. Four problems arise from this adoption. First, it assumes that correlations of punctuate events are representative of all factors present in the situations under study. This conceptual claim is yet to find empirical support. Second, descriptions of ongoing behavior must be formulated as sequences of punctuate events in time, with the postulation of filling-in mechanisms, such as chaining, conditional reinforcement, etc. Third, events not operationally or formally identified in a situation must be assumed not to intervene in functional relations between explicitly manipulated punctuate events, a highly improbable state of affairs. The implication here is that constancies exist in closed situations such that by virtue of manipulation of some features of those situations, some events are changed while others are not. And, finally, the reflex paradigm forces investigators to find experimental criteria that will produce previously defined relations. As Skinner has suggested:

> ". . . a reflex, then, is a correlation of a stimulus and a response at a level of restriction marked by the orderliness of change in the correlation (1935, p. 58).

Instances of this attitude are the articulation of stability criteria and the almost morbid concern to prevent "superstition."

AHISTORICAL DESCRIPTIONS OF BEHAVIOR. Reflex activity, as a phylogenically built-in mechanism, has no ontogenic history in biology. Rather, its history in the individual is its history of systemic integration with complex self-regulatory processes. Reflex activity is, in this sense, predetermined by the species history of the individual. This ahistorical description of behavior is a product of adopting a reflex conception of behavior.

When we refer to an ahistorical description of behavior, we mean two things. First, that in the analysis of individual behavior, synchronic processes are not enough. Diachronic processes must be invoked in order to understand the development of the individual. Development can not be approached as a mere linear sequence of chained contingencies, however. Second, individual histories are always manipulated in experimental analyses of behavior, and changes in behavior represent this historical intermingling of factors in the individual organism's experience. However, no concept is put forward by which to identify history as a set of events, themselves requiring description, and the functional properties of this history with respect to subsequent behavior are not identified. Individual organisms' psychological history cannot be contained in a fatalistic print out of the past, but neither can it be understood as an empty concept referring to anecdotal episodes in an organism's lifetime. Formal properties must be given to history if theoretical analyses are to come to grips with the ontogenically constructed interactions that behavior represents.

NO PARAMETRIC IMPORTANCE GIVEN TO SPACE. Reflex activity always takes place in the same location: the effector, and through the action of stimulus energy that "travels-through" more or less invariant neural paths. Space, in being constant, is not relevant to the description of the reflex. Space is substituted for location, as in Cartesian Mechanics, in which bodies contact in place but not in space. Place is constant in the fixed neural pathways including receptors, central neurons and effectors. Thus, the reflex as a conceptual representation of stimulus-response covariations does not take space into account. Pavlovian techniques with a restrained organism are analogous to an isolated preparation of the neuromuscular plate. Behaviors occur only in time and space is barely mentioned as situation cues (in this regard, Kupalov's situational conditioning is actually similar to a discrete operant situation). On the contrary, in the free operant situation, the lack of restriction on responses in time is due to the fact that there are no constraints on the free moving of the organisms in the experimental chamber.

Nonetheless, it is surprising that no parametric importance is conceded to space. The "response" is virtually identified as the interception of the organism's movement on a fixed location (the operandum). Recent empirical findings seem to suggest that the geography and topography of behavior and stimuli need to be taken into account in order to "solve" apparent paradoxical effects, traditionally analyzed in terms of "responding" and "not responding."

LINEAR, UNIDIRECTIONAL RELATIONS. The reflex is articulated in a linear, unidirectional relation between stimulus and response. The relation ends with the response and no additional interaction follows. Recent discoveries in Neurophysiology have altered the one-pathway conception of the reflex in this science, but in Psychology, its paradigmatic influence has remained. The three-term contingency in operant conditioning is represented as a linear relation between the S^D, the response and the S^R. Thus, contingency relations between the elements are always depicted as forward, successive connections in time, and reinforcement is analyzed as having an effect on subsequent responding. No explicit analysis is provided of the functional properties involved in the contingency relation as such. Only the step-like occurrence of successive elements is taken into account.

In *Behavior of Organisms*, Skinner restricted his definition of behavior to those movements involving transactions with the environment. This was an attempt to differentiate the respondent type of covariation between responses and stimuli from the operant type. However, to the extent that responding became the dependent variable, response-stimulus relations, (i.e., the effect of responding on the environment) were not identified as the functional unit. Rather, these relations came to be regarded as operations allowing for an analysis of discontinuous stimulus effects on recurrent responses over time. As a result, practical analyses interpreted the "reinforcer" as a stimulus affecting subsequent responding, that is, as time-mediated S-R relationships in accordance with reflex tradition. This interpretation made it necessary to postulate a nonelicited character of emitted behavior, otherwise the reinforcer could not functionally substitute for the UCS of the respondent reflexive relation. This may explain why the operandum has never been conceptualized as a stimulus in the free operant situation. If the operandum were given the formal character of a stimulus then the operant relation would become a specific case of the second order type of law of the reflex, described as $R = F(S, A)$. Reinforcement would become one of the conditions affecting reflex strength but would be excluded as a defining property of the reflex itself.

This is not the only difficulty with the operant as a class of events in correlation, since by considering responses to be dependent variables, and reinforcers to be independent variables, it is not possible to define the class as a two-elements covariation. This is the case because the class must then be conceptualized as varying in accordance with the action of one of its own members. Reinforcers, as stimuli, cannot be conceptualized as both aspects of operants as well as conditions affecting the variations in strength and composition of the very same operants.

The noninteractive nature of the reflex paradigm is also observed in Skinner's analysis of verbal behavior. He points out that:

> "the behaviors of the speaker and listener taken together comprise what may be called a total verbal episode. There is nothing in such an episode which is more than the combined behavior of two or more individuals" (1957, p. 2).

However, the episode is isolated in two different segments, the behavior of the speaker and the behavior of the listener which are analyzed independently of each other. It is quite contradictory to assume that an analysis of an episode can take the form of separate accounts of the elements involved. An interaction as such can not be broken into pieces. The outcome of such a strategy, is that Skinner's *Verbal Behavior* does not embrace the essential property of language as behavior: its interactive character.

SHORTCOMINGS IN THE ANALYSIS OF HUMAN BEHAVIOR

Shortcomings in the analysis of human behavior have their origins in analyses of animal behavior studied in free operant situations, and before dealing with human behavior explicitly, it will be helpful to point out some of the inadequacies of analysis at the animal behavior level. Three sources of difficulty may be pointed out. First, even though the free operant situation of animal experimentation may be regarded as an extremely simplified experimental environment, the operant conditioning vocabulary is not extensive enough to describe the various kinds of events and conditions *operationally* taking place in that situation. In addition to the conceptual orphanage of the operandum, no conceptual description is provided of the interactive operant level (in fact it is never measured) or for the contextual factors involving organismic conditions (i.e., deprivation, drug administration, etc.) and the situational circumstances in the environment. These factors, which do not become a part of the "associative" process described by conditioning concepts, do play a role in the functional configuration of any particular interaction. Interactive history, and situational environmental and organismic factors act as setting variables, which not being discrete events, act as propensities or tendencies in the interaction. They operate as dispositional factors altering the probability of particular stimulus-response interactions. In summary, not only is there a conceptual gap in describing events and conditions taking place in the free operant situation, but the lack of appropriate terms for these events preempts a search for empirical relations that *do* participate in the situation.

Secondly, the three-term contingency relation prescribed by operant conditioning seems incomplete as a description of the actual mutual dependencies occurring in such situations. On one hand, contingencies account for occurrences of events in time, but not for the functional properties of those events. Thus, the S^D is a necessary condition if the S^R is to be presented when a response occurs. However, no dependency is *conceptually* specified among the properties of the S^D and the response with regard to the S^R and the response following the S^R. In fact, this last response, sometimes called the consumatory response, is virtually neglected in the description and exploration of the whole operant segment. The assumption appears to be that the "operant" response obtains its properties directly through its association with the reinforcer, or alternatively, that the response subsequent to the reinforcer presentation is just an instance of the operant class defined by a property of the experimentally measured and prescribed response.

Finally, something must be said in regard to the atomistic nature of the response definition. Two problems arise when experimental samples of interactions are assumed to be representative of behavior in general. One has to do with the fact that there are experimental phenomena which are difficult to reduce to the atomic type of descriptions and are thus unamenable to a description in terms of reinforcement as this term was originally defined. Instances of this problem are the "superstitions" patterns of responding discussed in Skinner's 1948 experiment, and the continuous, nondiscrete behaviors of wheel running, as in Morse and Skinner's 1958 experiment. A second problem concerns the punctuate, single-response in time, prescribed by free operant methodology. Even when two or more responses are analyzed, simultaneous interactions are not allowed in time. The atomic nature of the response-reinforcer relation requires non-contaminated independent relations, that tell us very little about actual interactions having a place in, for instance, simple concurrent schedules.

EPISODIC NATURE OF HUMAN INTERACTION. In examining the issue of human behavior, one general question arises from the problems just pointed out. The episodic character of most human behavior, as interaction with other individuals or with their behavioral outcomes, are hardly amenable to a description in terms of discrete events, in which the contingency relations end with a consequence to "the" speaker or behaver. Human interactions which inevitably involve substitutional processes (Kantor, 1977; Ribes, 1982) do not consist of atomic chunks linearly sequenced. Their episodic nature is difficult to reduce to a taxonomy such as the one developed in *Verbal Behavior* or to a synthesis of simple sequential components as proposed for social interactions (Skinner, 1962). The analysis of human behavior, in general, requires a set of categories able to describe situations involving (a) more than a single repetitive discrete response; (b) episodic interactions among two or more individuals; (c) functional properties not restricted to decreases or increases in response frequencies within a particular time period; (d) and reciprocal interactions that constitute the actual functional behavior segment. The categories derived from operant theory do not fulfill these requirements.

PRIVATE EVENTS. A second issue requiring reconceptualization concerns the topic of private events. This is a complex topic requiring an analysis beyond the scope of this paper; however, it may be instructive to pinpoint some of the problems arising when these events are interpreted in accordance with the paradigmatic influence of the reflex conception, as opposed to an interbehavioral, nonorganismic centered perspective.

The problem is that private events may become a "behavioral" surrogate of mental events. To refer to them as stimuli and responses does not prevent them from having mental status, as occurs in dualistic approaches. The reflex paradigm, because it originates in a dualistic philosophy, interferes, tacitly, with the possibility of a genuine behavioral analysis of these events. Kantor's (1973, 1981) discussion of privacy, as distinguished from internal or subjective worlds, has provided a general framework within which to deal with these events. Instead of reiterating Kantor's arguments here, we wish to stress the importance of approaching the problem from the standpoint of the behavioral genesis of so-called private events. From Skinner's (1945, 1953, 1957) perspective, the central issue to be addressed in this context concerns the characteristics of verbal responses to private events. Privacy gives rise to two problems. First, unlike the case for public stimuli, we cannot account for verbal responses to private stimuli by pointing to their controlling stimuli. Secondly, we must address the problem of how the verbal community achieves the necessary contingencies of reinforcement to bring about the acquisition and maintenance of verbal responses to private stimuli. In other words, the problem lies in how the individual is taught to be controlled by already existing physical, nonobservable, internal stimuli, arising from within the body. Skinner's solution to the problem is summarized in four tactics of reinforcement used by the verbal community: (a) identifying previously overt responses from which present covert responding to private stimuli have been derived; (b) identifying regular public accompaniments of the response to the private stimulus; (c) identifying collateral public responses to the same stimulus; and (d) stimulus induction.

However, the questions to raise are: How is it possible to postulate private stimuli without implying an internal world described by the person according to conventional language? How is it possible to formulate a description in terms other than that of recognition or expression of an internal world, or as it is usually phrased, of other minds? To call this internal world "private stimuli" does not depart from a dualistic world view at all. From an interactive standpoint, the dichotomy of private and public stimuli and responses has no meaning. Interactions between organism and environment embrace the organism as a whole. Essentially, what Skinner is doing in this regard is giving biological events, which are really responses or organismic states, the status of stimuli. The implication of this suggestion is that the individual is also possessed of an additional reactional system, consisting of responding to self-produced stimuli. However, what are these self-produced stimuli? Are they the biological events that continuously take place within the organism? We think not. Private events are really the linguistic responses of persons to conditions similar to those prevailing in their interactions with other persons. Linguistic responses refer to conditions affecting the individual, and to the extent that the stimulus products of these responses are accessible to this individual alone, they may be regarded as private stimuli. However, from this perspective, private stimuli are simply the products of linguistic responding, they are not internal biological states or responses. For example, when I talk about my toothache, the private event is not the ache or the physical process involved in the tooth alteration, but the fact that I do react to such a biological event in a conventional manner. In short, private events are stimuli produced by linguistic responding, not internal biological events.

To the extent that the referential function of linguistic behavior depends on the specific set of interactions which substitutes for concrete event contacts in a particular culture, we may assume that private events, in the sense that they are linguistic events, will be different in different cultures, and that this will be the case irrespective of the fact that the biological events in individuals across cultures remain the same. The problem of private events, as the idiosyncratic or individual character of personal reactional systems integration (individual differences), concerns how cultural institutions, to the extent that they prescribe the classes of interaction among individuals prescribe also the kind of individual interactions amenable to reference by conventional responding in the form of linguistic behavior. "Subjectivity" or "privacy," in this framework, is a consequence of linguistic interactions among individuals. Traditional views raise the obverse problem, that is, how language is associated with prevailing private events.

FINAL COMMENTS

We have tried to emphasize the fact that many of the present problems associated with operant theory are not possible of resolution by way of empirical investigation, or in the correspondence between particular concepts or hypotheses and data. On the contrary, it is the nature of the subject matter of behavior science as articulated by operant conditioners and the congruence of the conceptual paradigm with this subject matter, that is the source of the difficulty. No real progress may be achieved in science, if the fundamentals are not periodically revisited, to check out the correspondence between what we do and the tacit or embedded assumptions orienting our work.

The possibility of reconsidering operant conditioning theory as a nonlegitimate behavioral model, takes us to many other problems, that should be dealt with in depth, including: the notion of explanation as cause-effect or functional relationships versus interdependent field functions; the need for adequate observational and descriptive categories of behavior interactions; the monistic or algebraic interaction two-processes theory of behavior versus a hierarchical, nonhorizontal theory of processes, stressing inclusion and not exclusion of processes; the distinction between operations and true processes; the relation of a process theory with a genetic theory of individual and species development; and the relation between scientific theory and technology as extrapolation or as adaptation of knowledge.

To begin this analysis means at least to reject the possibility that a science of behavior already has the solutions required for a thorough understanding of its subject matter. Science, on the contrary, never raises solutions, but always new questions. It is the only way to depart from dogma.

Reference Notes

Ribes, E. Language and Symbolic Behaviors as Contingency Substitutional Processes. Read in the First Biannual Symposium on the Science of Behavior, National University of Mexico at Iztacala, February, 1982.

Shimp, C. Conceptual Interrelations between Language and Animal Learning Memory and Attention. Read in the First Biannual Symposium on the Science of Behavior, National University of Mexico at Iztacala, February, 1982.

REFERENCES

Bechterew, W. von. Objektive Psychologie oder Psychoreflexologie. Leipzig, 1913.

Kantor, J. R. Private data, raw feels, inner experience, and all that. *The Psychological Record*, 1973, *23*, 563-565.

Kantor, J. R. *Psychological Linguistics*. Chicago: Principia Press, 1977.

Kantor, J. R. Concerning the Principle of Psychological Privacy. *The Psychological Record*, 1981, *31*, 101-106.

Kuhn, T. *La estructura de las Revoluciones Científicas*. Mexico: Fondo de Cultura Económica, 1971.

Schoenfeld, W. N. The "Response" in Behavior Theory. *Pavlovia Journal*, 1976, *11*, 129-149.

Sechenov, I. *Los Reflejos del Cerebro*. Barcelona: Gontanella, 1978 (Spanish translation).

Skinner, B. F. The concept of Reflex in the description of Behavior. *Journal of General Psychology*. 1931, *5*, 427-458.

Skinner, B. F. The Generic Nature of the Concepts of Stimulus and Response. *Journal of General Psychology*, 1935, *12*, 40-65.

Skinner, B. F. *The Behavior of Organisms*. N.Y.: Appleton Century Crofts, 1938.

Skinner, B. F. "Superstition" in the Pigeon. The Journal of Experimental Psychology, 1948, *38*, 168-172.

Skinner, B. F. *Science and Human Behavior*. N.Y.: MacMillan, 1953.

Skinner, B. F. *Verbal Behavior*. N.Y.: Appleton Century Crofts, 1957.

Skinner, B. F. and Morse, W.F. Fixed interval reinforcement of running in a wheel. *Journal of the Experimental Analysis of Behavior*. 1958, *1*, 371-379.

Skinner, B. F. *Cumulative Record*. N.Y.: Appleton Century Crofts, 1959.

Skinner, B. F. Two "Social Synthetic Relations". *Journal of the Experimental Analysis of Behavior*, 1962, *5*, 531-533.

Commentary on RIBES'S PAPER

Hayne W. Reese

RIBES ARGUES that operant conditioning principles cannot provide a sufficient analysis of human behavior, defining sufficiency in terms of philosophical adequacy as well as empirical success. He does not argue against the empirical success of the analysis of human behavior; rather, he argues that because operant conditioning principles are based on Cartesian mechanics, they cannot provide a philosophically adequate analysis of human behavior. Three questions about Ribes's argument are addressed in this commentary: Is philosophical adequacy a legitimate criterion for evaluation of a scientific analysis? Are operant conditioning principles based on Cartesian mechanics? Is the use of these principles for the analysis of human behavior based on Cartesian mechanics? These questions are hierarchically related in the order given, and any later question in the series is meaningful only if the prior questions are answered affirmatively. Obviously, then, I agree with Ribes on the first two questions and, as one might infer, I disagree with him on the last question.

IS PHILOSOPHICAL ADEQUACY REQUIRED?

Wicksteed and Cornford remarked, in their translation of Aristotle's *Physics*, "it has been said of the 'Ancients' at large that 'they said everything, but proved nothing'" (Wicksteed & Cornford, 1929, p. xix). Along the same line, my father once characterized psychology as the science of proving what everybody already knew, which is reminiscent of George Bernard Shaw's comment, "Pavlov is the biggest fool I know; any policeman could tell you that much about a dog" (quoted in Payne, 1968, p. 16). However, without the proving, what the Ancients said and what everybody already knew was not *science*. (A further point, not relevant here, is that knowledge in psychology has in fact gone well beyond what the Ancients said and what everybody already knew, as Skinner [1974, p. 232] noted.)

Knowledge without proof is still knowledge, but it is not scientific knowledge. In fact, knowledge *with* proof is not scientific unless the proof meets two criteria. One criterion is methodological and the other is theoretical. Before these criteria are considered, a preliminary point is that "proof" is used here not in the sense of definite confirmation that a purported fact is true (or, worded more precisely, definite confirmation that a statement about a purported fact is true); rather, "proof" is used here in the sense of a test, or a judicious examination of a purported fact.

The *methodological criterion* refers to the source of the knowledge. For example, the source of commonsense knowledge is everyday experience, the source of literary knowledge is intuition, and the source of religious knowledge is revelation. The source of scientific knowledge is application of a scientific method. Different methods are employed in different sciences, but all scientific methods are basically the same in that they require careful observation of phenomena under known conditions. However, careful observation of phenomena under known conditions yields facts, or information, but in its fullest sense knowledge refers to understanding as well as information — knowing why as well as knowing what. Therefore, the information obtained by careful observation under known conditions needs to be interpreted or explained. In short, then, knowledge is scientific if it has the empirical proof given by use of a scientific method and the theoretical proof given by adequate interpretation or explanation.

An interpretation or explanation is adequate if it meets the *theoretical criterion* of scientific knowledge: The formulation of the interpretation or explanation must be consistent with an adequate cosmology (for rationales of this criterion, see Kuhn, 1970, chap. 2; Lakatos, 1978, pp. 47-52; Laudan, 1977, pp. 78-81; Overton & Reese, 1973; Pepper, 1942, chap. 4 and 5; Reese & Overton, 1970). Cosmologies are also called ontologies, paradigms, presuppositions, world hypotheses, world views and weltanschauungen, which means "world views." (In Langenscheidt's German-English dictionary [1970, p. 309], the meaning of *Weltanschauung* is given as "Weltanschauung".) Several adequate cosmologies are available. They do not, however, provide alternative approaches to the scientific collection of facts, which always involves careful observation under known conditions; rather, they provide alternative approaches to the interpretation or explanation of facts (Overton & Reese, 1973; Pepper, 1942). For this function, a cosmology is *adequate* if it has reasonably wide scope and reasonable precision. The scope of a cosmology is the range of facts that can be interpreted or explained within its confines; the precision of a cosmology is the extent to which its confines limit possible interpretations or explanations—a perfectly precise cosmology would generate one and only one interpretation or explanation for each fact within its scope.

The adequate cosmologies encountered most often in psychology are mechanism, contextualism, and organicism. Mechanism reflects Cartesian or, alternatively, Newtonian mechanics; contextualism reflects further development of American pragmatism; and organicism reflects Hegelian idealism (for discussion of these cosmologies, see Pepper, 1942). Examples are, respectively, Hull-Spence learning theory, Tolman's purposive behaviorism (Pepper, 1934), and Piaget's "genetic epistemology."

The point is that philosphical adequacy is required of scientific knowledge, and several different cosmologies are available to provide this adequacy.

ARE OPERANT CONDITIONING PRINCIPLES MECHANISTIC?

From the viewpoint of the foregoing considerations, the principles of operant conditioning are seen to be interpretations of certain facts. These facts were obtained by careful observation under known conditions; therefore, the principles have the required methodological proof. The interpretations are consistent with Cartesian mechanics, according to Ribes; if so, then because this is one of the adequate cosmologies, the principles of operant conditioning also have the required theoretical proof and consequently they qualify as scientific knowledge.

In Cartesian mechanics a system (or whole) consists of elements and their interrelations and is completely determined by (derivable from) these parts. A part as such cannot change qualitatively but can change quantitatively in location and in direction and speed of movement. Quantitative changes result from forces that are external to a part as such but that are contiguous with the part (because forces cannot act over a distance in this cosmology). Given the relevant laws and the state of the system at any moment, any future state can be predicted and any past state can be postdicted. (Heisenberg's principle of indeterminacy does not contradict this cosmological tenet of determinacy, it only makes the tenet untestable.)

This cosmology is reflected in the "push-pull" psychology of stimulus-response learning theory (Skinner, 1974, p. 6) and in the behavior analytic interpretation of respondent behavior. In the mechanistic cosmology the "push-pull" concept means that forces determine movement, the nature of which depends on the state of the system in which the force is applied. All behavior (according to stimulus-response learning theory) or respondent behavior (according to behavior analysis) is controlled by some antecedent stimulus, either as a result of genetically determined mechanisms or as a result of a particular history of contiguous presentations of two stimuli (the CS and UCS). However, current deprivation interacts with the genetic mechanisms and the history of stimulus presentations to determine the response. Thus, the antecedent stimulus is analogous to force; the respondent behavior is analogous to movement; and the genetic mechanisms and history of stimulus presentations, together with current deprivation, are analogous to the state of the system. The respondent system, then, is consistent with the mechanistic cosmology.

The principles of operant conditioning refer to a three-term contingency (antecedent stimulus — operant behavior — consequent stimulus) that is actualized concretely in a concrete setting. Operant behavior is said to be controlled by its consequences, and to be "by its nature . . . directed toward the future: a person acts *in order that* something will happen, and the order is temporal" (Skinner, 1974, p. 55; see also Bijou & Baer, 1978, p. 11). However, if the consequences are truly in the future, the operant system is consistent with a teleological purposivism. Behavior analysts consistently reject teleology; therefore, a better way to describe operant behavior is to say that it is controlled by antecedent stimuli as a result of a particular history of contingent presentation of reinforcing and/or punishing stimuli. The "purposivism" of operant behavior is merely a reference to this history (Skinner, 1974, pp. 56-57).

To be complete, the description needs to include definitions of the reinforcing and punishing functions, which in turn involve statements about deprivation. The standard functional definitions of effective contingent stimuli refer to whether the contingency is presentation or withdrawal and whether the consequence is an increase or a decrease in the (future) rate of the consequated behavior. Bijou and Baer (1978) noted that no other kind of observation is necessary or sufficient for the reinforcing/punishing functions (p. 46); but they also noted that these functions depend on deprivation — a stimulus can function as a reinforcer only if the subject has been deprived of the stimulus (pp. 93, 99, 103; see also Krapfl, 1977).

The operant system is consistent with the mechanistic cosmology in that the analogue of force is antecedent stimulation; the analogue of movement is operant behavior; and the analogue of the state of the system is the history of contingent stimulation, together with current deprivation. (The analogies are not the same for the operant and respondent systems, but the differences make no difference at the cosmological level because the analogue of force, for example, is not conceptualized as a *force* but as an analogue of force, that is, it is something in the system of interest that has a role like that of force in the mechanical system.)

Bijou (1979) argued that behavior analysis is not mechanistic because the reactive-organism model is rejected, along with other tenets, in favor of an active-organism model. In fact, however, the operant organism is reactive. A detailed discussion of the issue has been presented elsewhere (Baltes & Reese, 1977); the most relevant point here is that in the operant system the organism is the "source" of behaviors (Bijou & Baer, 1978, p. 26), or is the "host" of behaviors (Baer, 1976), but is not a "seeker of stimulation" (Bijou & Baer, 1978, p. 29), not a "true originator or initiator of action" (Skinner, 1974, p. 225; see also Skinner 1957, chap. 12).

In short, the principles of operant conditioning can be understood as mechanistic interpretations of the facts of operant conditioning. (They may also be understandable from the viewpoints of other adequate cosmologies. This issue is not considered herein because it is not directly relevant and anyway the required analyses have not been done.)

IS HUMAN BEHAVIOR ANALYSIS MECHANISTIC?

Although the principles of operant conditioning are mechanistic and are used in the analysis of human behavior, the analysis of human behavior is not necessarily mechanistic. Behavior analysis is not merely a scientific method, it is a scientific system. A scientific system includes a body of knowledge and the methodology and cosmology that provide the proof of the knowledge (Bergmann, 1956; Laudan, 1977, pp. 78-81; White, 1977). As such a system, behavior analysis includes the principles of conditioning, among other knowledge, operant-conditioning and other behavior-analysis procedures, and a cosmology. The question is whether this cosmology is mechanistic.

Skinner (1938) said, "A science of behavior cannot be closely patterned after geometry of Newtonian mechanics because its problems are not necessarily of the same sort" (p. 437). Presumably, he would have ruled out Cartesian mechanics as well. (In the same chapter, Skinner said that his system is "mechanistic," but he specified "in the sense of implying a fundamental lawfulness or order in the behavior of organisms" [p. 433]. This sense can be accommodated to contextualism.) He did not identify which cosmology would serve, but he noted that "Tolman has presented a system which is in many respects close to that described here" (p. 437). Tolman's system is consistent with pragmatism, or contextualism (Pepper, 1934), and therefore one might surmise that behavior analysis has at least an affinity to pragmatism. According to Day (1977) and Mapel (1977), Skinner's system is pragmatic. Mapel examined the six criteria used by Skinner (1974, pp. 214-217) to evaluate the relative merits of radical behaviorism and mentalism, and concluded that the criteria are pragmatic. Also, Skinner (1974) has cited, with evident approval, "an old principle that nothing is different until it makes a difference" (p. 31), which is the pragmatic truth criterion. As William James said, "There can *be* no difference anywhere that does not *make* a difference elsewhere—no difference in abstract truth that does not express itself in a difference in concrete fact and in conduct consequent upon that fact, imposed on somebody, somehow, somewhere, and somewhen" (James, 1907, pp. 49-50). This seems to be the "special sense" alluded to by Skinner (1974) when he said, "There is a special sense in which [scientific knowledge] could be 'true' if it yields the most effective action possible. . . . A proposition is 'true' to the extent that with its help the listener responds effectively to the situation it describes" (p. 235).

The mechanistic truth criterion is correspondence (or a refinement of correspondence—Pepper, 1942, pp. 221-231): the facts as described correspond to the real facts as they exist in the real world. The pragmatic truth criterion is successful working (or refinement of successful working—Pepper, 1942, pp. 268-279): the facts as described (or hypothesized) yield success in an enterprise of interest, which in behavior analysis is the prediction and control of behavior.

One might argue that if a scientific enterprise is successful, it is so because the facts as described correspond to the real facts, and that therefore the behavior analytic truth criterion is mechanistic after all. However, this argument goes beyond the successful prediction and control of behavior, and beyond what behavior analysts actually do. For example, knowing an organism's history of contingencies aids in predicting and controlling the organism's behavior, but positing a physiological trace of the history would be contrary to the principles of behavior analysis because (a) such a positing is reductionistic and (b) it adds nothing to the prediction and control of behavior (Skinner, 1984, p. 949).

On the basis of its own ground rule regarding truth, the use of operant conditioning principles in the analysis of human behavior must be judged on how successful it has been in the prediction and control of behavior. It has been extremely successful in basic as well as applied domains (e.g., as shown in many of the reports in Etzel, LeBlanc, & Baer, 1977; Lattal, 1984; Parrott & Reese, 1985; and the present volume). Therefore, the conclusion must be that operant conditioning has been sufficient to cope with much human behavior. Whether it will be sufficient to cope with *all* human behavior remains to be seen, but nothing in the approach *precludes* success.

REFERENCES

Baer, D. M. (1976). The organism as host. In H. W. Reese (Ed.), Conceptions of the 'active organism' (pp. 87-98). *Human Development, 19,* 69-119.

Baltes, M. M., & Reese, H. W. (1977). Operant research and operant paradigm: Contradictions are apparent but not real. In B. C. Etzel, J. M. LeBlanc, & D. M. Baer (Eds.), *New developments in behavioral reseach: Theory, methods, and application. In honor of Sidney W. Bijou* (pp. 11-30). Hillsdale, NJ: Erlbaum.

Bergmann, G. (1956). The contribution of John B. Watson. *Psychological Review, 63,* 265-276.

Bijou, S. W. (1979) Some clarifications on the meaning of a behavior analysis of child development. *Psychological Record, 29,* 3-13.

Bijou, S. W., & Baer, D. M. (1978). *Behavior analysis of child development.* Englewood Cliffs, NJ: Prentice-Hall.

Day, W. F. (1977). On Skinner's treatment of the first-person, third-person psychological sentence distinction. *Behaviorism, 5*(1), 33-37.

Etzel, B. C., LeBlanc, J. M., & Baer, D. M. (Eds.). (1977). *New developments in behavioral research: Theory, methods, and application. In honor of Sidney W. Bijou.* Hillsdale, NJ: Erlbaum.

Krapfl, J. E. (1977). Dialectics and operant psychology. In N. Datan & H. W. Reese (Eds.), *Life-span developmental psychology: Dialectical perspectives on experimental research* (pp. 295-310). New York: Academic Press.

Kuhn, T. S. (1970). *The structure of scientific revolutions* (2nd ed.). *International Encyclopedia of United Science, 2* (No. 2). Chicago: University of Chicago Press.

Lakatos, I. (1978). *The methodology of scientific research programmes.* In I. Lakatos, *Philosophical papers* (Vol. 1; J. Worrall & G. Currie, Eds.). Cambridge: Cambridge University Press.

Langenscheidt's German-English English-German dictionary (rev. ed.). (1970). New York: Pocket Books.

Lattal, K. A., & Harzem, P. (1984). Future directions for the experimental analysis of behavior. *Journal of the Experimental Analysis of Behavior* (in press).

Laudan, L. (1977). *Progress and its problems: Toward a theory of scientific growth.* Berkeley: University of California Press.

Mapel, B. M. (1977). Philosophical criticism of behaviorism: An analysis. *Behaviorism, 5*(1), 17-32.

Overton, W. F., & Reese, H. W. (1973). Models of development: Methodological implications. In J. R. Nesselroade & H. W. Reese (eds.), *Life-span developmental psychology: Methodological issues* (pp. 65-86). New York: Academic Press.

Parrott, L. J., & Reese, H. W. (Eds.). (In press). *Advances in behavior science.* Hillsdale, NJ: Erlbaum.

Payne, T. R. (1968). *S. L. Rubinštejn and the philosophical foundations of Soviet psychology.* Dordrecht, Holland: Reidel.

Pepper, S. C. (1934). The conceptual framework of Tolman's purposive behaviorism. *Psychological Review, 41,* 108-133.

Pepper, S. C. (1942). *World Hypotheses: A study in evidence.* Berkeley: University of California Press.

Reese, H. W., & Overton, W. F. (1970). Models of development and theories of development. In L. R. Goulet & P. B. Baltes (Eds.), *Life-span developmental psychology: Research and theory* (pp. 115-145). New York: Academic Press.

Skinner, B. F. (1938). *The behavior of organisms: An experimental analysis.* New York: Appleton-Century-Crofts.

Skinner, B. F. (1957). *Verbal behavior.* New York: Appleton-Century-Crofts.

Skinner, B. F. (1974). *About behaviorism.* New York: Knopf.

Skinner, B. F. (1984). The shame of American education. *American Psychologist, 39,* 947-954.

White, S. H. (1977). Social proof structures: The dialectic of method and theory in the work of psychology. In N. Datan & H. W. Reese (Eds.), *Life-span developmental psychology: Dialectical perspectives on experimental research* (pp. 59-92). New York: Academic Press.

Wicksteed, P. H., & Cornford, F. M. (1929). General introduction. In Aristotle, *The physics* (P. H. Wicksteed & F. M. Cornford, Trans.; Vol. 1, pp. xv-xc). London: Heinemann.

Section Two
REFINEMENTS OF KEY LANGUAGE EVENTS

Chapter Four

ON THE DIFFERENCES BETWEEN VERBAL AND SOCIAL BEHAVIORS

LINDA J. PARROTT

VERBAL AND SOCIAL behaviors are two closely related psychological phenomena which have not been adequately identified or differentiated by behavior analysts up to this point. The aim of this paper is to further clarify the character of these events such that the scientific operations of prediction and control may be applied to them more fruitfully than in the past. Before doing so, however, it is necessary to examine the nature and role of defining operations and their products in science, and it is in this exposition that the logic of the present attempt to construct more adequate definitions of verbal and social behaviors may be understood.

THE NATURE AND ROLE OF DEFINING OPERATIONS AND THEIR PRODUCTS

Scientific definitions are verbal constructions articulated for the purpose of isolating the events of interest to particular investigators, and their articulation thereby serves to focus investigative efforts on the unique character of particular events and their points of departure from other events. When satisfactory definitions are lacking, events involving different factors tend to be approached as though they were instances of the same general type of event, and manipulative investigations into their nature and operation turn up anomalies and contradictory findings. Additional investigations may ameliorate this situation and are, in fact, widely held to be the only means by which valid scientific definitions are both originally constructed as well as undergo change. The assumptions upon which this belief rests are that events are best isolated and defined on the basis of their operations with respect to other events, and that these operations are more likely to become apparent through manipulative contacts with events than by way of any other less intrusive mode of investigation.

Process Analysis

Scientific definitions constructed in accordance with these assumptions and by this procedure, are sometimes called "functional definitions," although this may be a misnomer. A functional definition of this type is one which identifies an event by reference to its role in the transformation of event fields from one in which the event of interest is a participant to one in which it is not. For example, reinforcement is defined as a response-produced stimulus change which has the effect of bringing about the recurrence of the productive response, given an opportunity afforded by the recurrence of original setting conditions, and irrespective of its own recurrence. Definitions of this sort depict processes of change in event fields, and the character of the postchange field is taken to be the means by which the nature of the process is identified. That is, processes are identified by their effects.

The products of process analysis, namely an understanding of the means by which event fields are transformed, give rise to the scientific goals of prediction and control. If we know that particular configurations of events have eventuated in outcomes of a known sort, then it is possible to predict the outcomes of similar configurations were they to occur. Further, by deliberately manipulating events such that they resemble prechange configurations having known outcomes, we may actually bring about those outcomes. That is, we may control the occurrence of particular events.

It is this ability of scientists to predict and control the transformations of event fields that give rise to the claim that the definitions of events derived by this means are functional in character. The constructional procedure involves dividing salient field factors into two types: those that bring about transformations and those that are present when transformations are complete. The latter, which in behavior science are always response events, are held to be a function of the former, which, in turn, are always stimulus events (including the stimulus products of prior responding.) Because "to be a function of," as here conceived, can only be interpreted as "to be an effect of," we may assume that the role of stimulus events in event field transformations is regarded as causal. This assumption is made explicit by Skinner (1953, p. 23) in his suggestion that a "cause-and-effect connection" is essentially synonymous with a "functional relation." The outcome of this procedure and this hypothesis concerning the nature of functionality, is to define response events in terms of their stimulational causes. For example, a set of contingencies (i.e., causal variables) defines an operant (Skinner, 1969, p. 131). Likewise, a verbal operant is defined in terms of the manner in which a particular causal variable, reinforcement, is brought into play (i.e., through the mediation of another person) (Skinner, 1957, p. 2).

A causal interpretation of the nature of functionality, as is characteristic of scientific enterprises working toward goals of prediction and control, is not without technical value: It is the basis of an applied science. Still, however, a causal interpretation of functionality is not warranted in theory, and to confuse the conventions required of technical application with an understanding of the nature of events as they are observed to occur may serve to hinder the progress of science. From a theoretical perspective, a functional relation is merely a commutative relation, implying the absolute equivalence of variants and no existential or causal dependence or independence (Kantor, 1970).

Pattern Analysis

One implication of a commutative interpretation of functionality is that functional definitions may be constructed without reference to the contributions of particular salient factors in the transformations of event fields. Indeed, the defining characteristics of a given event are not exhausted in such descriptions. Missing are descriptions of the broader range of factors participating in a given event at a particular point in time, as well as their pattern or organization. For those inclined toward process analysis, a pattern analysis of this sort may appear to have a structural as opposed to a functional character, as though it were the aim of such analyses to merely enumerate the factors present in a given field without regard to their interrelations. This is not, of course, the aim of such attempts at definition. Rather, it is assumed from the outset that all factors present in a given event field *participate* in that field, and that this participation is a functional, not a structural affair. The misunderstanding here stems from the causal interpretation of functionality underlying efforts to analyze processes, which a pattern analysis does not presuppose. The difference is one of focus, not function. Process analyses focus on the evolution of event fields, while pattern analyses focus on the configurations of interdependent factors participating in given event fields.

To deny the functional character of definitions derived from descriptions of the large number of factors participating in the occurrence of events is to confuse the events as they are observed to occur with our technical operations with respect to them. To reiterate, a causal interpretation of the concept of functionality is simply a convenient way of expressing relations among events for the purpose of predicting and controlling their occurrence. Causality is a convention adopted out of technological considerations; it is not a property of confrontable events nor of the relations sustained among them. As such, functional definitions are not the products of manipulative operations exclusively. When the functional interdependence of factors present in a given event field is assumed, a description of those factors and their pattern or organization constitutes a functional definition of that event.

It is not my intention to suggest that pattern analyses are always more adequate or more profitable as defining operations than are process analyses. On the contrary, they are complementary operations, both of them relevant to an understanding of events. It *is* my intention to suggest that pattern analyses are more fruitful as preliminary attempts at definition than are process analyses. This is the case because pattern analyses are made in the absence of manipulative contacts with events and, as such, allow for consideration of a broader range of simultaneously participating factors, both as they are configured in the unique instance as well as in the class of events of which that instance may be regarded a member. Once preliminary event definitions have been constructed by this means, the role of particular factors in the transformations of event fields may be assessed through a variety of manipulative contacts with them. These contacts have the effect of refining the original definitions of events for practical purposes, and this is, in fact their proper role in the scientific enterprise as a whole.

Hence, it is my aim in this essay to differentiate between verbal and social behaviors, not on the basis of the contributions of particular salient factors in the transformations of event fields of these types, but rather on the basis of the factors participating in their occurrence at a given time.

VERBAL AND SOCIAL BEHAVIOR

Having completed an account of the nature and role of defining operations and their products, we may now employ these operations in the construction of satisfactory definitions of verbal and social behaviors.

Why Adequate Definitions Are Lacking

Social and verbal event fields share a number of common factors, resulting in their being approached as though they were the same type of event. Significant in this regard is the presence of at least two persons in some form of perceptual contact. In other words, social as well as verbal behaviors typically involve the activities of two persons with respect to one another, and this similarity may have been a source of confusion. In addition, because the circumstances giving rise to both forms of behavior are concurrently or in close temporal proximity, the task of distinguishing one from the other may have been further complicated. Other similarities are to be found in the contributions of common factors in the transformations of event fields. In both cases each person may be regarded as a source of stimulation for the other and the consequences of responding for each tend to be mediated by the activities of the other. Likewise topographical features of responding do not provide a basis for their differentiation, since verbal behavior may be executed with the same musculature and have roughly the same form as social behavior, and vice versa.

It is very probable that the inadequacy of preliminary attempts at differentiating social from verbal behavior may be traced to one or the other or all of these similarities between them. These similarities cannot be regarded as solely responsible for the failure of more satisfactory definitions to have been developed, though. After all, continued contact with events of these types may be expected to result in finer discriminations with regard to their differences, and there has been no shortage of contact. Nonetheless, substantial refinements in the definitions of these events have not been made. They remain essentially unchanged from those originally proposed by B. F. Skinner (1953, 1957) some thirty years ago.

We must attempt, then, to account for the failure of satisfactory definitions to emerge by reference to factors other than those inherent in the events themselves. In doing so it is helpful to consider the influences of our verbal constructions about events upon our observations of them. It is a well known fact that our observations of events comport with our descriptions of them and this comportment is as much a product of our descriptions as it is our observations. In other words, what we see is as much a product of what we expect to see as the other way around. When what we expect to see becomes formalized as the definition for a particular type of event, the influence of our expectations upon our observations is intensified. Definitions circumscribe observations and provide an exclusive focus for investigative contacts. As such, the broader range of factors participating in event fields, and through consideration of which definitions might be altered or modified, are legislated out of consideration. This is the case irrespective of the adequacy of a particular definition, and it is not a situation that may be avoided if events are to be approached in a scientific manner. Neither is it *necessarily* a hindrance, since there is no other way to proceed. Still, it points to the influence of our verbal constructions upon our observations and suggests that when these constructions *are* in need of refinement they may be exerting a harmful influence from the standpoint of scientific progress.

It is quite possible that our preliminary definitions of verbal and social behaviors are having such an influence. That is, they may be serving to thwart the development of more satisfactory definitions. In short, not only are verbal and social behaviors inherently similar enough to create confusion, our preliminary definitions of these events may be having the effect of obscuring their differences even further, with the result that more satisfactory definitions have no observational basis upon which to be constructed. In other words, the differences between events of these types are not being observed, and as such they do not provide a basis for the refinement of the definitions of these events.

When observations of differences between events are lacking, it is possible to make these differences more salient by the very means by which they were originally obscured. That is, one may construct differences verbally, formalize these constructions into definitions of events, and then reapproach the events of interest armed with these new definitions. If the definitions are proper ones, which is to say, if the differences to which they point are to be found among the events, we may conclude that progress has been made. It is in accordance with this plan that we proceed in the following sections of this paper.

Similarities Between Verbal and Social Behaviors

Verbal and social behaviors are similar in many respects, as previously indicated. Obviously, these similarities do not provide a basis for the differentiation of these two classes of events. Still, features shared in common by these classes may serve as criteria for distinguishing them from events involving neither verbal nor social behavior; and further, in attempting to establish criteria by which verbal and social behaviors may be unambiguously distinguished, it is necessary to first rule out of consideration their similarities. It is the purpose of this section, then, to enumerate and describe the ways in which verbal and social behaviors are alike.

INTERPERSONAL ADJUSTMENTS. Verbal as well as social behaviors typically occur in circumstances involving more than one person. As Skinner (1957, p. 2) has pointed out, verbal behavior is reinforced through the mediation of one another person, without whom it would have no effect on the environment and would most certainly cease to occur. Likewise, social behavior is widely assumed to involve more than one person, in fact, it is the interpersonal character of such behavior that gives this class the name "social." On the contrary, behavioral events of other sorts may readily occur in the absence of other persons.

Nonetheless, it is clear that we frequently engage in verbal behavior when no one else is present. Reading and writing occur while alone, and we often talk to ourselves. Social behavior, on the other hand, appears to *require* another person for its execution. We don't hug ourselves or hold hands with ourselves, and we don't play tennis alone. (At least if we do, we are unlikely to call the occurrence an instance of social behavior.) The notion that social behavior necessitates the involvement of at least two persons in the physical presence of one another, while verbal behavior does not, appears to establish a criterion upon which these two classes of events may be differentiated. This criterion is a spurious one, however, arising from a failure to distinguish between stimulation and sources of stimulation. In Kantor's (1924) terms, it indicates a confusion of stimulus functions with stimulus objects. Persons are objects, not functions, and objects are of no immediate psychological interest. What *is* of interest is the stimulation arising from person-sources, and whether or not it is transferable to inanimate objects. In short, the physical presence of a second person is not required for an instance of social behavior, provided that stimulus functions having their origins in second person sources continue to operate through their attachment to other objects. Moreover, this is precisely how and why *verbal* behavior occurs in the absence of a listener. In summary, while both verbal and social behavior typically occur under circumstances involving more than one person, both may also occur in the absence of another person so long as the stimulational properties of another person inhere in an inanimate object present at the time of occurrence of these events. (For a more detailed discussion of these issues, see Parrott, 1983.)

INTERPERSONAL ORIGINS. While neither social nor verbal behavior require the participation of another person for its continued execution, both are unquestionably products of circumstances involving more than one person. That is, neither would be acquired under conditions of life-long solitary living, nor would it be possible to execute these behaviors in the absence of another person had they not originally been performed under interpersonal conditions. With regard to the latter issue, it is only because inanimate objects have accompanied, resembled, or existed in some other significant relationship with respect to other persons that they are able to acquire the stimulational properties of those persons. With regard to the former issue, namely conditions of acquisition, lifelong solitude, if such were even possible, provides no opportunity for the acquisition of social behavior and no reason for the acquisition of verbal behavior. In addition, verbal behavior has other characteristics which would make its development under such conditions impossible, to which characteristics we will turn momentarily.

The fact that both verbal and social behaviors are originally acquired under interpersonal conditions does not unambiguously distinguish these classes from other classes of behavior, however. While it is possible that some form of ambulation, self-stimulation, ingestion, elimination, and other activities closely related to biological maintenance and survival would occur under conditions of total isolation, most of what we do of a nonverbal and nonsocial sort as adults would not be acquired under such conditions. This is not because these activities require another person for their execution (i.e., another person is not a necessary participant in their occurrence), but rather because our activities as adults are complex coordinations of simpler forms of responding that are organized through the guidance and instruction of other persons. Other persons are thereby necessary for the acquisition of such activities, but they are not participating factors in the eventual occurrence of such activities. This distinction is subtle, subject to controversy with regard to the issue of participation, and probably not worthy of further comment.

VARIABILITY OF RESPONDING. Because neither verbal nor social behavior require the participation of another person for their execution, these behaviors do not always exemplify reciprocal exchanges among persons. Still, however, when two persons are involved in a reciprocal exchange of either sort, a great deal of variability in response forms is introduced, and this variability is of a sufficient degree to distinguish these classes of events from other classes. This variability is the product of two circumstances. In the first place, persons are sources of a larger number of stimulational functions than are inanimate objects. That is, our repertoires with respect to inanimate objects are far more limited than are those coordinated with animate objects. This difference is not entirely a matter of animation, since some inanimate objects may have rapidly changing characteristics and, as a result, may be endowed with an unusually large number of stimulational functions. A computer is an object of this sort, at least for particular persons. In general, however, animate objects are sources of more stimulational functions than are inanimate objects. Consequently, responding with respect to stimulation arising from animate sources is more variable than that arising from inanimate sources. Moreover, because of the phenomenon of stimulus generalization (or stimulus function transfer), the enormity of our repertoires with respect to any particular person does not depend on that person currently or ever having responded with respect to us as stimuli. In other words, persons are sources of a greater number of stimulational properties than are inanimate objects even when there is no mutuality of stimulating and responding at a given moment.

A second source of variability in responding is introduced when a mutuality of stimulating and responding does prevail, however, as is the case in reciprocal exchanges between two persons. To illustrate this point, we must examine the means by which functional relations undergo change and development.

Change and development in functional relations occur as a consequence of subtle variations in the nature of responding and stimulating over the course of repeated instances of their coordination. Changes in stimulation arising from inanimate objects, considered apart from their associations with persons, occur as a result of a small number of object conditions such as their physical deterioration or malfunction. Similar conditions make for changes in the stimulational properties of person-objects. However, persons are also sources of response functions, hence their stimulational properties are influenced by their reactional biographies as well, a condition not in effect for inanimate objects. Animate objects thereby embody significantly greater possibilities for the evolution of functions obtained between responding and stimulating. Consequently, functions involving animate objects evolve more rapidly than those involving inanimate objects; and this situation is exacerbated when mutual stimulation and responding characterize an episode of social or verbal behaviors.[1] Skinner (1953, pp. 298-299) makes a similar analysis, arguing that social behavior is more extensive than nonsocial behavior, and that it is "more flexible, in the sense that the organism may shift more readily from one response to another when its behavior is not effective" (1953, p. 299).

In summary, two person episodes of social or verbal behaviors differ from those involving only one person in two ways: First, because persons are typically endowed with more functions than are inanimate objects, our behavior with respect to them is more variable than that with respect to objects. And, second, because inanimate objects make relatively few independent contributions to the evolution of functional relations, functions involving inanimate objects evolve more slowly than those involving two persons. Moreover, when social or verbal functions obtain between two persons responding with respect to one another as stimuli, they may be even more variable and more changeable than when only one person is participating in this manner. This is because the functional relations obtained in these cases are influenced by subtle changes in responding and stimulating over repeated occurrences on the parts of *both* persons participating in such relationships.

When the possibilities for variance and change in social and verbal functions are enlarged to this extent, it becomes very difficult to predict which function will be obtained between two persons at a given point in time. This feature of reciprocal social relations is described by Kantor (1924, pp. 301-309) as "spontaneous unpredictability" and I would venture to say that, for reasons to be discussed below, verbal exchanges illustrate this property to an even greater degree. Inasmuch as our interactions with inanimate objects are less variable, this criterion serves to distinguish the social and verbal classes from other classes of behavior.

Summary of Similarities Between Social and Verbal Behaviors

Due to the conditions of communal living characteristic of the human

---

[1]There are circumstances in which social functions involving inanimate sources evolve very rapidly. We cannot account for rapid change in these cases by appeal to inanimate objects, however, because objects of this type make few independent contributions to the evolution of functional relations. We may appeal instead to frequent opportunities for stimulus function transfer from animate to inanimate sources, occasioned by frequent associations of inanimate objects with original person sources. In short, the vitality of functions involving inanimate sources depends on the vitality of functions involving persons from which the former were derived.

species, most of our behavior is acquired under interpersonal circumstances. Other members of our communities play a pedagogical role in the acquisition of our behavior, whatever be its particular type. Social and verbal behavior may be distinguished from other types of behavior, however, in that other persons are not only involved in teaching us how to perform these behaviors, they are also participating factors in their occurrence. For example, while other persons may teach us to tie our shoes, tying laces is something one does with respect to one's shoes, not other persons. On the contrary, waving goodbye, while also acquired through the instructional activities of other persons, is, in addition, something that one does with respect to other persons. That is, another person is *required for the occurrence* of social and verbal behaviors, at least initially.

Social and verbal behavior do not require the participation of another person for their execution once initially acquired, however, since responding of these types may occur with respect to inanimate objects which have taken on the stimulational properties of persons through association with them in the experiences of particular individuals. As such, the presence of a second person as a *source* of stimulation in a given episode of behavior cannot serve as a criterion upon which to differentiate these classes from other classes of behavior. Still, social and verbal behaviors may be differentiated as involving *stimulation originally arising from person sources*. Other activities do not have this characteristic, and it is, therefore, a criterion upon which the verbal and social classes may be differentiated from other classes of behavior.

We have also noted that when social and verbal behaviors constitute phases of reciprocal interpersonal adjustments (i.e., when two persons are responding with respect to one another), they occur with much greater variation of form than do other kinds of behavior, and these variations evolve at a much faster rate than do their nonverbal/nonsocial counterparts. The former characteristic was regarded as an outcome of the larger number of stimulational functions invested in animate sources as opposed to inanimate sources. The more rapid development of variations was attributed to the fact that in two-person episodes both persons contribute to the variation, and the variability in the coordinated actions of each. The potential for variable responding resulting from these peculiarities of reciprocal interpersonal exchanges, makes it extremely difficult to predict which response form will occur at any particular moment. Nonsocial and nonverbal behaviors, occurring with respect to stimulation arising from inanimate sources, are not as variable, and more precise predictions of their forms at any given time is thereby enabled. For this reason, variation of response form may also serve as a criterion by which the social and verbal classes may be differentiated from other classes of behavior.

Putative Differences Between Verbal and Social Behaviors

Before dealing with what this author believes constitute the fundamental differences between verbal and social behavior, we may first examine four potential criteria for their differentiation as proposed by other workers. These criteria concern the precise means of response acquisition, the conventionality of response forms, the meaning of responses, and the manner in which consequences for responding are introduced.

EXPLICIT CONDITIONING. In refining his definition of verbal behavior, Skinner (1957, pp. 224-225) adds the provision that the behavior of the listener, in reinforcing the speaker's behavior, must have been *explicitly conditioned* for the purpose of *creating a means of control* (emphasis his). These statements constitute a deliberate attempt on Skinner's part to differentiate verbal behavior from other kinds of behavior, social behavior in particular. They do not embody an unambiguous and thereby useful criterion, however. There are two sources of ambiguity. First, presumably all operant behavior is conditioned behavior, hence the issue becomes one of distinguishing between explicit and nonexplicit conditioning of the listener's behavior, about which not enough is said to provide for a distinction. In this regard Skinner (1957, pp. 225-226) suggests that the listener's behavior is conditioned in a "special" manner; however there is nothing particularly special about the process he describes. Specifically, he argues that the speaker's behavior occasions behavior on the part of the listener which serves as reinforcement for the speaker's behavior, and that this behavior of the listener is shaped and sustained by means of negative reinforcement supplied by the speaker (1957, pp. 225-226). Much of our behavior is conditioned in this manner, however, and not all of it is usefully described as verbal. For example, if A holds a gun to B's head, and B surrenders his wallet to A, followed by A withdrawing the gun, then B has just undergone this special process of conditioning and the behavior of A may thereby be considered verbal in kind. While there would be no controversy as to the suggestion that an instance of this sort exemplifies the social class, few would be willing to include such behavior in the verbal class, as to do so would allow this class to become so expanded that workers would be obliged to isolate subclasses for explicit study, raising the same problems of identification that led to the original attempt to define verbal behavior as a unique class of events.

Before abandoning this criterion as a means of distinguishing verbal behavior from other kinds of behavior, we must also take note of the outcome of this process of conditioning, as conceived by Skinner. It is possible that the outcome may suggest useful criteria. In this regard, Skinner (1957, p. 226) claims that: "This special process of conditioning (of the listener) eventually imparts to the behavior of the (speaker) properties of special interest." He does not elaborate as to the nature of these properties nor why they are of special interest, however. Hence we may conclude that unless some further clarification is forthcoming, neither the special process of conditioning nor its product, as identified by Skinner, may serve as useful criteria for distinguishing verbal behavior from other kinds of behavior, including social behavior.

Because the nature of "explicit conditioning" lacks clarity in Skinner's exposition, we may attempt to provide a more general description of this process, by means of which a substantive criterion for distinguishing among behavior classes may emerge. To this end, if we assume that explicit conditioning simply implies the involvement of an agent, such that conditions are deliberately arranged by an agent in order to bring about changes in the behavior of one exposed to those conditions, then the issue becomes one of determining whether the behaviors of a listener in mediating reinforcement for a speaker's behavior are any more or less explicitly conditioned than any of the listener's other behaviors.

A second source of ambiguity is introduced at this point because observers are unable to agree as to how linguistic development, of both speakers and listeners, comes about. Parents *do* make deliberate efforts to bring about the acquisition of speaking and reacting to verbal stimulation on the parts of their children (Cruttenden, 1979; Bijou, 1983); however, according to Kantor (1977, p. 191), linguistic development also occurs under conditions which are not contrived by others for this purpose. In fact, language development may occur primarily through such casual means. If this is the case, this criterion does not serve to distinguish verbal behavior from other behavior, at least it does not do so exclusive of other criteria.[2] Furthermore, even if linguistic development did come about *solely* as a result of explicit conditioning, it is not alone in this regard. Much of our behavior comes about by this means, including social behavior.

CONVENTIONAL RESPONDING. Skinner (1957) goes on, however, to

---

[2] It is likely that operant conditioners will find this suggestion unacceptable in that it violates the premise that all operant behavior is shaped and sustained by way of operant conditioning, and verbal behavior is most assuredly operant behavior. Nonetheless, the criterion is not a particularly useful one if observers cannot agree as to whether or not speaking and mediating reinforcement are adequately characterized by this means.

make one final point regarding the definition of verbal behavior. In his words:

> Verbal behavior is shaped and sustained by a verbal environment—by people who respond to behavior in certain ways because of the practices of the group of which they are members. These practices and the resulting interaction of speaker and listener yield the phenomena which are here considered under the rubric of verbal behavior," (1957, p. 226)

In other words, verbal behavior as well as responding to verbal stimulation are conventional forms of conduct acquired under group auspices. Kantor (1982, p. 164) makes a similar point, arguing that linguistic behavior is a type of cultural behavior which he identifies as follows:

> We recall that two types of criteria characterize cultural responses and mark them off sharply from other types of psychological behavior. In the first place, cultural reactions are correlated with common or conventional stimuli (institutions). When such an institutional stimulus function is in operation it is quite independent of the natural properties of the stimulus object. It must be added, too, that the commonness of the stimulus function of a cultural object is not an accidental result of two or more persons reacting in the same way to it. Rather, cultural stimulus objects have common functions because persons have endowed them with special properties. In the second place, we mark off cultural from noncultural responses because they are acquired through a culturalization process operating under specific group circumstances.

Verbal behavior *does* have this character and it *is* differentiated from other behaviors not sharing this property; however it is not a useful criterion for distinguishing among verbal, social, and behaviors of neither class because conventional responding does not respect these lines of demarcation. In other words, social behavior as well as behaviors of a nonsocial and/or nonverbal sort may exemplify conventional conduct in one instance but not another. For example, the manner in which persons greet one another, apart from their linguistic acts of greeting, may be taken to exemplify behaviors of the social class. These behaviors may be highly conventional, indicating a process of culturalization characteristic of verbal responding. As a result, greeting forms differ from group to group: American greetings take the form of a handshake; Asians traditionally bow to one another; and Europeans have adopted a style of grasping and kissing on both cheeks. These styles are not an accidental result of two persons reacting in the same way for personal and idiosyncratic reasons. They are the results of explicit conditioning occurring under specific group circumstances.

Likewise styles of eating and dressing which involve actions of neither a social nor verbal sort may share the property of conventionality. For example, Americans don't eat dog; Indonesians do. Asians eat with their hands; Europeans use utensils. Pakistani men wear skirt-like garb; Indian men wear trousers. Christian women do not cover their faces; Moslem women wear veils. In short, conventional conduct is not restricted to behaviors of the verbal class, and cannot thereby serve as an unambiguous criterion for the identification of verbal behavior.

Verbal behavior does differ from other kinds of behavior in this regard, however, in that *every* instance of verbal behavior shows this property, while particular instances of social and other response classes may exemplify idiosyncratic responding. For example, the behaviors of two lovers with respect to one another may be regarded as highly idiosyncratic forms of social conduct. Similarity, whether one wears synthetic or natural fibers in circumstances where both are available may be understood as an outcome of a personal, rather than a group, learning history. On the contrary, verbal behaviors, as well as reacting to verbal stimulation, are always instances of conventional conduct. It could not be otherwise, since there is nothing about the stimulation "close the door" that could give rise to the behavior of closing the door unless such stimuli had been endowed with this function by members of a group for purposes of social control, as suggested by both Skinner (1957) and Kantor (1982).

We may conclude this section, then, by suggesting that many kinds of behavior, including both verbal and social responding exemplify conventional forms of conduct acquired under group auspices, but that only verbal behavior may be said to have this characteristic in all instances of its occurrence.

MEANING. It is sometimes argued that verbal behavior embodies "meaning" in a manner not shared by other behavior. Meaning is said to be communicated by way of verbal behavior. It is not the behavior itself but rather some independent entity that is expressed by behavior and further is responsible for the occurrence of particular verbal topographies. As Skinner (1957, p. 7) points out (disparagingly): "A meaning explains the occurrence of a particular set of words in the sense that if there had been a different meaning to be expressed, a different set of words would have been used." Social behavior may have meaning in this sense as well, but because social behavior is relatively less varied in form (i.e., it has a smaller vocabulary), fewer meanings are able to be expressed in this manner and with less precision. Verbal behavior is thereby taken to be the preferred form of communication.

As here conceived, "meaning," like its predecessor "idea," has no physical dimensions. It is a fiction invented for the purpose of explaining the occurrence of particular verbal forms, and has the effect of bringing further inquiry into the observable and potentially observable conditions participating in the occurrence of particular verbal responses to an end. A workable criterion upon which to distinguish between verbal, social, and other response types cannot be derived from a fictional entity. Hence we must look to other conceptualizations of the nature of meaning if we are to use this argument for our purposes.

Skinner has addressed this issue in the context of verbal behavior, arguing that: "The meaning of an utterance is either some feature of the occasion upon which it is uttered or some effect on a listener," (1969, p. 11). In other words, the meaning of a response is not a property of the response, but of the contingencies responsible for its occurrence. However, Skinner does not restrict his account in this regard to responses of the verbal class. For example, he discusses lever presses maintained by food and water as having different meanings (1974, p. 90). Therefore, we may assume that social behaviors also have meaning in Skinner's sense of this concept: The meaning of social behavior is to be found in the contingencies responsible for its occurrence at a particular time. As such, verbal and social behaviors cannot be distinguished on the basis of this conception of meaning.

FACTORS INVOLVED IN THE TRANSFORMATIONS OF EVENT FIELDS. To complete an account of the differences between verbal and social behaviors, as claimed by other workers, we must take note of the factors which figure prominently in the transformations and evolutions of these two types of event fields. As previously indicated, a pattern analysis of a particular type of event, as I have been attempting to provide by characterizing the factors participaing in given events at given points in time, is complemented by an analysis of the processes through which those events evolve into other kinds of events.

Skinner (1957) has suggested that verbal behavior may be differentiated from other behaviors on the basis of the factors presumed to be responsible for the recurrence of events of this type. Specifically, verbal behaviors are held to be acquired and sustained by way of consequences mediated by other persons, while other kinds of activities produce consequences by more direct means. We may, then, turn to the issue of what factors are responsible for the recurrence of events to see if, by this exposition, a criterion for distinguishing among verbal, social, and other behaviors may be established. There are really two issues to be addressed here: First, is it reasonable to assume that any particular factor is responsible for the recurrence of events; and, second, if it is reasonable to make this assumption, do these factors differ to a sufficient enough degree to allow for the establishment of an unambiguous criterion by which to differentiate among social, verbal, and other behaviors.

The first issue concerns the law of effect. More specifically, do the consequences of actions determine subsequent actions? Space does not permit a consideration of this issue, neither is it necessary to address it in the present context.

The second issue is more pertinent to the task at hand, namely, is it possible to differentiate among classes of behavior on the basis of how consequential factors are introduced into event fields?

In this regard, Skinner (1957, p. 1) contends that the consequences of verbal action are introduced indirectly by the activities of other persons while the consequences of other types of behavior are introduced by more direct means, namely by altering the environment through mechanical action. Clearly it is the case that verbal behavior has no direct effect upon the nonsocial environment: The door does not close upon being asked to do so. However, the consequences of social behaviors as well as behaviors of other classes are also mediated by other persons in particular instances. Moreover, consequences are not mediated by others for many instances of verbal behavior because no action on the part of a listener is implicated in such instances. In this regard Kantor (1977, p. 72) distinguished between expressive and communicative language, arguing that in the former case a linguistic act may not operate beyond an individual's own immediate adjustment, while in the latter case, the subsequent activity of another person constitutes an integral phase of the interaction. Still, however, when the consequences of actions are integral and consummatory phases of those verbal actions, these consequences are always mediated by others. On the contrary, the consequences of other kinds of behavior may or may not be mediated by others. This criterion for distinguishing among social, verbal, and other foms of responding is, then, not entirely ambiguous, but it does point to a peculiarity of verbal responding, which may, in combination with other criteria, serve as a defining characteristic of such responding.

Summary and Conclusion

The serviceability of four potential criteria for differentiating between verbal, social, and other classes of behavior were examined, including: the precise means of response acquisition; the conventionality of response forms; the meanings of interactions; and the manner in which consequences for responding are introduced. These criteria were not found to be useful in distinguishing social and verbal behaviors from other classes of responding for a variety of reasons. With regard to the conventionality of response forms, this feature is not restricted to responding of these two classes alone. Further, social behavior may also exemplify unconventional responding acquired as a product of an idiosyncratic learning history. Likewise, personal mediation of consequences may exist for any behavior, not just for instances of the social and verbal classes. Moreover, the consequences of social behavior are not always personally mediated.

With regard to the issue of how these activities are acquired, by virtue of some special process of conditioning or by some more casual means, we have been unable to identify anything special about the means by which verbal behavior is acquired and, regardless of how "explicit conditioning" is conceived, we have encountered some disagreement among workers as to whether verbal behavior is any more or less explicitly conditioned than any other behavior.

Finally, meaning, at least as this concept is interpreted by Skinner, is a characteristic of all behavior, irrespective of type, hence it does not serve to distinguish among response classes.

These features of interaction, while not constituting criteria for the differentiation of the social and verbal classes from other classes of behavior, do have some potential for distinguishing *between* social and verbal behavior. More specifically, verbal response forms are *always* conventional; consequences for verbal behavior are *always* personally mediated, and, at least in some quarters, meaning is regarded as a characteristic of verbal responding which is *not* shared by responses in other classes. Still, however, these criteria cannot serve to distinguish verbal behaviors from all other types of behavior in the absence of other criteria. This is the case because particular instances of behavior which would not be considered verbal by anyone may share these characteristics, and because the concept of meaning upon which this assertion might be made is without scientific value.

Genuine Differences Between Verbal and Social Behavior

To differentiate between social and verbal responding, we must begin by examining instances of responding which exemplify the features previously identified as being common to both types of responding, as well as other features which may serve as criteria upon which one type may be distinguished from the other. These instances, then, must be able to be characterized as having been acquired by means of the pedagogical activities of others; another person (or substitute stimulus for another person) must constitute a participating factor in their occurrence in the immediate situation; and they must be capable of considerable variation in form from one occurrence to the next. Moreover, because particular instances of social behavior may resemble verbal behavior along other dimensions, we may avoid confusion by selecting instances for comparison which exemplify these other similarities. Among them are conventionality of response forms and social mediation of the consequences of responding. Likewise, because we have previously denied the possibility of distinguishing among social and verbal behaviors on the basis of the particular muscle groups figuring prominently in their execution, it will be helpful to select examples of social and verbal behaviors executed by the same musculature. Given these stipulations, we may construct representative instances of behavior for comparison.

As an example of social behavior we may use the following: A sees B across a street and waves, followed by B waving back. Waving to another person is acquired through the instructional activities of others. It is also an activity which typically occurs in the physical presence of another person, which is to say another person constitutes a participating factor in such events. Further, responses of this sort may vary in from from one occasion to the next along dimensions of magnitude and duration, for example. Still, however, the range of variability may be relatively small, given that gestural greeting forms tend to have a conventional character, differing markedly only *across* cultural groups. Finally, this episode of behavior exemplifies the feature of social mediation of consequences, in that the subsequent activity of B may be considered the relevant consequence of A's greeting action. This instance of behavior thus satisfies our criteria for a representative and serviceable example of social behavior.

As an example of verbal behavior, we may use the following: A signs to B in American Sign Language to pass the salt, followed by B passing the salt shaker to A. In this example, A's signing is obviously a product of instructional activities on the part of others. Likewise signing typically occurs in the physical presence of another person, which is to say another person may be considered a participating factor in the occurrence of this event. Further, the magnitude and other aspects of such responding may vary from occasion to occasion, although the form is conventional in the sense that it is acquired under specific group auspices and has significance to members of this group alone. Finally, the consequence of A's action, namely the receipt of salt, is mediated through the activities of person B.

Having constructed instances of social and verbal behaviors which exemplify the features held in common by these two classes of behaviors, we may attempt to distinguish them on the basis of their unique characteristics. Before doing so, however, it may be helpful to reiterate the goals of a pattern analysis and the interpretation of psychological events implied by such analyses.

As previously indicated, a pattern analysis is essentially a description of a particular event field in terms of the factors participating in it, without regard for the contributions of particular factors in the transformation of that field into a succeeding one. An event field may be conceived as a collection of interdependent factors isolated out of the continuous stream of psychological happenings. It consists, essentially, of a relation between the responding of an organism and the stimulating of an object, event, or other organism, occurring through a medium of contact, such as air or light, and taking place in a setting consisting of many other factors. Because a particular object, event, or person, may have more than one stimulational property, responding occurring with respect to a given object, person, or event at a particular moment in time varies in accordance with the configuration of other factors making up the setting in which the interaction of interest is taking place. That is, the setting determines which of a number of possible coordinations of stimulating and responding will occur at a given time. Further, the stimulational properties of objects, events, or persons, as well as the influence of particular setting factors with regard to the property exerting itself in a given occasion, have their origins in the interbehavioral histories of particular organisms, in a general as well as specific sense.

With this clarification at hand, we may now attempt to identify the factors involved in instances of verbal behavior which are not shared by typical instances of social behavior.

UNISTIMULATIONAL VERSUS BISTIMULATIONAL BEHAVIOR SEGMENTS. In the social example described above, the responding of person A is coordinated with stimulation arising from person B. This interaction obviously occurs in a context of a large number of other factors, among them the street and its various aspects and the organismic condition of person A (ie., restfulness or fatigue, deprivations or satiations of various sorts, etc.) However, these other factors constitute the setting in which A's greeting with respect to B takes place; they are not stimulational factors in this event. That is, when A greets B, A is interacting in that moment with stimulation arising not from the street and its numerous aspects, but with stimulation arising from person B. In short, a social interaction is one in which a single response function is coordinated with a single stimulus function, and the event may thus be characterized as unistimulational in nature.

On the contrary, in the verbal episode described above, two sources of stimulation are relevant to the occurrence of the interaction between A and B. As in the social example, one of these sources is person B. The other is the shaker of salt. That is, person A is interacting not only with stimulation arising from person B but also with stimulation arising from the salt shaker. The salt shaker is not a setting factor in this event, because its role is not to determine which of a number of stimulational properties of *person B* is activated in the moment, but rather to call out a particular response function coordinated with stimulation arising from the salt shaker. Neither is person B acting as a setting factor in this event, since the role of person B is not to determine which of a number of stimulational properties of *salt shakers* is activated in the moment, but rather to call out a particular response function coordinated with stimulation arising from person B. Person B stimulates a response of asking for something; while the salt shaker stimulates a response of asking for salt. In short, a verbal interaction of this type consists of two response functions coordinated with two stimulus functions occurring simultaneously, and the event, thereby, may be characterized as bistimulational.

DIRECTNESS VERSUS INDIRECTNESS OF ADJUSTMENT. The concept of psychological adjustment may be taken to mean the coordinated operation of the response functions of an organism with the stimulus functions of objects, events, or other organisms. A psychological adjustment is simply the interaction obtained between a responding organism and a stimulating environment at a given time. A direct adjustment is one in which the action of an organism with respect to a source of stimulation is accomplished in the absence of mediation by another object, event, or other organism. For example, a person may interact directly with the salt shaker by reaching for it. Similarly, one person embracing another may occur in the absence of mediation by other stimulus objects, events, or persons. In such cases, responding operates directly upon the stimulus coordinated with it, such as to produce some change in this stimulus. In the former example the change occurs with respect to the location of the stimulus object in space. In the latter example, where the source of stimulation for an embracing response is another person, the change in this source is likewise a modification of the spatial position of the body and its parts effected by the first person's embrace.

Much of our nonverbal behavior, including social behavior, may be characterized as a direct adjustment in this sense. Verbal behavior, on the other hand, does not share this property for reasons to be discussed below.

Many reactions do not operate directly upon sources of stimulation (i.e., objects, events, or other persons) such as to effect changes or modification in them, however. Feeling reactions, for example, result in changes or modifications in the reacting person, not the stimulus events with which they are coordinated. (For a detailed discussion of feeling action, see Kantor, 1924.) Other adjustments are of a mediate or indirect sort because the stimulus objects with which reactions were originally coordinated are not present in the immediate situation. In such cases, a stimulus object which *is* present, and which has by one of a variety of means acquired the function of an absent stimulus, brings about a reaction normally occurring under other circumstances (i.e., when the stimulus with which reacting was originally coordinated is present in the immediate situation). For example, a multitude of reactions to the enormous number of events making up a past summer vacation may occur through the operation of a small number of immediately present photographs and other mementos. In this situation there is no possibility of these reactions effecting changes in the stimuli with which they were originally coordinated (i.e., the events of the summer vacation) because these events are no longer present. Hence, whatever changes *are* effected by these reactions must occur with respect to the photographs and mementos. However, these objects, *as objects*, are insignificant features of this event. That is, their function is significant but not their formal characteristics. Thus adjustments of this sort may be considered mediate in character.

This sense of mediation applies to nonverbal behavior as well as verbal behavior. Just as we may speak of things in their absence through the operation of other things, we may also see, hear, or smell things in their absence. Likewise, should we smile upon spotting a friend's car in a parking lot or kiss a photograph of a lover, we are engaging in social behavior mediated by stimuli other than those originally coordinated with these actions.

Verbal adjustments are mediate in another sense as well, which is peculiar to events of this sort exclusively. Verbal adjustments have a mediate character not because the stimulus objects with which reactions were originally coordinated are absent and effectual action is thereby impossible (although this may also be the case), but because verbal action is necessarily ineffectual with regard to one of the two sources of stimulation relevant to its occurrence. More specifically, a speaker's request for salt operates to effect change in the listener but not in the salt shaker. A change in the spatial location of the salt shaker *may* occur as a subsequent event, but if it does it is the listener and not the speaker who effects this change. In such cases we may say that the speaker's action operates directly upon the listener and indirectly upon the salt shaker, and it is this indirectness of contact which gives verbal action its peculiar mediate character.

In summary, nonverbal adjustments may be direct or indirect. As indirect adjustments they constitute circumstances in which actions occur in the absence of the stimuli with which they were originally coordinated through the operation of other immediately present stimuli. By contrast, verbal adjustments are *always* indirect because verbal action, by nature, is ineffectual with respect to the nonsocial environment. In addition, verbal adjustments may be indirect in the same sense in which nonverbal adjustments have this character. That is, they may occur through the operation of stimuli other than those with which they were originally coordinated.

REFERENTIAL VERSUS NONREFERENTIAL ADJUSTMENTS. The bistimulational character of verbal adjustments and the fact that verbal responding is ineffectual with respect to the nonsocial environment make for another peculiarity of verbal action which is, in fact, its most distinguishing feature. Specifically, verbal stimuli (i.e., the auditory, tactual, or visual products of verbal responding) acquire the functions of other stimuli more readily than do nonverbal stimuli and as a result they serve to extend both the speaker's and listener's contact with the environment beyond its stimulational capacity at a given moment. It is by means of verbal action that we are able to react in a *highly specific way* to events in their absence. Events may be absent from immediate circumstances for a variety of reasons. They may have occurred at some previous time and are no longer existent as events with which current action may be coordinated. Likewise, we may react to events as yet to occur by means of verbal action. Further, while events may be both existent and immediately present they may lie outside the boundaries of observation by virtue of their size or separation from observers in space, and it is through verbal action alone that they may be implicated in the current circumstance. For example, no one would deny that atoms or smaller particles constitute features of any given situation, yet we do not interact with these events directly except under unusual circumstances involving sophisticated amplifying technologies. Nonetheless, we may still react to such events in their observational absence through the operation of verbal behavior. And, finally, events may be absent from the immediate situation by virtue of the fact that they do not have nor ever had any actual existence. Deities and the minds of men, while having no actual existence — from a scientific standpoint at least — are constructed in the effective present by means of verbal behavior. In short, verbal action enables us to respond to the *past*, the *future*, the *remote*, and the *nonexistent* and it is our capacity to do so that underlies the development of human civilization and distiguishes it from the comparable, though simpler, present-bound social organizations of animal species.

To substantiate these claims we must address the operation of verbal action and the reasons for its facility in acquiring the functions of other stimuli, beginning with the latter issue.

Verbal stimuli are able to acquire the stimulational functions of other stimuli more readily than nonverbal stimuli for two reasons. First, because verbal responding is ineffectual with respect to the nonsocial environment, verbal responding with respect to nonsocial stimuli does not interfere withthe execution of nonverbal behavior coordinated with the same stimuli as much as does other nonverbal behavior. For example, we may say "window" while washing a window more easily than we may hang a curtain rod while washing a window. As a result, verbal action occurs in conjunction with other response events more often than do nonverbal actions coordinated with the same stimuli. Furthermore, because perceptual (i.e, seeing, hearing, etc.) activities are inevitable components of all nonverbal responses, verbal responses occur in conjunction with perceptual activities more often than with any other type of nonverbal responding. In other words, saying "window" is likely to have occurred more often in conjunction with seeing a window than with washing a window, or hanging a curtain rod, or any other response coordinated with the object window. This is the case because seeing a window is involved in each of these other activities and occurs as well in the absence of any of them. (For a more detailed discussion, see Parrott, 1984.) Frequent conjunctive occurrence of verbal and perceptual responding has important implications. Specifically, whenever different types of responding occur in conjunction or close temporal proximity with sufficient frequency, the subsequent occurrence of one type of responding may give rise to reactions of the other type such that upon saying "window" (or hearing it said) one may also have a tendency to see a window even if there is no window to be seen in the immediate situation. Likewise, upon seeing a window, one may have a tendency to say "window" despite the absence of an appropriate social context for this action. While this process is not peculiar to conjunctions of verbal and perceptual action, for example we may have a tendency to hear thunder in its absence upon seeing lightning for the same reasons, the effect is more prevalent in the verbal field because of the ineffectual character of verbal action and its resulting lack of interference with the occurrence of other behavior. Moreover, because of a second feature of verbal responding our actions with respect to things in their absence may be especially precise and differentiated in form. We may now turn to this second feature.

Verbal responding displays an arbitrariness of form not shared by its nonverbal counterparts. This is the case because verbal responding is ineffectual with respect to the nonsocial environment and its form is thereby not conditioned by the physical properties of nonsocial stimuli in the same way as is nonverbal responding (Parrott, 1984). As a result, verbal response forms exist in enormous variety. This variation in form allows for a greater degree of specificity of correspondence with aspects of the physical environment, such that each physical object or event, as well as each of its aspects or properties may become coordinated with a verbal response having a form peculiar to that object and that object alone. Consequently, verbal responding not only allows for the occurrence of actions historically occurring in conjunction with it, but because of the specificity of correspondences between verbal response forms and features of the physical environment, these conjoint actions may be more precise and differentiated. In short, upon saying or hearing said the word "chair," we may see a chair in its absence with unusual clarity. On the other hand were we to attempt to produce chair-seeing in another person by means of fanciful sitting responses, seeing a chair would be no more likely than seeing a sofa or a bench. This difference between verbal and nonverbal response forms, with regard to their serviceability as substitute stimuli as here conceived, underlies the game of charades. If nonverbal response forms were as effective in bringing about reactions to things and events in their absence there would be no game of charades. In summary, we are able to engage in actions with respect to things in their absence, notably perceptual reactions, and to do so in a highly specific way by means of verbal stimulation. Stimulation of other sorts employed for this purpose cannot produce such highly differentiated action, and is less effective for this reason. Combining this feature of verbal stimulation with the fact that verbal adjustments are bistimulational and involve indirect adjustments, the concept of reference may be understood as follows: when a speaker produces verbal stimulation for a listener, the listener's response to such stimulation is not merely audient activity. It consists as well of reacting in a characteristic way to the things spoken of. If these things are present in the immediate situation the effect of verbal stimulation is to orient the listener with respect to things in a direct manner. If the things spoken of are not immediately present, the listener may react to them indirectly by means of historically associated perceptual activity. It is this orientation of the listener with respect to things spoken of that is implied by the concept of reference, and it is only by way of verbal stimulation that it may come about. Speaking is the act of bringing a listener into contact with things and events of the physical world; it is the act of referring a listener to the things spoken of.

SUMMARY OF DIFFERENCES BETWEEN VERBAL AND SOCIAL BEHAVIORS. Social adjustments involve coordinations of single response and stimulus functions. Social responses typically have an effectual character, producing some change in the source of stimulation with which they are coordinated, although they may occur in the absence of original sources of stimulation through the operation of historically associated stimuli. They have no referential function, which is to say they do not have the effect of orienting another person to stimuli other than those constituting the stimulus products of social responding.

Verbal adjustments, on the other hand, are bistimulational adjustments involving two response and two stimulus functions occurring simultaneously. Verbal responding is effectual with respect to only one of the sources of stimulation participating in its occurrence, however. That is, verbal responding is effectual only with respect to the social environment. Hence, in order for verbal responding to produce change in the nonsocial source and thereby have utility and significance, it must operate such as to bring a listener into effectual contact with this source of stimulation. This operation is what we are calling the referential function of language which is not duplicated in any other type of responding, and which is, above all, the defining characteristic of verbal behavior.

CONCLUSION

My attempt has been to distinguish verbal from social behavior by way of an analysis of the factors participating in their occurrence at a given moment. In doing so certain similarities between these two classes of responding have become apparent. Both are acquired by means of the pedagogical activities of others and, in both, another person (or substitute stimulus for another person) constitutes a participating factor in their occurrence. Further, both are capable of wide variation in form, although verbal behavior is considerably more variable than social behavior. Likewise both show a conventionality of response form and social mediation of the consequences of responding, although these conditions do not prevail in all instances of social behavior. Finally, both may be executed with the same muscle groups and cannot be differentiated on these grounds.

With regard to their differences, verbal responses produce reactions on the part of listeners with respect to stimuli other than the stimulus products of verbal responding, while social behaviors produce reactions only to the stimulus products of the social response itself. In other words, verbal responding has a referential function not shared by social responding, and this is the principle difference between these two classes of responding.

REFERENCES

Bijou, S. W. (1983). The initial development of linguistic behavior. In N. W. Smith, P. T. Mountjoy, and D. H. Ruben (Eds.) Reassessment in Psychology: The Interbehavioral Alternative. Washington, D.C.: University Press of America.

Cruttendon, A. (1979). *Language in Infancy and Childhood*. New York: St. Martin's Press.

Kantor, J. R. (1924). *Principles of Psychology (Volume 1)*. Chicago: The Principia Press.

Kantor, J. R. (1977). *Psychological Linguistics*. Chicago: The Principia Press.

Kantor, J. R. (1982). *Cultural Psychology*. Chicago: The Principia Press.

Parrott, L. J. (1984). Listening and Understanding. *The Behavior Analyst, 7*, (pp. 29-39).

Skinner, B. F. (1953). *Science and Human Behavior*. New York: The Free Press.

Skinner, B. F. (1957). *Verbal Behavior*. New York: Appleton-Century-Crofts.

Skinner, B. F. (1969). *Contingencies of Reinforcement: A theoretical analysis*. New York: Appleton-Century-Crofts.

Commentary

ARE THEY REALLY SO DIFFERENT?: COMMENTS ON THE DIFFERENCES BETWEEN VERBAL AND SOCIAL BEHAVIOR

PHILIP N. CHASE

LINDA J. PARROTT'S chapter is worth reading for three reasons. First, the chapter is an original attempt to distinguish between two classes of behavior that heretofore have not been distinguished by behavior analysts. Second, the chapter is pedagogic, it shows the complexity of the issue and establishes the need for further study, description, and elaboration. Third, the chapter suggests a descriptive methodology that focuses on distal environmental relations as well as the proximal relations that have been studied traditionally by behavior analysts. With some elaboration, this methodology might be a worthwhile adjunct to current experimental methodologies. However, from this author's point of view, the chapter erroneously criticizes other behavioral attempts to distinguish verbal behavior from nonverbal behavior (e.g., Skinner, 1957), and erroneously establishes three criteria for distinguishing verbal from social behavior. Though both of these problems deserve comment, I will restrict my comments to Parrott's criteria for differentiating verbal and social behavior. I believe that is the more important issue at hand.

VERBAL AND SOCIAL BEHAVIOR

If differences do exist between verbal and social behavior, as common sense indicates, then psychological scientists should determine these differences through one of two routes. We can try to find the biological structures that are involved in verbal behavior that are not involved in other forms of social behavior or we can try to discover the different learning experiences or conditions under which verbal behavior occurs rather than some other type of social behavior. Obviously, a behavior analytic psychologist should look at the latter. Therefore, it is the last part of Parrott's chapter that is most critical to the goals of behavior analytic science; the part where she begins to elucidate some of the behavior-environmental conditions that differentiate verbal from social behavior.

Parrott describes three critical differences between verbal and social behavior. She claims that social behavior is unistimulational and verbal behavior is bistimulational, that social behavior has both direct and indirect effects on the environment, whereas verbal behavior is always indirect, and finally that social behavior is not referential and verbal behavior is referential. I would like to comment on these three criteria in turn.

UNI VERSUS BISTIMULATIONAL

Of the three sets of criteria that Parrott describes, the uni versus bistimulational distinction is the most difficult to understand. I do not see how counting effective stimuli can help us to differentiate between classes because the number of critical stimuli that effect behavior across situations varies both within and across classes of responding. For example, Parrott presents two examples of behavior. The social example involves a person waving at another person across the street; Person A sees person B, and waves. The verbal example involves signing for salt at the dinner table; Person A sees salt and Person B, and signs to Person B to pass the salt. The problem with these examples is that the social example can be shown to have bistimulational properties and the verbal example can be shown to have other stimulational properties. The presence of B is not sufficient for A to wave. B must be present, but B also should be looking in the direction of A or should be waving also. If A saw Person B, and Person B was facing the other direction, waving would not be effective. Similarly, it is not necessary for the salt to be present in order for A to sign for salt. In fact, the absence of salt may be more of a motivational condition to ask for salt than its presence (see Skinner's analysis of mands, Skinner, 1957).

I do not believe that these are nit-picking examples. They simply point out that counting stimuli does not distinguish between these two classes of behavior. Like most complex instances of behavior, both of these examples involve conditional discriminations: in the presence of a particular set of conditions, a stimulus will set the occasion for a particular response.

Though it is always difficult to isolate a single controlling stimulus, uni versus bistimulational distinction can be further damaged by providing examples of verbal behavior that are unistimulational. Skinner defined a whole subclass of verbal behavior that has this property called verbal behavior controlled by other verbal behavior. The intraverbal is one example of this class; my conversational behavior is controlled primarily by the verbal behavior of others. In addition, some types of tacts may be seen as being unistimulational. I see a desk and I say it is a desk. This behavior does not always require stimulation from another person. In sum, there are many examples of verbal behavior that might be unistimulational and other social behavior that have bistimulational control. Thus, this distinction does *not* function as a useful criterion.

DIRECTNESS VERSUS INDIRECTNESS

Parrott claims that the effect of verbal behavior can be direct or indirect, but that verbal behavior always has an indirect effect. In part, this is the same distinction that Skinner (1957) described when he stated that verbal behavior requires the mediation of another person. Therefore, Parrott agrees with Skinner. Though this agreement is made clear with the salt shaker example on pg. 43, Parrott tries to make an additional point. She says that verbal behavior often has both a direct effect and an indirect effect. Other types of social behavior may have a direct effect on another person or an indirect effect on other relevant stimuli, but they do not have both a direct and indirect effect in the same situations. This forces the question: can we think of any examples of nonverbal, social events that have a direct effect on a person, but an indirect effect on other relevant stimuli? If we take indirect to mean that a behavior changes one aspect of the environment which in turn changes another aspect of the environment, then most examples of complex social behavior include indirect effects. Food gathering and preparation is a useful example. If I am standing over a stove and Karen gives me a tomato that she has picked in the garden, then her picking the tomato has a direct effect on me. If I then cut the tomato and put it into a sauce, then the tomato affects the sauce. Karen's picking and giving the tomato, however, have an indirect effect on the sauce. Again, I do not think I am stretching the point. The point is that both common examples of verbal examples and common examples of social behavior have direct and indirect effects. Therefore, we can not use the directness of effect as a criteria for distinguishing between verbal and social behavior.

REFERENTIAL VERSUS NONREFERENTIAL

Parrott comes the closest to distinguishing between verbal and social behavior when discussing the criterion of reference. She claims that verbal behavior references other events and nonverbal behavior does not. Parrott defines reference as one set of events acquiring the function of another set of events and thereby extending the behaver's contact with the environment. Verbal behavior does acquire the functions of other events and does extend our contact to past, future, remote, and nonexistent events. However, so do other kinds of social behavior. If a friend shows us a picture of a beach, this event may evoke "vacation" responses. The waving example that Parrott provides extends a greeting response across environmental circumstances that do not promote vocal greetings. Division of labor extends the contact of social animals to many sources of stimulation: food, heat, shelter, and so on. Therefore, extension per se does not differentiate verbal from social behavior. However, the extent of extension that is allowed by the conventional forms of verbal behavior may be sufficient to claim a distinction.

Within this argument lies the true distinction between verbal behavior and other social behavior: that the conventional verbal forms of speaking, writing, and signing provide a greater variety and flexibility for extending an individual's contact with other aspects of the environment. If we concentrate on variety and flexibility, then we should go back to the earlier set of comments that Parrott made about variability of responding. Interestingly, Palmer and Chase make similar observations in Chapter Two and the commentary on Chapter Two of this book. Palmer claims that the development of vocal musculature that are sensitive to reinforcement contingencies may be significant because these muscles are free of other demands and because the responses they allow stimulate other people exactly as they stimulate ourselves. Chase added to this by describing four features of conventional verbal behavior that facilitate their effectiveness.

The conclusion drawn from these discussions is that verbal responses are particularly effective social events. Conventional verbal behavior is particularly effective because of the extent that it can extend our contact with other aspects of the environment. In fact, it may be the particular effectiveness of vocal and written stimuli to acquire the functions of other stimuli that distinguishes the social repertoire of humans from other animals. Humans have the musculature that makes possible these specific fine-grained extensions.

In sum, I agree with Parrott that there is a critical difference between verbal and social behavior, and that this difference lies in the referential character of verbal behavior. However, this referential character is not functionally different for other social behavior, in any absolute sense. Social behavior is bistimulational, it has both indirect and direct effects on the environment and it does acquire the functions of other stimuli. The difference is that some forms of social behavior, talking, signing, and writing, are particularly effective in extending our contact with other features of the environment. It is these forms of social behavior that we usually refer to as verbal behavior.

REFERENCES

Skinner, B. F. (1957). *Verbal Behavior*. Englewood Cliffs, NJ: Prentice-Hall, Publishers Inc.

Commentary

CAN VERBAL BE NONSOCIAL?
CAN NONSOCIAL BE VERBAL?

PHILIP N. HINELINE

APPROPRIATELY, Dr. Parrott begins by making explicit her stance and the tradition within which she is writing. It is the stance of an interbehaviorist, in a tradition that derives more frm the work of J.R. Kantor than from that of B.F. Skinner, which is the more typical antecedent for behavioral accounts of human action. Thus, Parrott's opening section prepares us for reading in terms of "participation in event fields," "interpersonal adjustments," and the like, rather than in the traditionally behavioral terms of stimuli, responses, and consequences. *A propos* of this, it should be noted that Skinnerian interpretations are sometimes elaborated in terms of behavioral situations and repertoires. Discussed in such terms, both interpretive traditions become more easily discriminable from the connectionistic, S-R psychologies with which they are often confused. Skinnerian and Kantorian approaches seem reasonably compatible in the relationships they emphasize, and Parrott's discussions in terms of "configurations of event fields," and transformations of such fields, capture some of the reciprocity and dynamic characteristics of behavioral process that are not so readily apparent in strictly Skinnerian accounts. Still, Kantorian prose continually strikes me as odd and wordy, and Parrott writes of "cause" in ways that I find puzzling. Of course I would not be surprised if a Kantorian found my prose in the Skinnerian tradition to be odd in its own way.

Given that the chapter includes discussion of definitions in general, as well as of specific definitions, the particular discriminanda for our speaking and writing are very much at issue. Yet Parrott does not precisely identify the discriminda that control her defining of social and verbal behavior. It is clear that the definitions themselves are offered to facilitate rule-governed behavior within the scientific community. Consistent with this, in most parts of the chapter the community whose contingencies are discriminanda for the definition, seems to be the community of behavior analysts. If this were consistently the case, the chapter would discuss "social" and "verbal" as purely technical terms. But in some passages, Parrott seems to be attempting to characterize vernacular usage—in which case, the discriminanda controlling the definition are contingencies of the community at large, even though the definition itself is to function in discriminative control within the scientific community.

The relevance of the above distinctions became evident in my trying to resolve another key item that I found missing from Parrott's essay: a clear indication of the coordinate/superordinate relationships of the social and verbal categories. To be sure, features common to social and verbal behavior are discussed in detail. Also, it seems fairly clear that Parrott views social and verbal behavior as mutually exclusive categories. There are no necessary embarrassments in this; birds and mammals have many features in common and yet are mutually exclusive categories. However, if contingencies of vernacular usage are relevant to these definitions, there is a problem. Surely, to the community at large, some verbal behavior is social behavior. Indeed, if one accepts functional origins of a class of behavior as relevant to its being defined as verbal, then all verbal behavior may be social behavior—although not all social behavior is verbal behavior, which seems to be the main point that underlies Parrott's chapter.

Putting aside vernacular usage, there is still a problem. If social and verbal behavior are mutually exclusive categories, to what superordinate category do they belong (corresponding to vertebrates, in the case of birds and mammals)? An appropriate superordinate term will be sorely needed, since many behavior-analytic discussions will involve collectively the two sets that Parrott has apparently chosen to keep distinct. Also if these are to be taken as purely technical, behavior-analytic terms, it should be clearly noted that Parrott's definition of verbal behavior is distinctly different from Skinner's definition of the same term, for unlike Skinner, Parrott seems to exclude all instances that would not be said to involve language. This is basic to her social-verbal distinction. I wonder whether she might have achieved a cleaner distinction by defining verbal behavior as the linguistic subclass of social behavior.

The touchstone that Parrott finally identifies for the social/verbal distinction is that of "unistimulational" vs "bistimulational," with bistimulationality being the crucial defining property of verbal behavior. Her supporting examples are the purely social case of two people waving to each other, and the verbal case of "Pass the salt." According to Parrott, the former case is social and nonverbal because there is only "a single response function coordinated with a single stimulus function." The "Pass the salt" example includes both a direct function (that is, salt is a reinforcer, and one might interact with the shaker directly, making the vocal utterance superfluous) and an indirect function, whereby the vocal utterance involves mediation "by other stimulus objects, events, or persons" as well as the direct involvement of salt with one's behavior. Parrott points out that one person embracing another would exemplify a direct, unistimulational relation. But how about an episode involving "Give me a hug?" Presumably this is verbal—yet on the verbal/social dimension, it is not clear why it would differ in that respect from one person's wave prompting another person's wave, or one person's puckering lips prompting another person's kiss. Further, there are many multistimulational relationships that are neither social nor verbal. Under the rubric of "multiple causation," behavior-analytic interpretation has always allowed for a single bit of behavior participating in two or more concurrent relationships.

While I do not find that it enables us to distinguish social from verbal behavior, Parrott's unistimulation/bistimulational distinction is an interesting one. It relates to the basis that Zettle and Hayes (1982) offer for a definition of rule-governed behavior. They refer to related but distinguishable sets of response-consequent relations which are in the same domain as the event fields that Parrott discusses. A difference is that in the adherence to pattern analysis rather than functional analysis, she captures the reciprocity of the relationships, but loses clarity with respect to the source of orderliness in the patterns.

To delineate these relationships—between verbal behavior, social behavior, rule-governed behavior, and the like—it is important to avoid confusions between vernacular and technical usage of terms. Failure to do so is certain to compromise the internal consistency of our interpretive system and result in diminished conceptual elegance, mis-characterized functional relationships, and even in misunderstanding of what we claim to explain. The first two of these costs have been spelled out by Catania (1975) and by Goldiamond (1976) with respect to the vernacular/technical hybrid, "self-reinforcement." The misunderstanding of what is claimed, can be seen in common reactions to Skinner's analysis of verbal behavior.

Skinner (1945) explicitly rejected vernacular definitions as delineating the interpretive concepts of behavior analysis. Furthermore, in the early pages of *Verbal Behavior* (1957) he was unequivocal in providing an explicit, technical definition that did not accept the approximate vernacular equivalence between "verbal" and "linguistic:"

> In defining verbal behavior as behavior reinforced through the mediation of other persons we do not, and cannot, specify any one form, mode, or medium. Any movement capable of affecting another organism may be verbal. We are likely to single out vocal behavior, not only because it is commonest, but because it has little effect upon the physical environment and hence is most necessarily verbal. But there are extensive written languages, sign languages, and languages in which the 'speaker' stimulates the skin of the 'listener.' Audible behavior which is not vocal (for example, clapping the hands for a servant, or blowing a bugle) and gestures are verbal, although they may not compose an organized language. . . . Pointing to words is verbal—as, indeed, is all pointing, since it is effective only when it alters the behavior of someone. The definition also covers manipulations of physical objects which are undertaken because of the effect upon people, as in the use of ceremonial trappings. In the case of any *medium*, the behavior is both verbal and nonverbal at once—nonverbal in the effect upon the medium—verbal in the ultimate effect on the observer (p. 14).

Skinner's defining a technical term, verbal behavior, in this way, was an ingenious stroke, but its subtlety appears often to have been lost upon both critics and proponents. Too often it is taken as a behavioral definition of language, which it clearly is not. Its focus is not upon the grammar and structure of languages, which have been the traditional foci of linguistic theories, but rather upon what is involved when we speak of meaning. "But meaning is not a property of behavior as such but of the conditions under which behavior occurs. Technically, meanings are to be found among the independent variables in a functional account, rather than as properties of the dependent variable" (Skinner, 1957, pp. 13-14).

Even with its terms this precisely introduced, Skinner's account of verbal behavior has often been taken for something it is not. Although it would be cumbersome, we could perhaps remedy this by always invoking the phrase "when we speak of," when not engaged in strictly technical usage. Similarly, my reading of Parrott's worthy contribution would have been aided if I could have clearly and consistently discriminated social behavior and verbal behavior as technical categories, from what is involved when we commonly speak of social behavior and language.

REFERENCES

Catania, A. C. (1975). The myth of self-reinforcement. *Behaviorism, 3*, 192-199.
Goldiamond, I. (1976). Self-reinforcement. *Journal of Applied Behavior Analysis, 9*, 509-514.
Skinner, B. F. (1945). The operational analysis of psychological terms. *The Psychological Review, 52*, 270-277.

Skinner, B. F. (1957). *Verbal Behavior*. New York: Appleton-Century-Crofts.

Zettle, R. D. & Hayes, S. C. (1982). Rule-governed behavior: A potential theoretical framework for cognitive-behavioral therapy. In P. C. Kendall (Ed.) *Advances in Cognitive-Behavioral Research and Therapy, Volume I*. New York: Academic Press.

Chapter Five

INTRAVERBAL BEHAVIOR[1]

E. A. Vargas

INTRODUCTION

VERBAL BEHAVIOR[2] was published in 1957 after Skinner worked twenty-five years on it. Prior versions were presented as the William James Lectures and for a language course at Columbia.[3] Reactions seemed favorable though perhaps puzzled. Then a great silence ensued, broken only by Chomsky's (1959) bombastic review which when not missing the point misunderstood the analysis. Thereafter it appeared to be the book's fate to be trotted out and roundly scolded when any of a variety of those of the psycholinguistic or cognitive persuasion wanted to show the inadequacy if not sheer ineptness of a behavioral analysis of language. The only attention obtained was of an honor so fashioned that it would have been best to have forgone it.

Few of those who scorned the book appeared to have read it. They preferred to quote prior critics. Sadder yet, not many behaviorists seemed to understand Skinner's formulation of verbal behavior or if they did, to be affected by it. Behaviorists made rare use of the analysis even when they investigated verbal behavior in the laboratory, interpreted it in daily life, or taught it in the classroom. The question immediately poses itself: why? No answer can be very satisfactory, indulging as it must in post hoc speculation.

---

[1] I wish to thank Phil Chase, Lawrence Fraley, John Humphrey, B. F. Skinner, Julie Vargas, and Margaret Vaughan, for helpful comments on earlier versions of this article.

[2] Unless otherwise noted all later quotes are to *Verbal Behavior* (Skinner, 1957).

[3] "Ralph Hefferline's stenographic version circulated fairly widely *after* the course." (Skinner, 1984, Personal Communication)

Three reasons suggest themselves. One reason seems immediately apparent. Few instructors taught an analysis of language behavior using Skinner's formulation. This was true even in those departments in which one or two behavior analysts resided. One encounters the second reason daily: The grip the common culture maintains on the reasons given as to why we talk. Many of the prevalent theories of language promote common language conceptions but they are gusseted in sophisticated terms. A central axiom seems hard to abandon: the human being as prime actor in speech making, rather than as locality. The third reason is easily at hand: Skinner's analysis of verbal behavior is hard to understand and his book difficult to read.

The book, though condensed as it is, sometimes obscures its arguments behind the rush of detail it presents for the benefit of the reader. Even with such detail Skinner demands a lot from the reader. What he argues against must in some way already be known (Skinner stated that too much of the book began to be a review of the literature and he dropped a good third of it), what he argues for is often strange unless the reader abandons preconceptions, and what his argument implies readers must tease out by themselves. Such effort is only reasonable. Not everything could be said or said in the usual way, at least not when the aim is no less than to take a radically different approach to the analysis of language behavior. Most importantly, the analysis is the first of its kind and from one person. It thus carries the virtues and faults of originality. The prime virtue is it seminal quality. It will provoke many more words than it contains and easily more studies than it mentions. But its original quality signifies an author struggling to say what has not been said before and against a tradition for saying it a certain way. Skinner at times does not "know" his own design or at least does not clearly present it; (a common occurrence in radically new formulations). Then, of course, what he does say is only a beginning.

This chapter extends Skinner's analysis, that portion called "verbal behavior under the control of verbal stimuli." It provides an exposition so the reader may discriminate more precisely the framework of Skinner's analysis; clarifies a few issues (for example the difference between textual behavior and reading); and furnishes terms to facilitate speaking more exactly of the verbal relations currently delineated, thus promoting their experimental assessment and the further analysis of other verbal relations not yet well distinguished conceptually.

Skinner's Analysis of Verbal Behavior: An Overview

Prior to understanding well any aspect of his analysis, Skinner's overall analytic design must be understood. Skinner concentrates on and interprets the controls on a complex type of human behavior specifically mediated by other humans (and taught to do so) whose actions reinforce the speaker's behavior; and isolates this type under the rubric of "verbal behavior." He assumes that always an event, or set of events, controls our verbal behavior. The events may be physical or physiological, but the dimensional level of analysis with which he concerns himself is behavioral, with controlling events resulting from the individual's interaction with the immediate environment, an environment which may include that enclosed within the skin. Skinner's book demonstrates that thesis by systematically describing those behavioral and environmental controls and their dynamic features within a framework derived from the experimental analysis of behavior.

Skinner classifies three sets of events as controlling verbal behavior: (1) events that are themselves verbal behavior; (2) events in the physical environment or due to conditions of deprivation or aversive stimulation; (3) and events produced when verbal and nonverbal stimuli combine. Control thus resides: (1) in verbal behavior; (2) in occurrences independent, that is outside, of verbal behavior; (3) and in a combined interaction of verbal and nonverbal events. Skinner labels these controls as: (1) "verbal behavior under the control of verbal stimuli"; (2) "tacts" and "mands"; (3) and "autoclitics".

A broader, and perhaps more convenient, labeling might be: intra (or within) verbal; extra (or outside) verbal; and auto (or self) verbal. Each of these labels attempts to capture the salient feature of the control relationship: "intra" or "within" for verbal behavior controlled solely by other verbal behavior; "extra" or "outside" for verbal behavior controlled by environmental events; and "auto" or "self" for controls that are nonverbal and verbal concurrently and whose locus is the individual.

Imagine a continuum of control from verbal events to nonverbal events, and now place intra (within) verbal at one end, extra (outside) verbal at the other, and auto (self) verbal in the middle. Each type of control occupies a certain sector of the continuum, and the autoverbal type begins where intraverbal and extraverbal controls blend toward the middle. Skinner emphasizes the prevalence of multiple controls over our verbal behavior, and though possible, it's doubtful whether any of the relations at either end of the continuum are ever found in pure form.

Table 5-I relates the classifying labels given above to the categories that Skinner uses for the types of verbal relations he discusses. In all cases the three-term contingency operates though priority of control varies between antecedent and postcedent stimuli as in, for example, the tact and mand.

Table 5-I

Intraverbal	*Autoverbal*	*Extraverbal*	
Verbal Behavior controlled by Verbal Stimuli	Autoclitics	Tacts	Mands
Echoic Textual Transcription "Intraverbal"	Descriptive Qualifying Quantifying Relational Manipulative	Extended generic metaphorical metonymical solecistic nomination Abstraction	Extended superstitious magical

This chapter reworks the intraverbal category, that is, what Skinner calls "verbal behavior under the control of verbal stimuli," hereafter designated "VS:VR."

Skinner's Analysis of the VS:VR Relation: A Synopsis

Skinner's brief but cogent treatment of the interactive relation in which verbal stimuli control verbal behavior provides an important foundation for many later analyses including those of multiple control and that of the autoclitic relation. He describes a number of different types of interactions in which verbal stimuli control verbal responses. The general model is not complex, and Skinner analyzes verbal episodes always from the perspective of the controls over the speaker.

In the verbal episode, the roles of the speaker and listener are quickly changing. (Figure 5-1 diagrams the shifting relation between speaker and listener.) For any of a number of reasons, a current speaker initially emits a verbal stimulus in the presence of a listener, an audience. The verbal stimulus may request that the listener, the speaker-to-be, repeat the statement. The new speaker emits the verbal response, under the discriminative control of the audience (the original speaker) and the verbal stimulus plus whatever establishes the motivative relation between statement and consequence, for example, a slight aversive threat. (Other operations may of course establish other consequences.) The speaker's response reinforces the prior verbal action of the current listener (the initial speaker) and becomes the discriminative stimulus for a response on the listener's part to withdraw or to reduce the threat. Withdrawing the aversive stimulus reinforces the speaker. This general case fits into Skinner's three-term contingency paradigm of an antecedent stimulus (almost inevitably a discriminative or establishing stimulus), a response, and a postcedent stimulus (either a reinforcing or punishing event).[4] (See Michael [1982a and 1984] for an account of establishing stimulus, establishing operations, and motivative relations.)

The underlying theme in Skinner's analysis of verbal behavior under the control of verbal stimuli is the degree to which verbal behavior, or its product, corresponds to verbal stimuli. As he states on page 55 of *Verbal Behavior*, "A . . . distinction may be made in terms of the resemblances between forms of stimulus and response." The correspondence ranges from complete identity to complete nonidentity. A further consideration is the type of medium, roughly the physical form of the verbal relation. He considers two forms, spoken or written (page 55), and mentions a third, gesturing (page 71), in passing. The medium of verbal interaction, while important for describing a particular type of verbal relation, is, as a classification criterion, subordinate to the correspondence principle.

Skinner examines three principal categories of VS:VR relations: "echoic, textual, and intraverbal" (p. 55) though he also briefly comments on a fourth, "transcription" (pp. 69 to 71). Table 5-II illustrates the interrelations of Skinner's principal categories.

---

[4] "Consequence" means those events that result due to prior conditions or actions. The word implies the necessary connection between the result and the prior action. However there are events that follow actions that aren't so connected. They may come to have a functional significance through adventitious conditioning, but otherwise would have no effect due to the absence of any prior relation. "Antecedent" categorizes events of this sort BEFORE an action occurs. It's a term neutral in its "causal" or "functional" implications since it simply designates events by their place in time. "Postcedent" is an equivalent term for events that take place AFTER an action occurs. It allows us to talk about events that follow actions without implying that these events are functionally or causally connected as the term "consequence" both denotes and connotes (Vargas, 1984).

Table 5-II
VS:VR

Correspondence

	matches	point-to-point	differs
same	echoic transcription: copying		
medium different		textual transcription: dictation	
irrelevant			intraverbal

Note that since "medium" is in a sense a residual criterion, a number of the cells remain empty. Some verbal relations could fit in more than one cell: the "intraverbal" relation could be placed in all the cells that intersect between the correspondence column "differs" and the three medium rows, "same," "different," "irrelevant."

In the discussion that follows, the organizing principle, correspondence, will be emphasized as well as the controls based on this principle. Specific verbal relations discussed serve to illustrate these controls. Many more types of verbal relations exemplify the control of verbal responses by verbal stimuli than those mentioned by Skinner. His list was not meant to be exhaustive, nor do those verbal relations later mentioned in this article exhaust the possibilities. A number of extensive systems of verbal behavior won't be covered such as braille, international flag code, morse code, music, and semaphore code.

INTRAVERBAL BEHAVIOR: A REORGANIZATION

INTRODUCTION

The critical feature of the VS:VR relation is the criterion for control that the verbal community uses either to reinforce or to punish.[5] As mentioned, the principle one is the degree of correspondence between the form of the stimulus and that of the response, or perhaps more often, that

---

[5] "Use of reinforcers and punishers can be very slight. The intraverbal 'house-home' is due to thousands of instances in which, having heard 'house' it is useful to say 'home', gaining a very slight reward." (Skinner, 1984, Personal Communication)

of the response product. (Though obviously it is not the effect of the response that is reinforced, a product, for example a written copy, but the response itself; it makes no sense to say that the verbal community reinforces a text though the text itself may be the discriminative stimulus for reinforcement.) The degree to which the criterion of correspondence applies varies in stringency. A correspondence continuum ensues from the verbal community's demand that all aspects of the verbal response or response product match the verbal stimulus to whatever degree is possible, to the verbal community's disregard for whether such a match occurs or not. When the correspondence criterion becomes irrelevant it drops out with others taking its place.

Using the degree of correspondence between verbal stimulus and verbal response as a first organizing principle, three primary groupings of verbal relations emerge:

Verbal episodes occur in which point-to-point correspondence in all dimensions must take place between verbal stimulus and verbal response or response product for the verbal community to provide reinforcement. Of necessity both verbal stimulus and response or product occur in the same medium. Skinner describes one type extensively, echoic, but others are possible such as duplicating a text or a gesture. The term "duplic" thus will denote those verbal relations due to reinforcing the formal identity of response to stimulus, to whatever extent that can occur.

In another large subset of verbal relations where verbal stimuli control verbal behavior, sequential point-to-point correspondence takes place between verbal stimuli in one medium and verbal responses in another. Textual and transcriptive (when dictated) verbal relations fall into this category. Maintenance of seriality between verbal stimuli and responses in different media is the critical feature here, and so the term "codic" will designate these verbal episodes.

Verbal relations occur in which a certain verbal response must follow a given verbal stimulus, but without regard to the degree of correspondence between them; (thus the medium in which verbal responses or verbal stimuli occur is irrelevant). Socially constructed sequality, based on certain criteria, provides the rationale to name these relations "sequelic".[6]

---

[6] I've adopted the terms "duplic" and "codic" from Jack Michael's designations of similar categories based on similar criteria (Michael, 1982b). The term "sequelic", with accent on the middle syllable, is coined on the same principle as the first two category labels. Each label is based on the primary feature that enters into all verbal relations falling within a specific category. The suffix "ic" means to have or consist of a particular characteristic and thus points to that primary feature. Also note later that the specifications for reinforcement become less stringent from duplic to codic to sequelic verbal relations with respect to their physical dimensions.

Table 5-III updates Table 5-I by substituting the new organizing labels for verbal relations in the intraverbal category. Terms not yet defined will be later in the manuscript.

Table 5-III

Intraverbal	*Autoverbal*	*Extraverbal*	
V.B. Controlled by V.S.	Autoclitics	Tacts	Mands
Duplic	Descriptive	Extended	Extended
echoic	Qualifying	generic	superstitious
identigraphic	Quantifying	metaphorical	magical
mimetic	Relational	metonymical	
Codic	Manipulative	solecistic	
textual		nomination	
Sequelic		Abstraction	

Duplic Verbal Behavior

In the duplic subcategory of the intraverbal relation, verbal stimuli and verbal responses (or response products) correspond point-to-point in all aspects of form. The physical dimensions of the response or response product duplicate those of the verbal stimulus. Verbal behavior matches in critical physical attributes the verbal stimulus, except possibly for scale. Thus, necessarily, both stimuli and responses occur in the same physical medium.

Duplic verbal behavior takes place within a variety of media. Skinner does not define "medium" directly but his use of the term connotes the means by which verbal behavior can take place. He says, for example (page 69), that "Writing . . . occurs only in a 'medium'." Skinner discusses only the vocal type or duplic interaction extensively, the echoic. However, two other common types occur through graphics and gestures: identigraphic, and mimetic.[7]

---

[7]The subcategory names, echoic, identigraphic, and mimetic reflect the critical feature of the various media in which a formal match occurs between verbal stimulus and verbal behavior. Skinner already supplied "echoic" and the Oxford English Dictionary provided "mimetic" and the basis for "identigraphic". This latter subcategory name presented the greatest difficulty. A term was needed that would convey the sense of exactly copying a graphic stimulus. None was available. "Copying" was too general. "Transcribe" ambiguous as it also refers to control by a
→

Echoic Verbal Behavior

A common type of verbal behavior is repeating, in more or less exact form, something just spoken. Skinner names this interaction "echoic," and describes it thoroughly (pp. 55-65). He portrays the duplicating relation between verbal stimulus and verbal behavior as follows in Figure 5-1.

SPEAKER

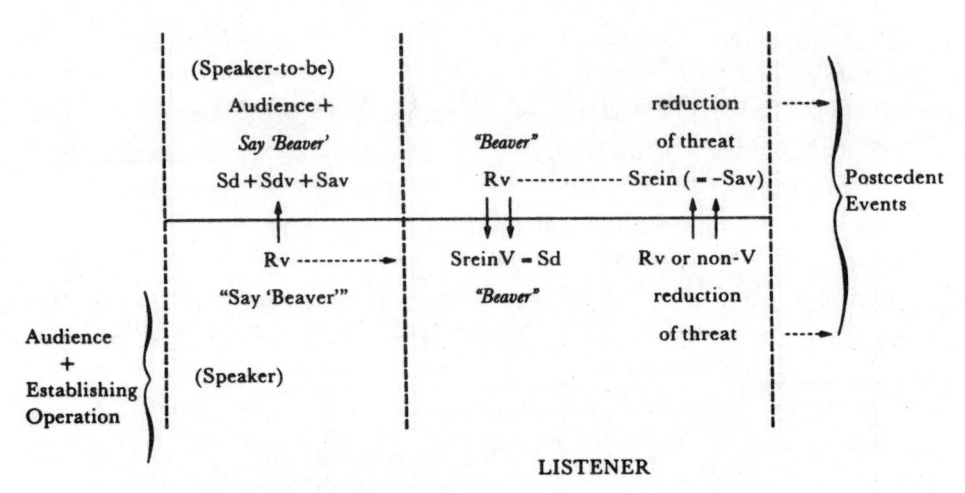

```
                (Speaker-to-be)
                Audience +                           reduction
                Say 'Beaver'        "Beaver"         of threat
                Sd + Sdv + Sav      Rv ----------- Srein ( = -Sav)   } Postcedent
                                                                       Events
                 ──────────────────────────────────────────────
                     Rv ────────▶    SreinV = Sd      Rv or non-V
Audience             "Say 'Beaver'"    "Beaver"       reduction
   +                                                   of threat
Establishing     (Speaker)
Operation
```

LISTENER

Where Rv = verbal response
Sd = discriminative stimulus
Sdv = verbal discriminative stimulus
Sav = aversive stimulus
Srein = reinforcing stimulus

Figure 5-1. (Modified slightly from page 57, *Verbal Behavior*)

Identigraphic Verbal Behavior

A text may also be duplicated. Someone writes something down and a second person matches it. Skinner mentions this relation in passing (page 70) and calls it "copying." The degree to which the verbal community applies stringent criteria to the response may vary but how correct it is, that is, how well it duplicates the verbal stimulus, always enters into the de-

---

vocal stimulus. "Graphic" was also too general. Although it carries the notion of a culturally mediated visual stimulus it doesn't restrict its meaning to the duplicating of text or picture. "Identigraphic" was etymologically permissible, "from ident(i), for L. idem 'same'" and "graphic" meaning "drawing" or "writing". (*Oxford English Dictionary*, p. 1368, subpage 19, column 1, and p. 1191, subpage 359, column 3).

livery of reinforcement. Penmanship exercises provide a common example. The standard maintained depends on a second party, who may be the original writer at a later time, responding as effectively to the copied material as to the original.

Verbal relations in visual terms are broader than simply that of duplicating textual material; copying a drawing, for example. Any sort of graphic stimulus may provide the occasion for the verbal community to reinforce an effort to copy it exactly. Often instruction may involve the copying of great works of art in order to learn the techniques of the "old masters." Thus students busily wielding their brushes may be found in the galleries of museums sitting on little stools in front of works of art. A copy may also be made to pass falsely as a Rembrandt or a Vermeer and receive the same value as if it were one of their works. Since art patrons may respond to the imitation as they would to the original such occurrences lead to discussions on the meaning of art, and deal with many of the same sort of considerations involved in the analysis of verbal behavior. In any case, such copying requires a fine grained repertoire of an order usually not necessary in the everyday duplicating of graphics for the effective behavior of others.

The difference in repertoire depends on the size of the minimal duplic unit shaped by the verbal community. In exemplifying that size difference, Skinner distinguishes between copying a familiar alphabet and one unfamiliar. In the latter the repertoire approaches the fine-grained type involved in copying a picture. In the former there are simply standard responses at hand for the copyist.

In a rough way an analogy could be drawn here between these two types of minimal unit repertoires and the two types of printing apparatuses for computer printers. In one, the daisy wheel, the printing font delivers a whole character; in the other, the dot matrix, the character is built up from a series of very small dot impressions. The daisy wheel automatically delivers a standard letter quality character. The degree to which the dot matrix printer prints a letter quality character depends on the density, the number of dots per unit space printed. The analogy is useful only for the type of response described. It breaks down with respect to how the response, mechanical or organic, is obtained and in how it is maintained. The fine-grained repertoire in the human response is self-corrective. The response of the dot matrix printer is not (though presumably it could be with a visual scanner and the proper feedback loops.) If the standard unitary response in, for example, copying a familiar alphabet gets too far out of line with the stimulus, the verbal community shapes it up again through punishment and reinforcement. When the daisy wheel font begins to make a mark no longer of good quality it is simply replaced with an equivalent unit. The distinction between the two processes is, of course, between that of a mechanical one where the action is present and an organic one where it is interactional and future responses depend on prior consequences.

Mimetic Verbal Behavior

Another relation in visual terms is that of motion or gestures which as verbal stimuli may control other motions or gestures. The interaction between "speaker" and "listener" is similar to that which occurs in echoic interactions. Gestures are duplicated in sign languge, and mimetic interactions constitute an important component of that language especially in teaching it. As Sundberg, Michael, and Peterson (1977) point out, mimicking the movements that people make facilitates coming under stimulus control of other gestural verbal relations. (Sundberg, et al. analyzed sign language as verbal behavior and through such an analysis developed an effective instructional technology to teach it. See Sundberg 1978a, 1978b, and 1980.)

Sign language is not the only system of verbal behavior in which a "speaker" duplicates prior motions. In ballet, for example, stylized techniques mediated by others must be learned in order to have specific effects on the audience. These gestures usually tell a story. At least in dramatic ballet they do; ballet may also consist only of dance steps to music—which in their own way may also be verbal behavior if an effect specifically "intended" by a verbal community occurs through more than mere mechanical action.

Codic Verbal Behavior

The codic relation depends upon a verbal community reinforcing the serial order between a verbal stimulus in one medium and a verbal response in another. A successive point-to-point correspondence across modalities characterizes a variety of verbal relationships and of those relationships three are quite common: textual, someone speaks from a written product; dictation, someone writes from speech; and, someone speaking and writing from gestures. Of the three, Skinner analyzes the first two in *Verbal Behavior*. No labels presently represent categories for the codic relations of the third. Other correspondences exist between verbal behavior in different media such as Braille with its tactual-written-spoken relation.

Skinner discusses the textual relation and that of dictation briefly and clearly. However, two points of confusion with respect to textual behavior often arise: that concerning reading and that which concerns other behavior under the control of a textual stimulus.

Reading[8] and Textual Behavior

Reading is not identical to the textual relation, though vocal verbal behavior under control of a textual stimulus constitutes an important component of the behavior called reading. The term "reading" is a label for such a wide variety of behaviors that it may be one of those terms that disguises rather than reveals what is happening. Be that as it may no educator or psychologist is content to have reading be mere control by a textual stimulus. People may vocalize a textual stimulus but unless they act appropriately in other ways with respect to it, such behavior is not accepted or termed as reading. Such other ways are said to show "understanding," "comprehension," "insight," and so on, and all these labels observationally turn out to be a set of behaviors from whose presence the labeled state is inferred or which are that state.

The distinction between textual behavior and reading lies in the narrowness of the control of the textual stimulus. Events other than the textual stimuli have their play and responses are more than mere vocalization. Skinner provides the following description,

> "The reader usually, though not necessarily, begins with . . . textual behavior . . .; his responses are made under the control of visual stimuli. He may then react to his own textual behavior as a listener. It is not necessary that he do so. In reading aloud to children one may not react beyond the merely textual stage, and in reading aloud in a barely familiar tongue, one may become so preoccupied with pronunciation as to neglect all other functions of reader or self-listener. On the other hand, nontextual responses may predominate" (p. 169).

In reading, then, the reader responds with more than merely point-to-point vocal responses to a textual stimulus. He responds in other ways either directly to the text or after he has responded vocally.

Collateral effects provide the evidence for the distinction between textual behavior and reading behavior. An example from Skinner's Notebooks (1980) labeled appropriately enough "Text and Context" points to the distinction indicated by collateral effects:

---

[8]For a wider discussion of reading and the teaching of reading behavior, see Moxley, R. A., *A Functional Analysis of Reading*, this text.

> Shortly after reviewing a section in *The Shaping of a Behaviorist* about L. J. Henderson, I drove down Brattle Street. My eye hung on the sign 'Willard Street' as I passed. I have passed it many hundreds of times. I noted my interest and then recalled that Henderson had lived on that street. I had dined with him there (p. 160).

What formerly Skinner responded to textually, he now read for the reasons given. Conversely, the absence of any collateral effect when responding to a text also demonstrates the difference between the two types of control. The common experience of "reading" and not knowing what one reads indicates textual behavior, but no other behavior of any consequence.

Collateral effects point to the fact that the same stimulus can give rise to more than one effect; (or its converse: that the same response can be controlled by more than one stimulus). *Notebooks* (1980) supplies another example:

> I frequently try to abbreviate PIGEON as PIG, as in PROJ. PIG., but my response to pig invariably intrudes, and I lengthen to PIGEON. I have noticed the same tendency in avoiding ASS for ASSOCIATION (AM. ASS. ADV. SCI.), ANAL for ANALYSIS, and CONT for CONTINUED. A friend tells me he uses PRO and CONTRA because the French CON bothers him (p. 32).

The same stimulus evokes two effects, one formal and one emotional. (Puns and other word play illustrate the same response controlled by more than one stimulus.)

These differing controls and their effects result from prior multiple correlation of stimuli and responses. Over time, verbal behavior occurs in many settings, in the presence of many audiences, and under the control of many variables. Due to prior pairing with many other events any verbal stimulus may produce concurrent responses—collateral effects—some of which are verbal and some not. As Skinner put it in a simple example (page 154),

> If a verbal stimulus frequently accompanies some state of affairs which is the unconditioned or previously conditioned stimulus for an emotional reaction, the verbal stimulus eventually evokes this reaction. Thus, if one is afraid of snakes and if the verbal stimulus SNAKE has sometimes accompanied real snakes, the verbal stimulus alone may evoke an emotional reaction (p. 154).

These differences in prior conditionals reflect themselves in the complex histories readers bring to a text and thus in the complexity of the subsequent interaction readers have with that text. In *Martin Eden* (1909), a thinly disguised autobiographical novel by Jack London, London's hero, a tough roughneck from the waterfront, meets an upperclass girl who's led a sheltered life. She begins to teach him grammar and to introduce him to the pleasures of poetry. London notes their different reactions.

> She read Browning aloud to him and was often puzzled by the strange interpretations he gave to mooted passages. It was beyond her to realize that, out of his experiences of men and women and life, his interpretations were far more frequently correct than hers (page 58).

The question is not that such multiple prior pairings occur but how they occur, what results from such pairings, what the classes of variables are, how to distinguish the control of one variable from another, and under what circumstances one variable seems to seize control. The distinction between reading behavior and textual behavior simply highlights one instance of the effect of the variety of conditioning of verbal behavior. In fact, the reading "response" may also occur to irrelevant stimuli—bordering lines, size of page, etc.—accompanying the text. (See Vargas, J. (1984) for a discussion of irrelevant stimulus control in the design of instructional material.)

Non-textual Behavior to Text

A text is a specified pattern of visual stimuli to which particular responses are shaped by a verbal community, some verbal and some not. While on the one hand that text may evoke complex responses (such as reading), on the other, no textual behavior may occur. Skinner's discussion is brief and to the point:

> "Nontextual responses . . . may come to be made directly to the printed text, and they may be conditioned in the absence of textual behavior. Thus, children may react appropriately to cards reading RUN, SIT, CLAP HANDS, and so on, without engaging in vocal behavior. . . . We react to many signs, such as SILENCE in a library or BARBER on a shop window, by taking appropriate action without necessarily engaging in textual behavior. We would make essentially the same reaction to a picture of a man with a finger on his lips and a revolving red-and-white spiral, respectively" (pp. 160-170).

In these examples the listener doesn't vocalize to mediate his or someone else's behavior and therefore is not engaging in verbal behavior.

Sequelic Verbal Behavior

The overall paradigm of control for sequeled verbal relations is the usual three-term contingency of verbal stimulus as discriminative stimulus (VSd), correlated with a verbal response (VR) and generalized reinforcement (S+). The verbal community shapes all verbal relations within the intraverbal category following that paradigm.

However, the difference between the three subcategories of intraverbal relations—duplic, codic, and sequelic—lies in the distinguishing characteristics of the verbal relation specified for reinforcement by the verbal community. So, for example, in duplic verbal relations, the VSd:VR contingency relation takes place within the same medium and for reinforcement a formal match must occur between the verbal stimulus and the verbal response; echoic as well as transgraphic and mimetic verbal relations exhibit those properties. The verbal community does not reinforce those characteristics in the other two intraverbal subcategories, nor are they even plausible in the codic subcategory due to the occurrence of responses and stimuli in different modes. The verbal community "applies" the three-term contingency differently for each of the three subcategories of verbal relations within the intraverbal category.

Sequeled verbal responses resemble neither the form nor the order of verbal stimuli. The distinguishing characteristic of verbal relations in the sequelic subcategory is that verbal responses do not share properties of prior verbal stimuli, except by accident. Reinforcement by the verbal community of point-to-point correspondence does not occur or occurs only as a by-product of reinforcement for other reasons. When asked to state the first thing one thinks of saying when given the word "blue," an individual may say "sky" or "grass" or "bird." Regardless of its seemingly free relation, a particular verbal response (or responses) must follow the immediately prior verbal stimulus (or stimuli)—therefore the label "sequelic" for the subcategory—but what determines the "must" presents a more complex case for analysis in this subcategory than in the others.

In sequeled verbal relations the verbal response is reinforced not just because it simply follows the verbal stimulus. All verbal responses follow verbal stimuli. It is reinforced when a specific response follows; the verbal community reinforces the correct verbal response, or type of correct verbal response, succeeding a particular verbal stimulus. The critical question then becomes, "what defines 'properly' or 'correct'"? (Such a question was pertinent for the other verbal relations discussed and the answers were rather straight forward: correctness for duplic responses lies in point-to-point correspondence in form between verbal stimulus and verbal response within the same medium, and for codic responses in point-to-point correspondence in the order of verbal responses to verbal stimuli in different media.)

Skinner defines the important characteristic of sequelic verbal behavior as that of verbal responses showing "no point-to-point correspondence with the verbal stimuli which evoke them" (page 71), that is, the verbal response must differ in form from that of the verbal stimulus. But this characteristic is not enough. It fails to distinguish why the verbal community reinforces one verbal response and not another when both lack formal correspondence with prior verbal stimuli. For reinforcement to occur the verbal community demands more than that "four" differ from "two plus two" either in sight or sound or that "blue" differ from "white" in "red, white, and . . .". "Five" and "green" differ also. As control of the verbal response by and large resides primarily in prior verbal stimuli and there appears to be no specific feature of this class of verbal stimuli by which the verbal community reinforces a particular relation of verbal responses, then we must look for the conditions that define "properly" or "correct." As current control resides in immediately preceding verbal stimuli these conditions were pertinent when the verbal response was acquired.

Since the labels for the subcategory relations capture their essential feature, the term "sequel" needs to be exactly defined. "Sequel" is used in its older sense of "that which follows as a result of an event or cause of action; an after consequence" (*Oxford English Dictionary*, p. 2733, subpage 484, column 2, definition 3). A quote from Hobbes, quite behavioral in its expression, in the *OED* provides an example of that meaning of the word: "The future being but a fiction of the mind, applying the sequels of action past, to the actions that are present." How have the "sequels of action past" that dictate current verbal relations in this subcategory been acquired? Skinner gives three ways (page 75). Sequeled verbal relations may be (1) "specifically acquired"; (2) acquired because they "frequently occur together"; (3) acquired due to a "special history."

One may argue that frequently occurring sequeled verbal relations are also specifically acquired, and that's true in the literal sense, but the difference lies in how. One set of relations is deliberately shaped by a social agency and the other through frequent pairing in typical social situations of a common culture. As the labels "specifically acquired" and "frequently occur together" do not clearly distinguish that difference, it may be best to use "formally shaped" and "informally shaped" to stand for these differing origins of sequeled verbal actions.

Formally Shaped

Sequeled verbal behavior that is specifically acquired may include such common verbal relations as the alphabet, the times table, poetry, definitions, pledges, and scientific formulas. Students dutifully "memorizing" a set of verbal stimuli considered important by the culture appears as a common sight in many classrooms. Teachers hand out exercise sheets in arithmetic that repeat the same procedures over and over again. Spelling bees celebrate the hours spent learning what letters follow others in a particular order. Many students flip flashcards to practice emitting a specific response, whether formula, foreign term, or definition, to a rapidly exposed verbal stimulus. The aim of these efforts is rigorous control by prior verbal stimuli as exemplified by lack of error and often as well by speed of response.

What is learned doesn't have to make any "sense" to the person acquiring the specifically sequeled verbal relation. University students correctly answer fill-in-the-blank questions or properly match terms though later can't "use" these same terms when conversing or writing. Such occurrences are common and Wouk provides such an example in *The Caine Mutiny*.

> "It happened that in the first week a terrible examination was scheduled in Ordnance, with the announced purpose of causing weaklings to go down. Everybody crammed feverishly, of course. Willie was as earnest as the rest, but one page of the book, composed in the worst Navy jargon, baffled him; a description of a thing called a Frictionless Bearing. . . . Willie had read the page seventeen times, then twice more aloud, and was on the point of quitting when he noticed that whole sentences had become embedded in his memory. He worked another half hour and memorized the entire page, word for word. The chief essay question on the examination, as luck would have it, was Explain the Frictionless Bearing. Willie happily disgorged the words, which meant no more to him than a Hindu chant. When the results of the test were announced he stood first in the school. . . .
>
> With a reputation to uphold, and dozens of questions to answer in every study period, Willie thereafter drove himself to a meaningless verbal mastery of all the details of naval cannons" (p. 41).

A poem may have no particular meaning, the times table no apparent logic, a scientific formula no significance, the spelling of a word no rule to it. Yet the speaker may recite them or write them down properly when asked to do so.

What is said may convey more meaning to others than it does to the speaker. What the speaker now acquires as a set of verbal responses following a set of verbal stimuli were acquired under other conditions by some subset of the verbal community. That subset may know the significance of the speaker's statements and thus demand that these statements be acquired. But for the speaker they are simply a set of sights and sounds and gestures, learned in a particular sequence, to which he emits no other collateral behavior (except possibly emotional depending on the circumstances of reinforcement and punishment when acquired). Eventually from such sequeled verbal behavior the speaker, as well as the community, derives practical effects.

The verbal community formally shapes and maintains specifically acquired sequeled verbal behavior. Its organization may be so extensive that it constitutes a large part of what is usually called "bodies of thought." The times table was given as an example but sequeled verbal relations may be, and often are, much more elaborate. Though large portions of the following verbal behavior may be under multiple control, sequeled verbal behavior may consist of any or all the verses and phrases in the Bible or Koran or Torah, Shakespeare's sonnets or the entirety of one or more of his plays, the taxonomic arrangements of any of various animals or plants, or the tightly constructed links in so-called truth tables. The verbal community teaches the individual sequeled verbal relations from and in specific sets, of whatever size, of verbal stimuli.

Informally Shaped

Sequeled verbal responses that "frequently occur together" are exemplified by common everyday sayings such as: "good morning"—"hello"; "how are you?"—"fine, how about yourself?"; "goodbye"—"so long"; "gotta go now"—"well, take 'er easy"; "we must get together sometime"—"yes, let's do." Most sequeled verbal responses that "frequently occur together" do so in a social context. Sequeled verbal behavior occurs frequently in greetings and departures, in conversational starters and enders, in statements of seeming friendliness.

The strength of verbal behavior under informal sequeled control becomes apparent when one makes a mistake with respect to the social context in which the sequeled verbal response is uttered. For example, visiting someone in the hospital, immediately hearing that person launch into a long detailed rendition of his misery and then in the small silence that follows when that person says, "Well, I've talked too much. How are you?", saying, "Fine. How are you feeling?" Or bumping into someone greeted and talked to an hour or so before and when she says, "Well! Hi again", saying, "Hi. How have you been?" If the reader said "good morning" to people in the evening, he or she would find a goodly number replying "good morning." Puzzled looks usually result when verbal responses occur that are only appropriate to the prior verbal stimuli (that is, under strong control by them because they usually follow and are usually reinforced), but not appropriate to the social situation in which they occur.

The verbal community informally shapes and maintains frequently occurring sequeled verbal behavior. The particular linking of verbal stimuli and responses result from "contiguous usage" (page 75) in a common cultural or social context. "A penny for the Guy" is a typical saying on

Guy Fawkes Day in England and it would be expected that most English people would "automatically" think or say the rest of the phrase if part were stated to them. Similarly an American would hardly ever think of other than the usually stated month if one said, "Fourth of . . . . Certain verbal communities may have sequeled verbal relations of greeting, departure, chit-chat, and conversational filler that are cliches with them, that is, control resides exclusively in prior verbal stimuli, but which interest outsiders for a while, for example, Valley Girl talk. The verbal responses that people most often encounter will be those that they will most likely emit if reinforced for doing so.

Idiosyncratically Shaped

Sequeled verbal behavior acquired with a "special history" almost seems to be a residual category, but comprises in a sense simply the formally-shaped or informally-shaped cases where usage is low, the verbal relations unique, and the subset of people involved as possibly only one. An individual in speaking to himself, or herself, may bring certain forms of speech purely under the control of prior forms so that verbal responses occur only as the result of prior verbal stimuli. Skinner in *Particulars of My Life* (1976, p. 280) mentions the effect when younger. "My notes also show idiosyncratic usages and turns of phrase which suggest the autodidact." Anxiety and other emotional states may promote certain verbal forms which become tightly linked to verbal stimuli and which then appear even in the absence of those states or the conditions that predispose to them. "Verbal tics" may be examples here such as saying "o.k." in those social circumstances when obviously neither approval nor permission is being requested.

What is called "style" partly results from sequeled verbal relations shaped through the special history unique to every person. Most of the sequeled verbal behavior in a person's speech or writing would have been constructed formally or informally, for example: how words are spelled, which ones follow others, and how those are typically grouped. Some types of sequeled verbal behavior associated with certain occupational and social groups are so discriminable that they are used to add color or veracity in drama or fiction when identifying individuals by features of social class. However, other sequeled verbal behavior would have been the result of uncommon events so that regardless of the occupational or social group to which the individual belongs certain aspects of his verbal behavior stand out. These sequeled relations dominate enough of what is said or written so that whatever the individual composes, if he writes or speaks extensively, the idiosyncrasies of his verbal behavior lead to easily identifiable imitation. They are, as it were, the fingerprints of the special events in his verbal history. Analysis of obscure, ambiguous, or controversial writings make use of these special verbal stimulus response links through statistical counts of their frequency.

Sequeled verbal relations due to a "special history" originate in circumstances unique to the individual, and later are maintained by reinforcement produced by that verbal behavior or received under typical social contingencies. The scope may be as large as style or as small as nonsense phrases or sounds. Any idiosyncracy of speech independent of composition effects or control by extraverbal variables could belong in this subcategory. What may sound fresh, immediate, and creative to a new audience may simply be habitual speech.

Sequelic Subcategories

It is difficult to say whether there are various subcategories of sequeled verbal relations. The variety of response forms to a particular verbal stimulus is not restricted as in duplic and codic relations. This restriction calls for certain topographic features in the verbal responses of the latter two categories correlated with those of the verbal stimulus. In one case, the duplic, the physical form of the response product must match that of the verbal stimulus, and in codic relations, the response product must correspond point-to-point with the serial order of the verbal stimulus.

However, restriction can and does occur in sequeled verbal behavior. Contrast "two plus two equals" as a verbal stimulus with "red." To the verbal stimulus "two plus two equals," only the verbal response "four" is reinforced as a correct response form by the verbal community, whereas it may reinforce a variety of verbal responses that follow "red": "white," "bloody," "sky," "color," "line," "car," "apple," and so on. Only in very special circumstances would the verbal community permit and reinforce a response form other than "four" to follow "two plus two equals," and current control for the differing response form would reside as much elsewhere as in the prior verbal stimulus. Sequeled verbal behavior thus ranges from "nonspecified" to "specified," and the latter category approaches the restrictive characteristic of duplic and codic verbal behavior but without the feature of point-to-point correspondence in form or sequence.

Skinner argues "complexity" as the reason for the restriction of verbal forms.

> "The nature of the stimulus control . . . is shown by responses to verbal stimuli containing more than one word. The stimulus 'red' in the usual word associa-

tion experiment may yield 'green,' 'blue,' 'color,' or any one of many other responses, for there are many different circumstances under which it appears as part of the occasion for the reinforcement of such responses. Similarly, the stimulus word 'white' will yield 'black,' 'snow,' and so on. But in an American verbal community, the absence of other specific determiners, the compound verbal stimulus 'red,' 'white' . . . will yield 'blue' in preference to any other. The compound stimulus is a much more specific occasion than either part taken separately, and it is an occasion upon which the response 'blue' is characteristically made and reinforced. In the same way, such an expression as 'That has nothing to do with the . . .' will produce 'case,' or one or two other forms to the exclusion of all others, although these words, taken separately, would produce a great variety of responses. The more complex the stimulus pattern, the more specific the verbal occasion, and the stronger the control exerted over a single response" (p. 76).

It certainly appears to be the case that "the more complex the stimulus pattern, the more 'specific' the verbal occasion, and the stronger the control exerted over a single response." However, "a very good morning to you" appears to be as complex a verbal form as "two plus two equals" and a variety of response forms (even though limited) follow which the verbal community reinforces: "thank you," "good morning to you," "well! how are you?", "how have you been?," "good to see you," and so on. Complexity is not the critical factor in whether the verbal community restricts a response or not. Specificity is; (and Skinner indicates that in the quote above and in other places of his analysis). Complexity indirectly but specificity directly addresses how many response forms are grouped with the verbal stimulus. With increased specification fewer forms become permissible to the speaker. The speaker emits an improper form at his peril. Mark Twain describes such a scene in *Tom Sawyer* (1876):

"... That is what you will say, Thomas—and you wouldn't take any money for those two thousand verses—no indeed you wouldn't. And now you wouldn't mind telling me and this lady some of the things you've learned—no, I know you wouldn't—for we are proud of little boys who learn. Now, no doubt you know the names of all the twelve disciples. Won't you tell us the names of the first two that were appointed?"

Tom was tugging at a button-hole and looking sheepish. He blushed, now, and his eyes fell. Mr. Walter's heart sunk within him. He said to himself, it is not possible that the boy can answer the simplest question—why did the Judge ask him? Yet he felt obliged to speak up and say:

"Answer the gentleman, Thomas—don't be afraid."

Tom still hung fire.

"Now I know you'll tell me," said the lady. "The names of the first two disciples were. . . ."

"DAVID AND GOLIATH!"

Let us draw the curtain of charity over the rest of the scene (pp. 36-37).

The importance of specificity in restricting response forms ensues from the multiple conditioning of stimulus and response forms in the history of the typical speaker. Sequeled verbal relations result from

> ". . . hundreds of thousands of reinforcements under a great variety of inconsistent and often conflicting contingencies. Many different responses are brought under the control of a given stimulus word, and many different stimulus words are placed in control of a single response. . . . 'Four' is part of the occasion for 'five' in learning to count, for 'six' in learning to count by twos, for 'one' in learning the value of 'pi,' and so on. On the other hand, many different verbal stimuli come to control the response 'four,' e.g., 'one, two, three' . . . or 'two times two make' . . . Many different connections between verbal responses and verbal stimuli are established when different passages are memorized and different "facts" acquired. The word-association experiment shows the results. . . (I)n general the response which will be made to a verbal stimulus when no other condition is specified can be predicted only in a statistical sense. . ." (p. 74).

Minimal specificity allows the play of extensive multiple conditioning to take place.

OVERVIEW

"Intraverbal," as defined in this article, labels the category of verbal behavior under the control of verbal stimuli. Verbal relations in this category fall into three subcategories: duplic, codic, and sequelic. Each subcategory groups a number of differing verbal relations that share a common, primary feature implied by the subcategory name. The subcategory, duplic, contains the "echoic," "identigraphic," and "mimetic" verbal relations and all other types in which the verbal response or product must mirror the verbal stimulus; the subcategory, codic, groups "textual" and other types of verbal relations in which the serial order between stimulus and response in different media must correspond; and in the subcategory, sequelic, the verbal response or response product must follow the verbal stimulus in specified or nonspecified fashion.

The verbal community shapes, maintains, and alters those verbal relations. The criteria it uses differ for each of the primary subcategories, but are based on the degree of correspondence between verbal stimulus and verbal response or response product. A further factor is the degree of restriction with respect to the verbal response or response product that follows the verbal stimulus. While the necessity of identical point-to-point correspondence between form or order automatically restricts the verbal responses or response products that follow verbal stimuli in the duplic or codic relations, the verbal community specifies response forms through social demands for a large subclass of verbal responses or response products in the sequelic category.

While intraverbal relations—duplic, codic, sequelic, and subcategories—are not as complex as those verbal relations of multiple control that later build on them such as the autoclitic, their analysis still addresses much that occurs in typical speech episodes. Additional conceptual and experimental work would continue to clarify the relations between verbal stimuli and verbal responses, and prompt increased use of radical behavioral terms in practical and applied work drawn from such an analysis. Further, delineating intraverbal relations emphasizes the fact that for many verbal actions and products control resides exclusively in prior verbal stimuli and that no other causal agent need be postulated or inferred.

REFERENCES

Chomsky, N. (1959). *Verbal Behavior*, by B. F. Skinner. *Language*, 5, 26-58.

London, J. (1909). *Martin Eden*. New York: Airmont Publishing Co. Edition (1970).

Michael, J. (1982a). Distinguishing between discriminative and motivational functions of stimuli. *Journal of the Experimental Analysis of Behavior*, 37, 149-155.

Michael, J. (1982b). Skinner's verbal operants: Some new categories. *Verbal Behavior Newsletter*, 1, 1.

Michael, J. (1984). Motivational relations in behavior theory: A suggested terminology. Unpublished manuscript in draft, 31 pages.

Oxford English Dictionary, Compact Edition. (1971). New York: Oxford University Press.

Skinner, B. F. (1957). *Verbal Behavior*. New York: Appleton-Century-Crofts.

Skinner, B. F. (1976). *Particulars of My Life*. New York: Alfred A. Knopf.

Skinner, B. F. (1980). *Notebooks*. Englewood Cliffs, New Jersey: Prentice Hall.

Sundberg, M. L. (1978a). A Program for Teaching Verbal Repertoires to Persons in Whom Language is Absent or Defective, Western Michigan Behavioral Monograph Series, Monograph No. 6, Kalamazoo, Michigan: The Association of the Experimental Analysis of Behavior, Western Michigan University.

Sundberg, M. L. (1978b). The Relevance of B. F. Skinner's Analysis of Verbal Behavior for the Deaf: New Directions for Deaf Education. Presented at The Fourth Annual Convention of the Midwestern Association of Behavior Analysis, Chicago, Illinois, May 13-16.

Sundberg, M. L. (1980). Developing a verbal repertoire using sign language and Skinner's analysis of verbal behavior. Dissertation. Kalamazoo, MI.: Department of Psychology, Western Michigan University.

Sundberg, M. L., Michael, J., and Peterson, N. (1977). Sign Language: A Behavioral Analysis and Applications. Presented at the Third Annual Convention of the Midwestern Association of Behavior Analysis, Chicago, Illinois, May 14-17.

Twain, M. (1876). *Tom Sawyer*. New York: Holt, Rinehart and Winston Edition (1961).

Vargas, E. A. (1984). "A New Term and Some Old Advice". *The Behavior Analyst*, 7, 67-69.

Vargas, J. S. (1984). "What are your exercises teaching? An analysis of stimulus control in instructional materials". In Heward, W. L., Heron, T. E., Hill, D. S., and Trap-Porter, J. (Eds.) *Focus on behavior analysis in education*. Columbus, Ohio: Charles E. Merrill.

Wouk, H. (1954). *The Caine Mutiny*. New York: Doubleday and Co., Inc.

Commentary

A NONDUPLIC DISCUSSION OF INTRAVERBAL BEHAVIOR

James G. Holland

AT FIRST APPROACHING Skinner's analysis of *Verbal Behavior* one might expect that the topic "verbal behavior under the control of verbal stimuli" would be less interesting than the tact, with its implications for semantics, or the mand, with its potential for current interest in pragmatics and the functions of speech, or the autoclitic, with the appearance of an upper level controlling a lower level (the "mind"); but intraverbal behavior (following Vargas's usage) plays a crucial role in the behavioral account of language. Vargas's analysis opens important new areas as yet undeveloped in the experimental analysis of behavior and answers some of the common naive objections to the behavioral analysis of language. The following addresses each of these contributions and suggests some minor improvements.

Much of the form of verbal operants is developed by "imitation." The description of the reinforcement of echoic behavior is an analysis of the basis for imitation of speech (and avoids the implication of an imitative faculty). Figure 1 of Vargas's chapter depicts the child acquiring an echoic. In the established operant there is a one-to-one correspondence between the sample presented to the speaker and the stimuli produced by the speaker's vocal behavior. With sufficiently precise reinforcement contingencies the speaker becomes proficient at quickly and easily mimicking the new combination of speech sounds. Ultimately a fine-grained, continuous repertoire develops in which small variations in the discriminative stimuli are closely matched by small differences in the responses that produce stimuli comparable to the discriminative stimuli. Continuous repertoires are not exclusively verbal and include other instances of a stimulus field controlling point-by-point variations in a response field, for example, drawing from copy, singing, driving a car, and a wide range of other motor skills. (For a discussion of continuous and discrete repertoires, see Skinner, 1953, pp. 116-122, and Holland and Skinner, 1961, pp. 167-180).

When echoic behavior is well developed, the form of new verbal operants can be shaped with ease and can proceed through vocal play or other vocal behavior without the intervention of another person. This is possible because of the automatic reinforcement by the produced sound matching the learned or heard standard or sample. The extent to which the speaker can discriminate the adequacy of the match determines the closeness of the approximation to the correct form that can be automatically reinforced. An interesting application of this analysis involves the correction of articulation deficits in children by use of a program which teaches the children to discriminate the correct sound from the incorrect in all of the phonetic contexts for the sound (A. Holland & Matthews, 1963). After completing the teaching machine program the children quickly learned to articulate the correct sound in previously misarticulated words. Much improvement in speech production appeared shortly after discrimination training even without direct training in production by a speech therapist. Having learned the correct sound, the production of that sound provided differential reinforcement of the correct vocal response. When a mismatch occurs there is the possibility of an immediate correction as the degree of mismatch provides corrective feedback.

The concept of a continuous repertoire is of enormous importance in programming a variety of educational tasks. Learning to draw from copy, handwriting, most motor skills, composition and many social skills are examples of behaviors which match a standard, are subject to automatic differential reinforcement, and the reinforcement criterion is set by the limits of the person's current ability to discriminate the differences between the sample or standard and the response produced stimuli.

Given the potential importance of the continuous repertoire in language acquisition and many other performances it is surprising that research on continuous repertoires is absent from the literature of the experimental analysis of behavior. This is but one of several important gaps in basic laboratory based knowledge revealed in *Verbal Behavior* and emphasized in Vargas's chapter.

Another example is the minimal repertoire learned in the process of echoic and textual behavior. The response unit developed in echoic behavior is not typically so small as a phoneme; rather the unit of behavior under specific functional control may be whole words or even phrases. However, when many echoic responses are formed which share common smaller elements (such as phonemes) these elements can become minimal units useful in the initial shaping of new forms. "Having acquired a dozen complex echoic responses all of which begin with the sound b, the child may correctly echo a thirteenth pattern which begins with b to the extent of beginning the larger response with b also. When this happens, we must recognize the functional independence of an echoic as small as b" (Skinner, 1957, p. 63). Minimal repertoires become very important in the rapid acquisition of new forms. Here again is an important fact of behavior noted in Skinner's analysis of verbal behavior that should have prompted some systematic research, but as yet has not.

The treatment of intraverbals is also important for dispelling some of the key myths common in discounting a behavioral account of language. The account does not require that each verbal form must be slowly and painstakingly shaped by another person. Much is acquired through echoic behavior ("imitation"); and much shaping occurs through automatic reinforcement. Moreover, the behavioral account does not portray speech as a S-R chain of phonemes. Indeed, the chaining of phonemes cannot account for normal utterances of words and phrases as it seems unlikely that each produced phoneme has time to serve as a stimulus for the next muscular response. The analysis of intraverbals makes clear that the first developed and most common response unit is much larger than the phoneme and the minimal repertoire develops as a result of repeated acquisition of larger units.

Vargas has provided a possible extension and elaboration of Skinner's analysis of "verbal behavior under the control of verbal stimuli." He has introduced a modification and addition to the vocabulary of the topic. Some of the proposed changes and additions may prove helpful as new empirical bases are provided. This author, however, must confess to a bias against expansion of technical vocabulary unless there is a clear superiority in expressing a functional relationship or a previously unnoted relationship is being named. However, the suggested use of the term "intraverbal" for the whole class of verbal behavior controlled by verbal stimuli is especially welcome. This author already uses the term this way by mistake and must correct himself when confusion results. "Intraverbal" does naturally carry the meaning of the total class.

In *Verbal Behavior* Skinner uses the term "intraverbal" only for verbal responses that have no point-to-point correspondence between the discriminative stimuli and their responses. For this class Vargas has suggested the term "sequelic." However, some relatively more common words are available that would be more suited. Reasonable candidates would be "simple intraverbal", "arbitrary intraverbal", and "dysjunctive intraverbal."

Previously unnamed functional properties are designated by the suggested categories of "duplic" and "codic." Intraverbal behavior is duplic when the discriminative stimuli and the response-produced stimuli are nearly identical. This is most frequently the case when a continuous repertoire is developed, but "duplic" and "codic" refer to the relationship between the two stimulus fields and not the resulting grain of the repertoire. These terms may, therefore, contribute to the analysis of intraverbals.

Vargas also adds terms to designate the media in which the duplic relationship holds. The echoic behavior described by Skinner involves the duplic relationship in the aural-oral mode. Vargas's "identigraphic" would label drawing or writing from copy; and "mimetic" would label the duplication of gesture. Copying handwriting, however, varies considerably as for instance, copyists often follow their own style and may use box printing while "copying italic script," thus coming closer to the codic category. The problem is even worse for "mimetic" because the sample gesture or facial expression seldom, if ever, results in the same response-produced stimulus. The model and the copyist have such different vantage points that the similarity in the two stimulus fields is small or, as in facial expressions, totally lacking. One might also question the need for new specialized terms for different media when common phrases such as "drawing-from-copy" and "imitating gestures" serve well enough.

These minor criticisms aside, I hope that Vargas's chapter will stimulate greater interest in this important area which is full of potential for filling gaps in the experimental analysis of behavior and for correcting the misperceptions of psycholinguists, cognitivists and others concerning a behavior analysis of verbal behavior.

REFERENCES

Holland, A. L., & Matthews, J. (1963). Application of teaching machine concepts to speech pathology and audiology. *Asha, 5,* 474-482.

Holland, J. G. & Skinner, B. F. (1961). *The Analysis of Behavior.* New York: McGraw-Hill Book Co. Inc.

Skinner, B. F. (1953). *Science and Human Behavior.* New York: The Free Press.

Skinner, B. F. (1957). *Verbal Behavior.* Englewood Cliffs, NJ: Prentice-Hall, Inc.

Chapter Six

ETHICS AS A SYSTEM OF BEHAVIOR MODIFICATION

U. T. Place

THE FACT THAT the function of moral judgments is to modify the behavior of those to whom they are addressed is one of those facts that are so obvious and familiar that they seldom, if ever, attract attention, with the result that their implications are seldom considered and the importance of those implications is overlooked. In this chapter, I propose to examine the practice of making moral judgments and, more important, the practice of publicly uttering those judgments, from the standpoint of the scientific theory of behavior modification which has emerged in recent years from the experimental analysis of behavior as developed by Skinner and his disciples. It is my hope that this investigation will throw light, both on the psychological mechanisms involved in what is arguably the most effective and most widely practiced method of social control that human beings have yet devised, and on some of the peculiarities of moral psychology and moral discourse which have puzzled moral philosophers for centuries and in some cases for millenia.

MORAL JUDGMENTS AS IMPERATIVES

I said at the outset that it is an obvious fact that the function of moral judgments is to modify the behavior of those to whom the judgment is addressed. But is it all that obvious? Is it indeed a fact at all? In other words, is it true that all moral judgments have this function? Certainly those who enunciate moral rules or principles or tell other people what they have an obligation to do or not to do in a particular situation which currently exists or may arise in the future intend to influence their audience to conform to the principle they enunciate or to follow the more specific moral prescription they are making as the case may be. In such cases, as Immanuel Kant first pointed out nearly two hundred years ago, a moral judgment has the force of an imperative; and it orders or commands the individual to whom it is addressed to do or refrain from doing the action or variety of action mentioned in the judgment.

THE PROBLEM OF RETROSPECTIVE MORAL JUDGMENTS

But what about those cases where a retrospective moral judgment is passed on something the individual in question has already done—as when someone says *You did the right thing* or *You shouldn't have done that* or *You were wrong to do that*? It seems quite absurd to suggest, as Professor Hare does in his book *The Language of Morals* (Hare 1952, p. 189) that such judgments are retrospective or past tense imperatives. How can you order someone to do or not to do something they have already done? Nor can it be plausibly argued that to say *You did the right thing* or *You were wrong to do that* is equivalent to saying *do it again next time* or *Don't do it again*, since if that were the interpretation, why should anyone say, as they frequently do, *You did the right thing—Do that again next time* or *You were wrong to do that—Don't do it again?*

A slightly more plausible version of the imperative theory of retrospective moral judgments is that presented by Stevenson in his book *Ethics & Language* (1944). Stevenson argues that moral judgments in general express the speaker's approval or disapproval of the behavior mentioned in the judgment and urge the listener to share that approval or disapproval as the case may be. As applied to retrospective moral judgments with respect to the listener's own behavior, Stevenson's view would make moral praise into an invitation to the listener to congratulate him or herself on his/her past performance, while moral blame would come out as a similar invitation to join the speaker in disapproving of what one has done.

These awkward attempts to squeeze retrospective moral judgments into the straitjacket of the imperative theory overlook what must be obvious to anyone with the most elementary acquaintance with learning theory and the principles of behavior modification, namely that these retrospective moral judgments act, in the case of *You did the right thing*, as a reward for or reinforcement, and in the case of *You were wrong to do that* as a punishment of the behavior in question. Of course, from the fact that these retrospective moral judgments act either as verbal reinforcers or as verbal punishers, it follows that their function is indeed to influence the addressee in the direction repeating the kind of action that is praised and not repeating the kind of action that is condemned. But the way in which reinforcement and punishment produce their effect on behavior is quite different from the way in which a command or instruction produces its effect. Reinforcement and punishment are consequences which follow and increase or reduce the probability of the individual's emitting the response in question on future occasions, whereas a command or instruction is an antecedent which acts as a discriminative stimulus relative to the consequences of subsequent behavior. Therein lies part, at least, of the difference between saying *You did the right thing* and saying *Do that again next time*. Both utterances have the function of influencing behavior in the same direction, in the direction of repeating what has just been done, but the effect is produced in what are, from the standpoint of behavior analysis, two quite different ways.

MORAL JUDGMENTS PASSED ON THE BEHAVIOR OF THIRD PARTIES

So far we have only considered cases in which a moral judgment is made which applies, either exclusively or among others, to the person or persons to whom the judgment is addressed. But what about the cases where judgment is passed on the behavior of someone other than the person or persons addressed? In some of these cases, both where the judgment is prospective as in *What he ought to do is . . .* and where it is retrospective as in *He shouldn't have done that*, the point or function of uttering the judgment is to induce the person to whom it is addressed either to pass on the judgment to the individual concerned or, more commonly, to join the speaker in bringing moral pressure to bear on the individual concerned, thereby increasing the effectiveness of the moral judgment whether as a command, a reinforcement, or a punishment when it is subsequently addressed to him.

This explanation, however, can apply only in those cases where the person to whom the judgment is addressed is in a position to infuence the behavior of the person about whom the judgment is made. Where this is not the case, either because the person about whose behavior the judgment is made is too far removed in physical or social space to be influenced by the person to whom the judgment is addressed or because the judgment is made about someone who is dead or, in the case of a judgment passed on the behavior of a fictitious character, never existed, some other explanation of the point or function of uttering the judgment is required.

In the case where a moral judgment — almost invariably a moral condemnation blaming someone for some misfortune that has befallen the speaker — is made under circumstances where the person concerned is too far removed in physical or social space to be influenced by anything either the speaker or the listener might say about him, the primary function of the utterance would seem to be that it allows the speaker to give expression to and thereby discharge the pent up anger and frustration provoked by the misfortune and invites the person addressed to endorse his condemnation which, had the object of his wrath been more accessible would have increased its effectiveness as a verbal punisher.

An experimental analogue for this behavior is provided by the behavior of the pigeon in an experiment reported by Azrin, Hutchinson & Hake (1966).

When frustrated, as we should be inclined to say, by the onset of time-out when responding for food on a continuous reinforcement schedule, the pigeon in this experiment learned to peck a second key in the Skinner box when pecking this second key was reinforced by the appearance of another bird in its immediate vicinity. This second bird was prevented from moving by a restraining harness, thus providing a suitable object for the first bird to attack, and thus discharge its pent up anger provoked by the frustration involved in the sudden failure of pecking to produce food. But although the target bird in this experiment was clearly "a scapegoat" in the sense that it was in no sense "responsible" or "to blame for" the time out from reinforcement, its ability to function as a scapegoat for the experimental bird clearly depended on the physical presence of the target bird at or shortly after the onset of time out and by the obvious signs of pain shown by the target bird when attacked in this way. By contrast, in the case we are considering not only is the object of blame or condemnation absent from the situation in which the speech act of blaming or condemning him is uttered, but, except in the unlikely event of his coming to know what has been said about him, he is unlikely to be hurt by it. Even if he is, the suffering caused by the damage to his "ego" is unlikely to be visible to the original author of the judgment, whose anger may well, by that time, have long since subsided.

However, it has been shown by Azrin, Hutchinson, and Sallery (1964) that visible and tangible evidence that the victim is suffering from the attack directed towards it, though it helps, is not a necessary condition for the occurrence and persistence of experimentally-induced attack behavior. As this study shows, a stuffed dummy or even a soft leather ball which can be torn apart can be used as the target for attack in place of a live animal. We have here, I suggest, an analogy for the practice of burning effigies of people who are, or were once, objects of hatred, such as Guy Fawkes, which still survives as a harmless ritual in England long after the passions which provoked it in the first place have subsided.

Another function which is performed by the moral condemnation of people whose behavior either cannot or is unlikely to be influenced by them is also illustrated by the example of the burning of Guy Fawkes in effigy. This is the function of reinforcing the solidarity of the social group which the moral condemnation of those who are perceived as its enemies and outsiders appears to promote. Why joining together in an act of moral condemnation should have this effect is not completely explicable in terms of the current behavior theory, though part of the answer will become apparent later when we come to consider the role of the social group in giving moral commendation and praise its power to act as a reinforcer and in giving moral condemnation and blaming its power to act as an aversive event.

MORAL JUDGMENTS PASSED ON CHARACTERS IN HISTORY AND FICTION

Yet neither the displacement of pent up feelings of anger and frustration onto a scapegoat nor the reinforcement of social solidarity by asserting the moral turpitude of enemies and outsiders can account for those cases in which moral judgments are passed on the behavior of fictitious characters or persons long dead whose actions have no obvious relevance to the current misfortunes of either the speaker or the person or persons to whom the judgment is addressed. The case where moral judgments are passed on the behavior of fictitious characters in fictitious situations provides, I suggest, the best clue to the function of the moral judgment in all such cases whether factual or fictitious. For it is clear that where a moral judgment is passed on the behavior of a fictional character in fictitious circumstances in the context of a fable, parable, or other moralising tale, the point or function of the judgment and indeed of the tale as a whole is to influence the behavior of the listener or reader in the direction of following the example provided by the behavior of the characters whose actions are judged to be right or good and in the direction of avoiding those actions that are judged morally wrong on occasions when the listener or reader encounters similar circumstances in his own life.

That such tales and the judgments they contain do have, or at least are intended to provide, this kind of moral education is easily appreciated. What is much more difficult is to explain in terms of the accepted principles of behavior theory why such a procedure should have its intended effect, if indeed it does. The root of the problem here lies in the fact that behavior modification by means of moral verbal utterances on the behavior of those to whom the utterance is addressed; and the effect of verbal behavior on the listener is an aspect of behavior modification which is not well understood in terms of the conceptual scheme used in the experimental analysis of behavior as developed by Skinner and his disciples.

SKINNER'S *VERBAL BEHAVIOR* AND ITS DEFECTS

In his 1957 book *Verbal Behavior* Skinner has attempted to provide an account of verbal or language behavior in terms of the conceptual framework of Radical Behaviorism. Unfortunately, his account of verbal behavior in that book is heavily biased in favor of accounting for the verbal behavior of the speaker to the neglect of the problems presented by the response of the listener to what is said; added to which the book was effectively torpedoed on its maiden voyage by a devastating Review by Noam Chomsky (1959) from the effects of which in the eyes of all but Skinner's most devoted disciples, it has never recovered.

As I have argued elsewhere (Place 1981b), the principal source of Skinner's failure in *Verbal Behavior* to provide an adequate account of the listener's response to the verbal stimuli generated by the speaker's behavior is his refusal to draw the traditional grammatical distinction beween the unit of verbal behavior, the sentence, which is reqired in order to evoke a determinate response from the listener and the words and phrases of which sentences are composed. Without that distinction, Skinner is unable to appreciate the importance of the point to which Chomsky has repeatedly drawn attention, namely, that, unlike words and phrases, sentences are seldom repeated word for word, but are constructed *de novo* on each occasion of utterance in accordance with the syntactic and semantic conventions endorsed by the relevant verbal community.

When words and phrases are put together so as to form a grammatically complete sentence which, in that precise form, the listener may never have encountered before, they nevertheless acquire a unique property, the ability to evoke determinate responses from any listener who is a competent member of the verbal community constituted by the speakers and interpreters of the natural language or code to which the sentence in question belongs. But not only is the verbally competent listener able to decode sentences which he or she has never previously encountered, but the behavior which such a novel sentence is able to evoke may likewise be behavior which, in that precise form, the listener has never previously emitted.

THE CONCEPTS OF "DISCRIMINATIVE STIMULUS" AND "CONTINGENCY"

Although Skinner fails to address the phenomenon whereby novel sentences can evoke novel behavior on the part of the listener in *Verbal Behavior*, he does, it seems to me, point the way towards an effective account of this phenomenon in his "An operant analysis of problem solving" which forms Chapter Six of his book *Contingencies of Reinforcement* (Skinner 1969).

In order to understand that account we need to discuss the notions of "discriminative stimulus" and "contingency" and the relationship between the two. The term "discriminative stimulus" was first introduced by Skinner in Chapter Five of *The Behavior of Organisms* (Skinner 1938). It derives, evidently from Pavlov's (1927) notion of "the conditioned stimulus." However, Skinner's "discriminative stimulus" differs from Pavlov's "conditioned stimulus" in two crucial respects. In the first place whereas a conditioned stimulus is said to acquire its properties solely by virtue of its consistent association with the unconditional (reinforcing) stimulus, Skinner's discussion of the discriminative stimulus emphasizes the contrast between S^D, the stimulus in whose presence a particular response is reinforced, and S^Δ, the stimulus constituted by the absence of the S^D which is associated with the absence of reinforcement. Second, whereas the conditioned stimulus is said in Pavlov's terminology to "elicit" the conditioned response, Skinner's discriminative stimulus is said to provide "an occasion" for the emission by the organism of an operant which has been reinforced in the presence of S^D, but not in the presence of S^Δ.

Another way of putting the same point is to say that the discriminative stimulus acts as "a sign" of the existence in the environment of a particular contingency, in the standard case, the contingency whereby the emission of the operant in question is reinforced. This way of describing the role of the discriminative stimulus was not available to Skinner in 1938 because he had not then developed the notion of "a contingency." By "a contingency" is meant a causal relationship whereby given certain Antecedent conditions, the emission of a certain type of Behavior will have a particular set of Consequences. These three elements, Antecedents, Behavior, and Consequences (ABC) are said to constitute the three terms or "legs", as I prefer to call them, into which any contingency can be analyzed. As they affect the organism's behavior, contingencies in this sense are of two basic types depending on whether the effect of the Consequences is to increase or strengthen the probability that similar behavior will occur on relevantly similar occasions in the future, in which case the Contingency is "a Contingency of Reinforcement," or to decrease or weaken the probability that similar behavior will occur on relevantly similar occasions in the future, in which case the Contingency may be described, following the terminology suggested by Harzem and Miles (1978) as a "Contingency of Disinforcement."

"CONTINGENCY-SHAPED" AND "RULE-GOVERNED" BEHAVIOR

In Chapter Six of *Contingencies of Reinforcement* (1969) Skinner introduces an important distinction between what he calls "contingency-shaped" and "rule-governed" behavior. Contingency-shaped behavior is behavior which is shaped or moulded to the contingencies which govern its emission by repeated exposure to them. Examples of contingency-shaped behavior are the responding of a pigeon or rat in a Skinner Box after repeated exposure to one of the classical "Schedules of Reinforcement" (Ferster and Skinner 1957), or the tactical execution of a well developed motor skill like swimming, playing tennis, driving a car or constructing sentences. In the case of rule-governed behavior, by contrast, the organism's response to the relevant contingency is mediated by a verbal formula or "rule" which is described by Skinner (1969, p. 147) as "a contingency specifying stimulus." Rule-governed behavior may occur as a direct response to a verbal formula emitted by another speaker at the time or, indirectly, as a response to the "recollection" of a rule emitted by another speaker on a previous occasion. Alternatively, the individual organism may react to exposure to the contingency itself, or to observation of its operation in the case of someone else's behavior, by constructing an appropriate "hypothesis" as to the contingency involved or by "recalling" a previously constructed verbal formula which proved successful on some similar occasion in the past. The typical case of rule-governed behavior as conceived by Skinner is the case of problem solving behavior which he discusses in Chapter Six of *Contingencies of Reinforcement* (Skinner 1969) from which the notion of "rule-governed behavior" derives. However, if as I suggest we do, we equate Skinner's notion of "a rule" with the traditional grammatical notion of "a sentence," any behavior verbal or nonverbal which is under the control of a verbal stimulus in the form of a sentence, whether emitted by another speaker or self-directed in the form of a thought, would qualify as rule-governed.

SENTENCES AS DISCRIMINATIVE STIMULI

If we combine the suggestion that what Skinner calls "rules" are what grammarians and logicians call sentences or sentence utterances both with his suggestion that rules are contingency-specifying stimuli and with the suggestion made above that discriminative stimuli are signs which prepare the organism to encounter a particular contingency, we are inevitably led to the conclusion that sentences, as they affect the behavior of the listener, must be construed as discriminative stimuli. But if sentences act as discriminative stimuli with respect to the behavior of the listener, we need to recognize at least two respects in which they differ from the discriminative stimuli described by Skinner in Chapter Five of *The Behavior of Organisms* (1938).

One obvious respect in which sentences differ from the discriminative stimuli described by Skinner in *The Behavior of Organisms* is that the speaker's ability to construct novel sentences in accordance with the syntactic conventions endorsed by the relevant verbal community gives to such novel sentences the ability to act for the listener as discriminative stimuli with respect to contingencies the like of which the listener may have never before encountered. This contrasts with Skinner's S^D and S^Δ both of which acquire their ability to act as discriminative stimuli for the organism from a repeated association with a contingency in which an operant is followed, in the case of S^D, by reinforcement and in the case of S^Δ by nonreinforcement. In the case of the sentence, the repeated association in the past is between the constituent words and the sentence pattern on the one hand and the elements and form of the contingency on the other, rather than between the sentence as a whole and the contingency for which it nevertheless acts as a discriminative stimulus.

Whereas the ability to act as a discriminative stimulus with respect to a contingency which the listener has never previously encountered is a unique, if not a defining property of the sentence in its capacity as stimulus, the other respect in which sentences differ from the discriminative stimuli described by Skinner (1938) is more a matter of the difference between discriminative stimuli (defined as stimuli which prepare an organism to encounter a particular contingency) in general and those discriminative stimuli that are normally studied *under that description* in the laboratory, than a difference between verbal and nonverbal discriminative stimuli.

Skinner's S^D is a stimulus which prepares the organism to encounter a contingency of reinforcement, like a notice on the door of a shop or restaurant which reads *We are open*. Likewise his S^Δ is a stimulus, like the notice on the door *Sorry, We're closed*, which prepares the organism to encounter a nonreinforcement, time out or extinction contingency. By contrast not only are there sentences like the threat *Do that again and you'll be sorry* which prepares the listener to encounter a contingency of punishment, there are also sentences like the sentence *Joe is coming* which are wholly neutral with respect to the valence for the listener of the contingency they specify. The same form of words may be used by the speaker regardless of whether the appearance of Joe as consequence of the behavior of opening the door is welcome (positively reinforcing) or unwelcome (aversive or positively disinforcing) as far as the listener is concerned. This observation reinforces Jack Michael's (1982) emphasis on the importance of distinguishing the discriminative and motivational functions of stimuli and suggests that contingencies in the sense in which discriminative stimuli prepare the organism to encounter them should be regarded as neutral with respect to the valence for the responding organism of the consequences of the behavior in terms of which the particular contingency is defined.

BEHAVIORAL CONTINGENCY SEMANTICS

We have seen that by constructing an appropriate sentence in accordance with the syntactic and semantic conventions endorsed by the verbal community, the speaker generates a discriminative stimulus which prepares the listener to encounter a contingency the like of which he or she has not previously encountered. What we now have to consider is the behavioral mechanism whereby that effect is achieved. In a recent article (Place 1983) I have proposed the term "Behavioral Contingency Semantics" as the name of the behavioral mechanism I am proposing to account for the construction of novel contingency specifying stimuli or sentences. Behavioral Contingency Semantics is a version of Wittgenstein's (1922) Picture Theory of the meaning of sentences in which an atomic or single clause sentence, like the sentences *The baby is crying, Give it a bottle* and *It will go back to sleep*, is said to "map," "depict" or, to use Skinner's term, "specify," not as for Russell (1918/1919) and Wittgenstein (*op. cit.*) an atomic fact, but an event or state of affairs which constitutes one of the three "terms" or "legs" of a contingency, the Antecedent conditions (*The baby is crying*), the Behavior (*Give it a bottle*) and its Consequences (*It will go back to sleep*).

Given these three atomic sentences, we can now construct two compound *conditional* sentences of the form "If *pk* then *q*." The first of these, the sentence *If the baby cries, give it a bottle* specifies the Antecedent and the Behavior to be emitted. The second, the sentence *If you give it a bottle, it will go back to sleep* specifies the Behavior and its Consequences. Finally the three clause sentence, *If the baby cries, give it a bottle and it will go back to sleep* specifies all three legs of the contingency.

Although only the last of these sentences can be said to specify the contingency as a whole, any one of them with the doubtful exception of the consequence-specifying sentence *It will go back to sleep* can act as a discriminative stimulus for the contingency as a whole and can be used under appropriate circumstances as a way of inducing the listener to perform the behavior in question. Even the consequence specifying sentence can be used in this way, if it occurs in the form of the optative *I wish it would go to sleep* or the interrogative/optative *Why doesn't it go to sleep?*

MANDS, TACTS AND VERBAL MOTIVATORS

In Chapter Three of *Verbal Behavior* (1957, pp. 35-51) Skinner introduces the concept of "a mand," a type of speech act (Searle 1969) which embraces what we ordinarily talk about as commands, requests, and questions. In Skinner's terms a mand is a verbal operant whose emission by the speaker is reinforced insofar as it secures from the listener the emission of the behavior which it specifies. As he puts it (1957, p. 36), "the mand . . . works primarily for the benefit of the speaker." In this respect it contrasts with "the tact," the other major category of verbal operant distinguished by Skinner which, as he puts it, "works for the benefit of the listener by extending his contact with the environment" (Skinner 1957, p. 85). It does this, presumably, by providing the listener with advance information about contingencies which he has not previously encountered.

Unfortunately, partly because of his failure to draw the distinction between sentences and the words of which they are composed (Place 1981b), Skinner's use of the term "tact" is somewhat confused. It is clear, nevertheless, that what he has in mind when he contrasts mands and tacts in terms whether it is in the interests of the speaker or the listener that are served by the utterance is the contrast between those sentence utterances (mands) whose function is to direct the behavior of the listener in the direction required by the speaker and those (tacts) whose function is to provide the listener with information about the prevailing contingencies, without constraining the use to which that information is put. Moreover, just as mands are what we ordinarily talk about as "commands," "requests," and "questions," so tacts correspond approximately to what we ordinarily talk about as "statements" or "assertions."

However, when we consider examples like the sentences *The baby is crying*, *Give it a bottle* and *It will go back to sleep* discussed above, we see how difficult it is in practice to draw this distinction. For, by the normal criteria of grammar and logic, the sentences *The baby is crying* and *It will go back to sleep* are in the indicative mood and when uttered in the appropriate context constitute statements or assertions which are either true or false. In both these respects they contrast with the sentence *Give it a bottle* which is in the imperative mood and does not have a truth value. Nevertheless, since as we have seen their function in the situation we are envisaging is to induce bottle giving behavior on the part of the listener, rather than to supply information which the listener is free to make use of in whatever way best serves his or her interests, by Skinner's functional criteria they qualify as mands rather than as tacts. Yet it is only by virtue of their pragmatic function in inducing the listener to emit the required behavior that sentences like *The baby is crying* or *I wish it would go back to sleep* qualify as mands. At the semantic level, as well as at the syntactic level, the distinction between these statements and the imperative *Give it a bottle* is preserved. For it is only the latter sentence which actually *specifies* the behavior to be performed by the listener.

What this shows us, I suggest, is that the important difference between specifying the Antecedents of behavior as in *The baby is crying* or its Consequences as in *It will go back to sleep* rather than the Behavior itself, as in *Give it a bottle,* lies in the different functions performed by these sentences in controlling the subsequent behavior of the listener. This difference in function is another example of the distinction to which Jack Michael (1982) has drawn attention in a recent article between the discriminative and motivational functions of stimuli. In the case of these behavior inducing utterances, the distinction is between those sentences or aspects of sentences whose function is to indicate to the listener what behavior is to be emitted or omitted and those which provide the listener with an incentive to behave in this way. Thus of our three atomic sentences it is only the imperative *Give it a bottle* which actually specifies the behavior to be performed. The statement *The baby is crying* specifies what Michael has called "an establishing condition" whereby any behavior which reverses that state of affairs is reinforced. It thus implicitly promises the reinforcement of such behavior by the consequence specified by the other statement *It will go back to sleep*.

In the light of these considerations it would seem that we need to distinguish at least three distinct categories of functionally complete verbal operant or sentence utterance: (1) the mand which provides the listener with information about the behavior required of him by the speaker, (2) the tact which provides the listener with information which he requires for his own purposes and (3) the verbal motivator which provides the listener with an incentive to emit the kind of behavior required of him by the speaker and which is specified by the speaker's mand. Verbal motivators in this sense are of four main kinds: (1) promises of subsequent reinforcement, either verbal as in the case of *Please* or nonverbal as in *I'll make it worth your while* (2) threats of subsequent punishment which again may be verbal as in *I shall be very annoyed if you do that again* or nonverbal as in *Unless you behave, you won't watch television*, (3) verbal reinforcers like *Very good! You're absolutely right! Thank you!* etc. and (4) verbal punishers like *That was naughty!, No!, I don't agree, You shouldn't have done that*, etc.

KANT'S "CATEGORICAL IMPERATIVE" AND THE MOTIVATION OF MORAL CONFORMITY

Returning to the topic of moral judgments, it is evident that the distinction between mands which specify the behavior required of the listener and verbal motivators which provide the listener with an incentive to perform or repeat or not perform or not repeat the specified behavior helps us understand the difference, discussed earlier, between prospective moral judgments like the Ten Commandments and retrospective moral judgments in which the listener is praised or blamed for what he has just done. It also, I suggest, helps understand Kant's contention that a moral rule or prospective moral judgment is to be interpreted as what he calls "a categorical imperative."

When Kant describes sentences like *You ought not to steal* or *You ought not to tell lies* as imperatives, what he is saying is that, although grammatically indicative, the force of these sentences is that of an imperative. In Skinner's terms, they qualify as mands insofar as they specify behavior whose (in this case) omission by the listener reinforces their utterance by the speaker.

But the point that Kant is making when he describes these judgments as "categorical imperatives" is not that their imperative force is disguised behind an indicative grammatical structure. It is rather that they differ from what he calls "a hypothetical imperative" such as the sentence *Avoid dishonesty, if you want to be respected by others*, in that compliance with the imperative is not made contingent on a desire on the part of the agent, specified in the antecedent of a conditional which supplies an incentive for the listener to comply with it.

The reason why no such verbal motivator is required in the case of these prospective moral judgments, I suggest, is not that compliance with a moral imperative requires no antecedent incentive and no subsequent reinforcement. It is simply that a moral imperative requires no separate verbal motivator to supply an incentive for compliance with it. Moral imperatives carry with them their own incentive in the form of an implied promise of social approval in the case of compliance and an implied threat of social disapproval in the case of failure to comply. These implied promises and threats, moreover, are not just of approval or disapproval on the part of the speaker. They involve the approval or disapproval of the whole social group in whose name the speaker issuing the moral imperative is implicitly claiming to speak.

THE ROLE IN MORAL EDUCATION OF MORAL JUDGMENTS PASSED ON THE BEHAVIOR OF CHARACTERS IN HISTORY AND FICTION

While I think I can reasonably claim that this account of the way in which verbal operants are used to control the behavior of the listener goes some way towards remedying the defects of Skinner's account as presented in *Verbal Behavior*, it must be admitted that, as it stands, the theory only accounts for those sentence utterances which relate to the immediate behavioral concerns of the listener, to present circumstances which are liable to affect the listener's behavior, to the very recent past or to the immediate future. What it does not do is provide any kind of account of the effect on the listener of sentences relating to circumstances which are so far removed from him in space and/or time as to have no relevance to his immediate behavioral concerns or, to revert to the case from which our whole discussion of the effect of the sentence on the listener arose in the first place, where the circumstances referred to are entirely fictional and recognized to be so by both speaker and listener. What is required here and what I confess I cannot supply in terms of the existing armory of concepts developed for the purpose of the experimental analysis of events, whether historical or fictional, is able to vicariously experience those events not merely as a disinterested observer might do, but, by the mysterious process of identification with one or more of the characters in the narrative, to actually learn the contingencies of reinforcement and punishment which are represented as impinging on the character concerned, almost as if he or she had personally experienced those contingencies *in vivo*.

This problem of giving a behavioral analysis of the phenomenon of identification also arises in the case of narratives presented in the form of a play or a film, where the actual stimuli received by the audience is much closer to those that would be received by an actual participant in the events represented than is the case in a verbally-presented narrative. That, by itself, does not make the phenomenon of identification any easier to understand, but it does help to underline the fact that, given identification with the relevant character, many of the verbal operants that occur in the context of a narrative, including in particular the moral judgments that are passed on the behavior of a character in the narrative with whom the listener or audience identifies, have, in attenuated form, the same effect on the behavior of the listener or audience that they would have had, if they had occurred in the context of real life. Consequently the use of narrative, whether fictional or historical, is an effective way of helping the individual to learn the standard contingencies of reinforcement which he or she is liable to encounter in real life without incurring the risks that would be involved in actually experiencing those contingencies *in vivo*. Moreover, although it is often possible to learn those contingencies by learning an abstract verbal formula which states the causal law or moral rule involved, this method is only effective insofar as the learner can apply the causal or moral principle to the concrete instances to which in one or more examples of concrete instances in which it applies; and for this purpose, where the risks involved in practical experience are unacceptable, a historical or fictional narrative is the only feasible alternative. In the case of the inculcation of moral principles it is not so much the risk to life and limb which preclude the use of practical experience of the consequences of transgressing moral principles as the fact that in order to provide such experience it would be necessary to induce the very behavior which the moral principle in question is designed to prevent. It goes without saying that such a procedure would almost certainly defeat the very object it was designed to bring about. Hence, I suggest, the importance of moral judgments passed on the behavior of the characters in both historical and fictional narrative in moral education.

HOW MORAL JUDGMENTS ACQUIRE THEIR MOTIVATING PROPERTIES

Perhaps the most puzzling problem concerning this use of words to control the social behavior of other human beings is to explain how it is that retrospective moral judgments about the behavior of the individual to whom those moral judgments are addressed acquire the properties which they clearly do have of acting as motivators, i.e. as reinforcers in the case of moral praise and as punishers in the case of moral blame relative to the subsequent repetition by the listener of the specified behavior. These retrospective moral judgments, which constitute the speech acts (Austin 1962, Searle 1969) of praising and blaming the antecedent behavior of the listener, come into focus as the basic agents of behavioral change as soon as we begin to look at moral judgments as a system of behavior modification. This contrasts with the standpoint of the moral philosopher who takes the moral imperative and the universal imperative or moral principle in particular as his paradigm case of the moral judgment from which everything else proceeds. As we have seen, from the standpoint of behavior modification, these prospective moral judgments only affect behavior insofar as they effectively promise subsequent moral praise contingent upon the listener's compliance with the imperative and/or effectively threaten subsequent blame and recrimination contingent upon its transgression.

In this connection I shall devote special attention to the phenomenon whereby having to take the blame for something that one has done or failed to do constitutes one of the most powerfully aversive events in the experience of any but the most hardened and insensitive of psychopaths, rather than on the positively reinforcing effects of moral praise. I propose to concentrate on blame, in part, because praise in all its forms is widely recognized as a powerful social reinforcer by behavior modifiers and the principles governing its acquisition of those reinforcing properties are relatively well understood. By contrast the psychology of blaming has been almost totally neglected, despite the fact that the control of behavior through moral criticism and the attribution of blame is by far the most commonly used method of applying moral judgments to the control of behavior—so much so that the notion of passing a moral judgment has become synonymous with moral criticism, as, in the saying from the Sermon on the Mount: "Judge not, that ye be not judged"—itself incidentally a moral imperative. Another consideration is that, because of the importance we all attach to avoiding the aversive event of having to take the blame for something we have done or failed to do, an examination of blaming highlights the complex body of largely unwritten rules or conventions which determine whether or not the speech act of blaming someone for something succeeds in producing its intended effect and provides the potential victim with a number of loopholes or excuses by which he can avoid or at least mitigate the aversiveness of taking the blame. Although the same principles govern the applicability of moral praise, the recipient of moral praise does not have the same motive as the recipient of blame for disputing its application in his case. He may deny that he deserves the praise, but only because he has learned that self-depreciation in such circumstances is itself reinforced by further indications of moral approval.

AN ANALYSIS OF THE COMMON DOMESTIC QUARREL

Another reason for focusing on blame and criticism rather than praise is because of the remarkable analogy between the act of blaming someone for what he has done and the reflexive fighting or attack behavior exhibited by the animals in that remarkable series of experiments by Azrin and his co-workers in the 1960s to which I have already referred. This analogy between blaming and reflex fighting behavior in animals can be illustrated by the case of the common domestic quarrel, though the same principles apply to other more public forms of human quarrel whether between individuals, groups, communities, or countries. The starting point of any such quarrel, I suggest, is an initial act of moral censure or criticism passed by one party on the behavior of the other, which the accused cannot avoid by means of any of the standard excuses allowed in such cases. Finding himself, like the animal in the experiment described by Ulrich & Azrin (1962) in the situation of inescapable aversive stimulation, the accused party responds with a counter attack in which he criticizes or blames his accuser for something which the accuser in turn has done. This counter attack will only succeed, and hence be reinforced, insofar as the original accuser is likewise unable to avoid taking the blame for the action in question and is thus, like the immobilized target bird in the Azrin, Hutchinson & Hake (1966) experiment, visibly hurt by the consequent damage to his self-esteem.

Since the counter accusation constitutes an inescapable aversive stimulus for the original accuser, he in turn counter attacks with another accusation directed towards some other aspect of the original accused's behavior and so the quarrel proceeds, moving further and further away in both time and relevance from the original issue of dispute as each party searches for past misdeeds of the other for which they cannot avoid accepting blame. When the point is reached when neither party can any longer think of any more misdeeds which he can effectively pin on the other, this is often the point at which verbal quarreling is replaced by physical violence.

CONVENTIONS GOVERNING THE ASSIGNMENT AND AVOIDANCE OF BLAME

As a philosopher, what intrigues me about this example is that despite the apparent irrationality of the switches that take place within the quarrel from one topic to another, how very precisely each move in the quarreling game is constrained by the rules or, as I prefer to call them (Place 1981a), "conventions" which determine what constitutes a successful act of pinning the blame for something on someone else. In order to succeed in blaming someone for doing something the accuser must be able to show that

1. the individual concerned has performed or failed to perform the action in question,

2. he intended to do what he did,
3. he could have decided to do other than he did, if he had wanted to,
4. the consequences of his action or failure to act were harmful to others,
5. he ought to have done other than he did, either
   (i) because he had a specific duty to do so
or (ii) because he knew or could have known both (a) what the consequences of his action or failure to act would be and (b) that those consequences would be harmful to others.

Consequently in appropriate circumstances *any* of the following assertions, if substantiated and accepted as true by the individual to whom they are directed can succeed as an act of blaming:

1. "*You* did that!"
2. "You did that *deliberately*!"
3. "You didn't *have* to do that!"
4. "That *hurts*!"
5. "You shouldn't have *done* that!"
5-i "It's *your* job to see that things like that *don't* happen!"
5-iia "You could have *known* what would happen if you did that!"
5-iib "You could have *known* that that would hurt!"

Likewise blame can be successfully deflected or avoided by successfully denying any one of these assertions thus:

1. "It wasn't *me*!" — "*I* didn't do it!"
2. "I didn't *mean* to do it!"
3. "I couldn't *help* it!"
4. "It didn't do any *harm*!"
5. "I was *perfectly* justified in doing what I did!"
5-i "It wasn't *my* responsibility!"
5-iia "I didn't *realize* what would happen!"
5-iib "I didn't *think* it would do any harm!"

All of these counter assertions if substantiated and accepted would serve to deflect the blame from the accused. All of them except the first would constitute *excuses* for his having done what he did or for his having failed to do what he did not do.

FREEDOM AND DETERMINISM

It is in this context I suggest that the traditional philosophical disputes about the freedom of the human will need to be understood. What the libertarian is concerned to prevent is the situation in which the wrongdoer is allowed to get away with it by claiming that the social or psychological determination of his actions shows that he could not have done other than he did and that therefore he cannot be held to blame for what he has done.

By the same token, when you consider how easy it is when talking to another person about their past behavior to be taken as blaming them for what they have done, you begin to appreciate the significance of Freud's Principle of Psychic Determinism. In order to ensure that his patients were not deterred from making the kind of self-disclosure which is considered essential to the psychotherapeutic process, it was important to make clear at the outset that he was not going to blame them for anything they might have done in the past, since according to his theory they could not possibly have acted otherwise.

WHY DO WORDS HURT?

One question remains to be answered: how is it that for every normal human being, a mere string of words can have the behavioral properties of an inescapable aversive physical stimulus such as an intense electric shock? We can begin to understand how this can be, I suggest, if we think of the act of moral censure or blame as an act of social rejection — an act whereby the accuser breaks ties of affection, mutual support and cooperation not only between himself and his victim, but between the accused and the social group to whose accepted standards of moral conduct the accuser is implicitly appealing in making his retrospective moral judgment on the behavior of the accused. Clearly in the case where the personal relationship between the two people involved is very close the increase in social distance between the accuser and the accused is sufficient in itself to be highly aversive for the accused without an appeal on the part of the accuser to any wider social group to endorse his condemnation of the accused. In such a case there is no need to appeal to the standards of any social group wider than that constituted by the two people concerned. But since all human cooperation, however large or small the social group involved, depends on the acceptance of the basic moral principle of not pursuing one's own interest to the detriment of those of another member of the same social group, the same moral principles tend to govern the use of moral censure or blame when the effective social group is as small as two individuals as it does when a much larger group or community is appealed to. What I am suggesting is that the nature and size of the social group to which the accuser implicitly appeals to endorse his condemnation of the accused's behavior affects the nature of the moral principles which are appealed to in such a case very much less than is often supposed. The universality of the moral principles governing human social cooperation is important insofar as the act of blaming someone will only carry conviction as an act of the accuser speaking in the name of the wider social group insofar as it is clear to the accused that the moral principle appealed to by his accuser in condemning his action is one which is universally accepted by a social group to which he belongs and whose good opinion of himself he values and on which he depends for a wide range of both social and material reinforcement.

It is the importance of being able to appeal to a universally recognized set of moral principles in order to ensure the effectiveness of moral judgments in controlling the behavior of others, I suggest, which more than anything else accounts for our insistence on applying the law of the excluded middle, whereby either it is true or it is false that a given action is morally right or morally wrong to the case of moral judgments whereas in the case of other value judgments such as aesthetic judgments we are more ready to accept the principle enshrined in the Latin *de gustibus non est disputandum*, the French *Chacun à son gout* and the English *Every man to his taste*. Hence, the consequent temptation of many philosophers to assimilate moral judgments to purely factual statements or propositions where the law of the excluded middle properly belongs.

It seems that human beings become so dependent on the approval of other members of the social group to which they belong that an act of social rejection which the social group as a whole might be expected to endorse becomes highly aversive. This phenomenon no doubt has its roots, as has been suggested by the psychoanalysts, in the early experiences of the child in its dependence for all types of reinforcement on the affection of the parent, especially the mother. However, consideration such as those presented above together with evidence derived from social psychology and Piaget's (1932) study of the development of moral judgments in the child strongly suggest that while the parent-child relationship may provide an essential foundation, the experience of dependence on the solidarity of the peer group in later childhood and adolescence is an essential ingredient in the development of what is somewhat pretentiously described as "the moral consciousness of the adult."

MORAL JUDGMENTS AND THE ETHICS OF AVERSIVE CONTROL

One final point before concluding. It will be apparent from what I have already said that I do not hold the practice of modifying human social behavior by means of retrospective moral criticism and blame in very high esteem. It seems to me that like other more obviously violent methods of aversive control it is the source of untold human misery and suffering as anyone with the slightest acquaintance with the guilt feelings of the pathologically depressed knows only too well. If, as Skinner has consistently maintained, it is possible with a certain amount of ingenuity and expenditure of effort to replace aversive control of undesirable behavior in almost every case where it is used by a technique in which the corresponding desirable behavior is positively reinforced without any loss and with some gain in effectiveness, and if this principle applies equally in the case of the social control of behavior by retrospective moral judgments, as it does in other kinds of aversive control, it follows that a great deal of this misery and suffering could be avoided. And if it can be avoided, then it ought to be.

But what is philosophically interesting about *that* statement is that it is itself a moral judgment, a moral judgment like the moral imperative "judge not that ye be not judged" which is made about the practice of passing negative moral judgments on the behavior of others. And that in turn seems to imply a second order moral judgment, based on some kind of utilitarian principle, in terms which a critical moral judgment is passed on the practice of uttering first order moral judgments, or more precisely, on the practice of uttering negative or critical first order moral judgments which are specifically addressed to the individuals on whose behavior the judgment is passed.

REFERENCES

Austin, J. L. *How to do things with words* J. O. Urmson (Ed.) London: O.U.P. 1962.
Azrin, N. H., Hutchinson, R. R., and Hake, D. F. Extinction-induced aggression. *J. Exp. Anal. behav.*, 1966, 9, 191-204.
Azrin, H. H., Hutchinson, R. R., and Saller, R. D. Pain-aggression toward inanimate objects. *J. Exp. Anal. Behav.*, 1964, 7, 223-228.
Chomsky, N. Review of B. F. Skinner's *Verbal Behavior. Language*, 1959, 35, 26-58.
Ferster, C. B. and Skinner, B. F. *Schedules of Reinforcement*. New York: Appleton-Century-Crofts, 1957.

Hare, R. M. *The Language of Morals*, London: O.U.P., 1962.
Harzem, P. and Miles, T. R. *Conceptual Issues in Operant Psychology*, New York: Wiley, 1978.
Michael, J. Distinguishing between discriminative and motivational functions of stimuli. *J. Exp. Anal. Behav.*, 1982, 37, 149-155.
Pavlov, I. P. *Conditioned Reflexes*. English translation by G. V. Anrep. London: Oxford University Press, 1927.
Piaget, J. *The Moral Judgment of the Child*. M. Gabain (Trans.) London: Routledge and Kegan Paul, 1932.
Place, U. T. Skinner's *Verbal Behavior* I — why we need it, *Behaviorism*, 1981, 9, 1-24 (a).
Place, U. T. Skinner's *Verbal Behavior* II — what is wrong with it. *Behaviorism*, 1981, 131-152 (b).
Place, U. T. Skinner's *Verbal Behavior* III — how to improve Parts I and II. *Behaviorism*, 1982, 10, 117-136.
Place, U. T. Skinner's *Verbal Behavior* IV — how to improve Part IV, Skinner's account of syntax. *Behaviorism*, 1983, 11 (in press).
Russell, B. The philosophy of logical atomism. *The Monist*, 1918/1919, xxviii, 495-527, xxix, 32-63, 190-222, 345-380. Reprinted in B. Russell (1956). *Logic and Knowledge, Essays 1901-1950*, R. C. Marshall (Ed.) London: Allen and Unwin.
Searle, J. R. *Speech Acts*. Cambridge: C.U.P., 1969.
Skinner, B. F. The operational analysis of psychological terms, *Psychol. Rev.* 1945, 52, 270-277, 291-294.
Skinner, B. F. *Verbal Behavior*. New York: Appleton-Century-Crofts, 1957.
Skinner, B. F. *Contingencies of Reinforcement*. New York: Appleton-Century-Crofts, 1969.
Stevenson, C. L. *Ethics and Language*. New Haven: Yale U.P., 1944.
Ulrich, R. E., and Azrin, N. H. Reflexive fighting in response to aversive stimulation, *J. Exp. Anal. Behav.*, 1962, 5, 511-520.
Wittgenstein, L. *Tractatus Logico-Philosophicus*. English translation by C. K. Ogden and I. A. Richards, London: Kegan Paul, 1922.

Commentary

THE ROLE OF CONSEQUENCES IN A BEHAVIORAL THEORY OF ETHICS

Roger Schnaitter

FOR A BEHAVIORIST, the fundamental problem raised by ethics is the sheer possibility of a naturalistic account. Ethical naturalism, broadly construed, is the position that all matters of ethics and morals are susceptible to description and analysis in terms consistent with the description and analysis of the rest of nature. Naturalism is to be distinguished from the far more popular view that ethics requires reference to the interests of a divine being, or at least to some set of inexplicable transcendental principles. Historically, the rational appeal of antinaturalist positions has been based less on their own merits than the relative ease with which the antinaturalist has punctured the naturalist's best efforts. The sharpest arrows in the antinaturalist's quiver have usually been taken to be the several demonstrations purporting to show that derivations of moral imperatives from descriptive statements are always fallacious—the so-called naturalistic fallacy.

It shoud be fairly clear today why ethical naturalism could not be convincingly developed in, say, Aristotle's time, or even in Hume's time. A naturalistic account of ethics must be built on a naturalistic account of language, and a naturalistic account of language must be built on a naturalistic account of behavior in general. The scientific analysis of behavior itself has a history of less than a century, and only a recent fraction of that time has seen any significant advance in the understanding of language. Not surprisingly, then, the application of what has been learned about behavior and language to the fascinating problems of ethical behavior has hardly begun. Within this context, the contribution made here by Place is significant.

The central claim of Place's paper is that "the function of moral judgments is to modify the behavior of those to whom they are addressed." The modification of behavior can take place, according to the operant analysis of behavior, by manipulation of a discriminative stimulus antecedent to behavior, or by manipulation of a reinforcing or punishing stimulus consequent to behavior. In the former case, however, the control exercised by the discriminative stimulus is parasitic on the control by contingent consequences to behavior, in that if a response initially controlled by an antecedent stimulus is not subject to some type of differential consequence, the control by that antecedent will wane. The traditional approach to ethics has focused on the antecedent stimulus control properties of moral judgments, as seen in Kant's imperative theory. Place, on the other hand, brings our attention to the consequent relationship that the moral judgment can have to behavior.

The problems with analyzing moral judgments as consequences vary somewhat between the cases of retrospective and prospective moral judgments. The simplest case is the retrospective judgment where the party whose behavior is judged is present, and the judgment is immediately and directly contingent on behavior. The discouragements offered to a card player caught in the act of cheating illustrate such a case. Control by consequences is a less apt model where (a) the transgressing party is not present; (b) is dead; or (c) is a wholly imaginary character encountered in fiction, film, or moral tale. Place considers several possible accounts for such alternatives. For instance, one might judge the behavior of an absent party in hopes that the audience for the judgment will bring the judgment to bear on the protagonist at some later time. Proposals of this sort immediately cause one to consider what the contingencies are that maintain the act of offering the retrospective judgment, for the offering of judgments is itself behavior subject to controlling contingencies. But a simple consequence model seriously breaks down in cases (b) and (c) where there is no actual person whose behavior can be modified by any kind of consequence.

It is at this point that Place moves into consideration of prospective moral judgments: judgments offered before the occurrence of behavior on which judgment is passed. Moral judgments that may be retrospective in appearance but incapable of functioning retrospectively—paradigmatically, moral judgments passed on characters in history and fiction—are in fact a kind of moral education, suggests Place, in which case they function prospectively. But in order to develop an adequate analysis of the prospective moral judgment, Place believes it necessary to partially redesign

Skinner's analysis of verbal behavior.

A thoroughgoing critique of all that Place proposes concerning the revision of Skinner's analysis of verbal behavior runs well beyond what my limited space allows. Consequently, let me comment just on a few selected points. Place endorses Skinner's analysis of a rule as a "contingency-specifying stimulus," and then proposes that sentences be equated with rules. Shortly thereafter he proposes that simple sentences specify one or another among the "legs" of the three-term contingency of antecedent-stimulus/behavior/consequence. The latter claim seems inconsistent with the former: Skinner's notion of a rule includes a specification of at least two if not all three legs of a contingency, whereas sentences clearly can denote individual legs. Thus, while it may be (trivially) true that all rules are sentences, Place has not established that all sentences are rules.

Place introduces a new term into the taxonomy of verbal types proposed by Skinner, this new type being the "verbal motivator." It is clear that some verbal behavior can function as a reinforcing or punishing consequence, as seen in the effects of directly contingent praise and blame. The problem here is that this consequence function is often coextensive with what appears to be a tact, as seen in "You are a big help to me," "You did a good job," etc. But Place's real concern is with *promises* of praise and blame, as occur in prospective judgments of all kinds (e.g., "I shall be very annoyed if you do that again"). Promises are certainly complex instances of verbal behavior. The kind that Place uses to illustrate his argument are conditionals specifying the relation between the second and third legs of contingencies. This would seem to be a tact that "provides the listener with information which he requires for his own purposes." Some of that information is about motivational consequences. Place, however, sees advantage in invoking an incentive function above and beyond the descriptive function of the tact. Here again, I think the case has not been made sufficiently clear that such an advantage exists.

Place endorses the Kantian claim that prospective moral judgments are categorical rather than hypothetical imperatives. It should be noted that much of Skinner's discussion of values takes a hypothetical turn, however. Skinner has suggested that expressions of the form, "You ought to do x," can be interpreted as ellipses whose expanded form is, "If you are reinforced by y, then you will be reinforced for doing x, as you will find in doing x that y is contingent on x." By this reading (drawn from Chapter Six of *Beyond Freedom and Dignity*), a moral judgment would seem to be a hypothetical in Kant's sense. Moral behavior is complexly determined, and while it may be the case that speakers *state* imperatives categorically, it is worth considering that listeners may often *hear* them hypothetically.

Place's argument for the categorical nature of moral judgments turns on the role of praise and blame. While praise and blame may be the immediate regulators of moral conduct, to leave the behavioral analysis of ethics at such a point might imply that such an analysis necessarily takes the final arbiters of moral conduct to be those who possess sufficient authority to regulate the praising and blaming practices of the social group. Such a picture is misleading. Indeed, ethical contingencies ramify into a complex and subtle network of social contingencies in general. At least four sets of contingencies interlocked in the ethical valuing of behaviors would seem to provide the barest minimum for an adequate behavioral analysis.[1] Consider for purposes of illustration the contingencies involved in the prospective moral judgment, "You ought always to tell the truth."

I. *Contingency of personal advantage.* A person may lie rather than tell the truth because lying has the consequence of some advantage, or avoids some disadvantage. That is, lying is often reinforced (though not by praise), and truth telling is often punished (though not by blame).

II. *Contingency of social disadvantage.* Those who listen to a liar and act on the basis of what is heard are often at a disadvantage, while those who listen to a truth teller and act on the basis of what is heard are often at an advantage. But liars do not self-advertise, else they would not truly be lying.

III. *Contingency maintaining ethical sanctions.* When hearing the truth (particularly in situations where it would be to the immediate personal advantage of the truth teller to lie), praising the truth teller makes it more likely that one will hear the truth on similar occasions in the future; when hearing a lie, blaming and punishing the liar make it less likely that one will hear falsehoods on similar occasions in the future. Thus, the acts of praising and blaming are reinforced (positively in the former case, negatively in the latter) by their consequences on the truthfulness of other members of the society.

IV. *Ethics as a system of behavior modification.* Finally, we expect that truth telling, when praised, will be maintained or strengthened, and that lying, when punished, will be suppressed.

It is Place's claim that moral imperatives *directly* imply the contingen-

---

[1] A longer but somewhat more discursive treatment of this model was presented at the 1982 meeting of the Association for Behavior Analysis, under the title, "Good dope, fast cars, and long-legged women."

cies of this fourth category alone. About that he may be correct, and his discussion of the means through which this implication is carred out is always provocative, if not totally convincing to me. So far as advancing the program of a naturalistic ethics is concerned, however, I think it important to keep in mind the broader view of the contribution of ethical practices to the effectiveness of the culture as a whole, as sketched in the points above, even when focusing on one important component as Place has done.

REFERENCES

Skinner, B. F. *Beyond freedom and dignity*. New York: Knopf, 1971.

Section Three

AN EXAMPLE OF RESEARCH AND AN EXAMPLE OF APPLICATION

Chapter Seven

CORRESPONDENCE BETWEEN VERBAL AND OBSERVED ESTIMATES OF REINFORCEMENT VALUE

Daniel J. Bernstein

THE ROLE OF verbal behavior has become increasingly important to an operant account of human behavior. Although Skinner's (1957) *Verbal Behavior* has been available for nearly three decades, until recently there had been little empirical work exploring the functions of language from an operant perspective and using operant methods. Two visible examples are the use of correspondence training in the development of behavior modification programs (e.g. Risley & Hart, 1968; Israel & O'Leary, 1973) and the examination of the role of instructions in maintenance of human operant performance (e.g. Matthews, Shimoff, Catania, & Sagvolden, 1977; Lowe, 1979, 1983). The interaction of language and behavior has been the subject of intensive study in other areas of psychology, however, and researchers interested in both attitudes and personality have generated extensive empirical evidence. This chapter will briefly review some issues common to both research traditions and will report results from a procedure which draws from both personality and operant psychology. The chapter concludes by identifying potential research on individual differences from the perspective of behavior analysis.

This research was supported by Grant MH29806-01 from the National Institute of Mental Health to the author and by NIH Biomedical Sciences Support Grants RR-07055-09 and RR-07055-10 to the University of Nebraska—Lincoln. I am indebted to the late Theodore Mischel for his contribution to the conceptual development of this research and to Phil Chase for his comments on an earlier draft.

CORRESPONDENCE BETWEEN VERBAL AND NONVERBAL BEHAVIOR

Attitudes and Behavior

The social psychology research tradition has examined the correspondence between saying and doing as a central requirement for the effective use of data from attitude surveys. Both sociologists (e.g. LaPiere, 1934) and social psychologists (e.g. Ajzen & Fishbein 1977) have reported many cases in which verbal behavior is a poor predictor of overt action at a later time. Often verbal (or self-report) measures were not accurate indicators of behavior which has already occurred. These findings were so widely reported that there was substantial theoretical speculation on the reasons for the lack of correspondence (e.g. Nisbett & Wilson, 1977). More recently a new consensus has emerged (stimulated by Smith and Miller, 1978) which holds that it is more appropriate to identify the conditions under which there will and will not be corespondence than it is to argue whether or not correspondence holds in general. It is clear that there are limits to the conditions under which correspondence is to be expected. As detailed extensively by Fishbein (Ajzen & Fishbein, 1977; Fishbein & Ajzen, 1974; Fishbein, 1980), an attitude item must include a specific target of the attitude, a particular action with regard to the target, a time reference for the action, and a specific situation in which the action will occur. When the object of the question is carefully specified, there is ample evidence that there can be good agreement between aggregated self-reports and actual observation of both past and future actions.

Assessment of Individual Differences

The notion of psychological traits and their measurement has also been a prime source of research on the correspondence between self-report and observational measurement. In order to have an effective test for use in prediction there must be both a correct conceptual analysis of the relation between a trait and behavior and a valid measure of the trait. For decades people in "mental measurements" struggled in vain to obtain substantial correlations between trait measures and patterns of performance (see Vernon, 1964, and Mischel, 1968, for reviews). No amount of improvement in test construction and item analysis nor advances in the mathematical treatment of observations could substantially improve prediction. Finally the conceptual analysis of traits was challenged (Mischel, 1968), resulting in very different measures. Instead of looking for one scale to predict a wide range of specific activities, there was a trend toward narrowly focused items which made more limited predictions about the scope of the behavior which is in principle related to test scores. In a manner quite parallel to the change in attitude measures, personality inventories tailored to individual situations and activities demonstrated improved predictive utility (e.g. Goldfried & D'Zurilla, 1969; Goldfried & Sprafkind, 1974). There has been extensive development of measurement strategies among behavioral researchers interested in assessment, and situation-specific measures have emerged from theoretical traditions which did not include the trait concept (e.g. Goldfried, 1976; Ciminero, Calhoun & Adams, 1977; Cone & Hawkins, 1977).

Correspondence Training

A third area of research emerged as applied behavior analysts explored the use of language in behavior change procedures (e.g. Lovaas, 1964; Brodsky, 1967). Early studies (e.g. Risley & Hart, 1968; Israel & O'Leary, 1973) focused on the conditions under which correspondence would be maintained, and conceptual development in this area now recognizes the many potential relations between different parts of the parallel verbal and nonverbal chains of behavior (Paniagua & Baer, 1982). The potential for correspondence is made more complicated, however, by Catania, Matthews, & Shimoff's (1982) finding that shaped verbal responses maintain good control over nonverbal behavior whereas instructed verbal behavior has no consistent relation to its nonverbal referents. Accordingly a complete account of correspondence must analyze the establishment of the verbal responses.

The operant approach is different from social and personality psychology in that there is no assumption of necessary correspondence between verbal and nonverbal behavior. Skinner's (1945) analysis of the origin of self-descriptive verbal behavior suggests that verbal behavior will correspond to prior nonverbal behavior (do-say sequence) only if the language community uses agreement with nonverbal behavioral referents as the criterion for reinforcing verbal responding. Similarly, nonverbal behavior will correspond to prior verbal behavior (say-do sequence) only if the agreement with verbal behavior is the criterion for reinforcing nonverbal responding. Accordingly most operant research has been directed toward the synthesis (c.f. Catania, 1983) of such a reinforcement history. For example, Risley & Hart (1968) initially observed poor correspondence as a result of naturally occurring contingencies, but following explicit correspondence training the correspondence was much greater.

Strategies in Correspondence Research

It is possible to obtain qualitatively different results on correspondence depending on how the question is addressed. The entitites being measured (and therefore the measured used) can be either global or specific in nature. Correspondence between verbal and nonverbal behavior increases with the specificity of both the behavior and the self-report assessment instrument. There are also varying amounts of correspondence training included in the research procedures. An ethological approach studies the typical correspondence found under normal circumstances without specific intervention, while an experimental approach uses training to determine the maximum correspondence possible. This approach assumes that people can produce very accurate descriptions of their own behavior and its sources, and thus the appropriate research strategy is to maximize the potential correspondence between descriptions and their referents. The present research is of this latter type. It explores the importance of correspondence to a current model of personality assessment.

A Cognitive Social Learning Model of Assessment

Walter Mischel's (1973, 1978) conceptual analysis of personality departed radically from most traditional personality theories. The term "social learning" in the label indicates that the elements needed for prediction closely resemble a functional analysis of behavior. Mischel suggests that behavior from a person's basic repertoire occurs selectively as a function of the likely consequences of those actions in a given situation and the value of the consequences. Even though the elements are described in cognitive language, the essentials of a behavioral analysis are clearly included. Mischel even cites Premack's (1965) probability differential rule as a useful guide for identifying the value of consequences.

The term "cognitive" in the label also indicates a crucial feature of the model, namely that both behavioral and environmental elements are assessed verbally. The use of self-reports might simply have resulted from an assumption of good correspondence, implying only that verbal measures are an adequate and convenient substitute for detailed observation, but Mischel clearly implies that subjective perceptions of behavior and the environment are different from the experimenter's observations of the same events. Drawing from Rotter's (1954) social learning analysis and Kelly's (1955) personal construct theory, Mischel argues that subjective representations are necessary for prediction. The individual is portrayed as transforming past behavior and environmental interactions into idiosyncratic perceptions of that behavioral history. Whether it is the potential repertoire of behavior, the value of the consequence, the discriminative function of the stimulus, or the exact nature of the contingencies operating in the environment, Mischel qualifies observations by the active construction of subjective versions of these events. For this reason, verbal measurement of these properties after the transformation has taken place is crucial to the "cognitiveness" of his approach. He rejects the nomothetic assumption that observed environmental events are scientific constants, and instead verbal assessments of idiosyncratic perceptions are the primary elements for prediction of behavior.

An example of Mischel's analysis is found in his description of behavior-outcome expectancies. In discussing the necessity of a cognitive assessment strategy he provides the following argument:

> On the basis of direct experience, instructions, and observational learning, people develop expectancies about environmental contingencies. . . . Since the expectancies that are learned within a given situation presumably reflect the objective contingencies in that situation, an expectancy construct may seem superfluous. The need for the expectancy construct as a person variable becomes evident, however, when one considers individual differences in response to the same situational contingencies due to the different expectancies that each person brings to the situation. An expectancy construct is justified by the fact that the person's expectancies (inferred from statements) may not be in agreement with the objective contingencies in the situation. Yet behavior may be generated in light of such expectancies, as seen, for example, in any verbal conditioning study when a subject says plural nouns on the erroneous hypothesis that the experimenter is reinforcing them (Mischel, 1973, p. 269).

The Mischel model makes three predictions about the utility of verbal assessments. First the model assumes that self-reports are an adequate source of information for predicting the effect of a contingency imposed on a response repertoire, and a verbal measure should be an acceptable substitute for observing behavior. Second, the model predicts that there will be some discrepancies between environmental events and their subjective representations, due to subjects' use of personal constructs in forming perceptions. When the two assessment procedures make different predictions, however, self-reports should make a better prediction than observation of behavior about whether a contingency will have an effect. In this prediction the model is taking advantage of the idiosyncratic assessment inherent in verbal measurement, which should provide a better estimate of each individual's reactions to a given contingency situation. Third, the model predicts that verbal measures should make useful predictions even in complex circumstances for which there is no clear behavioral or environmental referent available. In a sense the cognitions measured by self-reports represent a substitute for a complete behavioral analysis of the person's entire reinforcement history. By tapping the end product of the subjective transformation (cognitions) the difficult and often impossible task of identifying that history can be avoided.

The research described here provides both verbal and nonverbal assessment of the reinforcement value of very specific activities and known contingency operations. The research procedures were designed to identify the maximum correspondence between verbal and nonverbal measures which these subjects could generate without explicit correspondence training. Several questions of interest could potentially be answered by the data. First, what kind of correspondence exists between people's estimates of the amount of time devoted to activities and the observed amount of time? Second, in those cases in which the subjective judgment differs from observation, which estimate of value makes a better prediction of performance under Premack-style contingencies based on those time estimates? Third, to what extent do people's subjective estimates of performance under deprivation contingencies correspond to the actual performance of people under similar constraints? The answers to these questions are important for evaluating Mischel's cognitive rationale for verbal measures and for evaluating the utility of verbal assessment as a substitute for observation in behavior analysis.

ASSESSMENT OF CORRESPONDENCE IN A LONG-TERM LABORATORY SETTING

Research Setting and Procedures

The basic procedures were similar to Bernstein & Ebbesen (1978) and Bernstein & Dearborn (1980). Four human subjects lived in a laboratory apartment for periods of three to four weeks, engaging in ordinary activities such as reading, sewing, artwork, and exercise. They remained in the lab 24 hours per day, being observed through a one-way mirror from 9 a.m. to midnight, and sleeping the remainder of the time. A detailed record of the exact duration of each burst of activity was kept, allowing for the calculation of frequency, average burst length, and total duration of each activity. As in previous work, contingencies were arranged between pairs of activities following the general guidelines of Premack's (1965) formulation of reinforcement value, as modified by Timberlake and Allison (1974). Time devoted to one activity would result in the availability of time for another activity. The nature of the contingency relations (but not the exact amounts) were explained to subjects, and contingencies remained in effect for several days. The exact contingency values were based upon the relative proportion of time devoted to the activities during several days of free-access baseline. According to Timberlake and Allison's model, response deprivation is a necessary condition for a reinforcer to be effective. The ratio of the instrumental requirement over the contingent allotment must be larger than the baseline ratio between the two activities. Adjusting the contingency ratio that is used results in predictions of either an increase or no change in performance of the instrumental activity.

Verbal Assessment of Value

At the conclusion of each baseline period in the present experiment there was also a verbal assessment of the amount of time devoted to each activity. Subjects used a psychophysical technique derived from Anderson's (1970) functional measurement to give precise and internally valid estimates of the amount of time devoted to each of the activities engaged in during their stay. Because it was assumed that correspondence would not be very good, it was important that the self-report measure be of the highest quality. Otherwise any lack of correspondence could simply be attributed to poor measurement rather than to a conceptual separation between verbal and nonverbal behavior. The strategy was to maximize potential correspondence by finding out the ability of people to make such judgments under ideal conditions.

Each subject repeatedly estimated the total amount of time devoted to a pair of the activities available in the laboratory. Subjects rated all possible pairs of activities several times using a 100 mm rating scale labeled "No Time" at one end and "All The Time" at the other. Training on consistency of judgment was provided, but no feedback was given on the correspondence between verbal and nonverbal behavior. This additive task provides a quick way to assess the internal validity of the ratings. If two sets of elements in a factorial design add together perfectly, for example the verbal ratings and the observed behavior, the data will plot as parallel lines (revealed as no interaction in a two-way analysis of variance). The data can show this pattern only if subjects can both perform the judgment task and use the response scale systematically.

At the conclusion of the experiment each subject also performed a different set of verbal ratings. In addition to giving time estimates for baseline periods of free-access to all activities, subjects also produced distributions of time when response deprivation contingencies were in effect. These distributions were produced by stacking poker chips for each activity. Subjects were given 60 chips representing 15 minutes each, and they were told to distribute all 60 chips to fill 15 hours of a typical day. In this distribution there was a requirement that for every so many minutes (chips) of time put into the contingent activity there must be at least another number of minutes (chips) on the instrumental activity. The instructions were very similar to those used in the actual contingencies the subjects had experienced during response deprivation conditions, and the instructions explicitly stated that no time needed to be devoted to either the restricted or the designated instrumental activity. Each subject generated distributions on four different pairs of activities.

Three different ratios were calculated for each pair of activities. One ratio was simply the baseline ratio as determined either by verbal estimate or by observation of behavior during the final baseline of the residential experiment. From a response deprivation perspective, a contingency with a baseline ratio should result in no increase in time devoted to the instrumental activity. The other two ratios were approximately two or four times larger than the appropriate baseline. In accordance with the response deprivation formulation, these sets of contingency ratios should result in more time being distributed to the instrumental activity. The distributions were done in a random series of trials over a period of an hour, and no subjects reported noticing any pattern to the constraint ratios when asked to describe the procedure afterward.

Evaluation of Correspondence

Correspondence between the measures of reinforcement value was evaluated three different ways. First, the percentages of time actually devoted to the activities in baseline were correlated with the verbal reports of time taken before and after each baseline. Second, the contingency ratios used in the residential experiment were selected so that either the verbal measure of value or the observation of time actually devoted to activities predicted an instrumental increase while the other measure predicted no increase. Third, the results of the purely verbal contingencies were compared with the results of contingencies placed on the amount of time actually devoted to the activities in this and previous residential studies. Details of the procedures can be found in Bernstein (1983).

COMPARISONS OF THE MEASURES

Validity of Verbal Measure

The advantage of Anderson's (1970) functional measurement is the opportunity to make an evaluation of subjects' use of the response scale without reference to the external criterion of observed behavior. Analysis of variance performed on the raw ratings yielded no interaction between factorial combinations of activities, so subjects were using the response scale systematicaly to add the pairs of activities. Algebraic decomposition of the rating matrix yielded estimates for the amount of time devoted to each category (Anderson, 1970). The scale was normalized with a total of 100 so that it was equivalent to the percent time measures obtained through direct observation.

Covariation of Baseline Values

The first type of analysis simply compared subjects' ratings of the time devoted to each activity with the actual amount of time observed for that activity. The first comparison was made by correlating the verbal estimate of value with the observed value from the baseline period preceding the ratings. The rank orders of activities by the two measures corresponded quite closely, with mean Pearson rank order correlations for four subjects ranging between .60 and .81 (with 4 or 5 pairs per subject). While one pair of ratings for a single subject had a correlation of only .07, most were in the range of the means, and all four subjects had at least one instance of rank orders with a correlation of .90 or greater. When exact ratings were correlated rather than ranks, the results were similar. For all individual categories a correlation was calculated between the rating time and the actual time from the preceding baseline.

This sample of 77 pairs yielded a correlation of .70, accumulated across subjects.

There were some systematic instances of low correlations. The first set of verbal reports were taken before the subjects actually moved into the laboratory and spent time with their activities. The four rank order correlations between those ratings and the first baseline period were .04, − .70, .75, and .78. For two subjects the rating task was virtually impossible without prior experience, and for the other two performance improved after having some experience with the activities. Following up on this observation, each set of ratings in the entire study was correlated (when possible) with both the baseline preceding it and the baseline following it. For all four subjects, the correlation was higher between ratings and the baseline which had already occurred, suggesting that the recent behavioral history is a crucial determinant of verbal reports.

The strong correspondence between verbal and observed measures of value gives reasonable support to the first assumption of Mischel's personality model. It is possible for people to provide useful and accurate descriptions of their own behavior, and in certain cases these self-reports may be substituted for observations of behavior. An operant account of verbal behavior would also anticipate this result, given the assumption that people have been exposed to contingencies on correspondence. One feature of the data suggests a primacy for nonverbal over verbal measures. Previous behavioral experience is sometimes necessary for the generation of accurate verbal behavior. Two subjects were incapable of making sensible ratings until after they had lived in the laboratory, and all subjects made more accurate reports about past behavior than about future behavior. In a cognitive model one might expect that self-reports of idiosyncratic value would make a better prediction of the behavior caused by the values than of the behavior which preceded the formation of those subjective values. A behavioral account (e.g. Skinner, 1945) holds that past behavior functions as the primary referent for verbal behavior in response to questions about value (e.g. liking, attitudes), and a higher correlation with previous behavior would be expected.

Functional Equivalence in Prediction

Eight contingencies were arranged in which time on one activity produced access time for another activity. The contingency ratios were picked so that either the observed baseline time or the ratings of time (but not both) would predict an instrumental increase due to response deprivation (Timberlake & Allison, 1974). To accomplish this, the activities used in the contingencies were those for which the two measures of reinforcement value were substantially different. Given that the correspondence between ratings and actual time was quite good, this selection was often difficult. For five of the eight contingency ratios selected, the observed behavior values predicted an instrumental increase and the verbal values predicted no increase. For the remaining three contingency ratios the verbal values predicted an instrumental increase and the observed behavior values predicted no increase. In each case the prediction of no increase was made for one assessment method because the schedule ratio was equal to that method's baseline ratio, and a condition of response deprivation was not produced.

All five contingencies in which response deprivation was based on observed time produced instrumental increases, with the change varying from 40 percent to 1050 percent of the baseline level of the instrumental response. Two of the three contingencies in which response deprivation was based on ratings also produced instrumental increases, being 23 percent and 93 percent over their baseline levels. The magnitude of the reinforcement effect was substantially larger when the response deprivation values came from observed behavior rather than from ratings. When observed and subjectively estimated reinforcement values differ from each other, it appears that the observed value makes a better prediction. This result would seem to provide a counterexample to Mischel's position that subjective estimates should be more useful than nomothetically derived measures for those cases in which they differ.

This conclusion must be considered tentative because there were instrumental increases in two of the three contingencies in which observed baseline values predicted no response deprivation. Variables other than response deprivation may also have contributed to instrumental performance in all of the contingencies. Either the observed measure of value did not correctly assess the absence of response deprivation, or the experimental procedure did not produce conditions under which response deprivation was a necessary condition for instrumental performance. The overall magnitude of the effect of the contingencies was larger under one set of conditions, however, and it is fair to assume that the difference was due to a larger contribution from response deprivation when observed behavior was used for the estimate of baseline value.

In general there was very good correspondence between specific ratings of time and the actual amount of time devoted to individual activities. While it would have been easy to arrange successful contingencies based on the ratings alone, Mischel's model makes a prediction for those few cases in which the two measures were different. The results of those contingencies suggest that behavioral observation was a better predictor of contingency performance than was the subjective representation of value. At least under certain circumstances an untransformed estimate of the controlling variables makes a better prediction than the perceived value of those variables.

It should be noted that the probability differential rule already encompasses the relativity of idiosyncratic assessment. As discussed by Premack (1965) and Timberlake & Allison (1974), the probability differential rule was an alternative to the nomothetic notion that an identified reinforcer will function the same way for all members of a species. By showing reversibility of the reinforcement relation within and between subjects, Premack made his model an example of idiosyncratic assessment. The identification of a reinforcing stimulus is most properly made on an individual basis, but the rules for identification have been shown to hold across subjects. Premack's model has both idiosyncratic and nomothetic characteristics.

Contingencies with Only Verbal Performance

When subjects used chips to estimate the distribution of time under contingencies, performance was very sensitive to response deprivation. For ratios based on both previous behavior and on ratings of time, there was no increase in the number of chips placed on the instrumental activity when the schedule produced no response deprivation (contingency ratio equal to baseline ratio). When the contingency ratio was either two or four times the baseline ratio, however, there were large increases in the number of chips placed on the instrumental activity. The data are shown in Table 7.I. All four subjects increased estimated instrumental time when the ratio was doubled, and two of four produced larger increases when the ratio was quadrupled. One subject consistently decreased instrumental performance in the latter condition. Since the chip distribution trials were randomly presented, it was not possible for subjects to compare their estimates to produce this pattern of verbal output, and none of them reported any prior knowledge of response deprivation during the debriefing and discussion of the experiment. Overall the verbal ratings were sensitive to the deprivation implicit in the constrained ratios imposed on the verbal repertoire, though they were not consistently sensitive to differing levels of deprivation.

Table 7-I

Distribution of time (in percent) on instrumental response in verbal contingencies for long-term subjects. Means of four sets of contingency ratings per subject (adapted from Bernstein, 1983)

Subject	Baseline 1	No Response Deprivation	Moderate Response Deprivation	Strong Response Deprivation	Baseline 2
HH	7.0	8.5	14.0	22.0	7.0
DB	12.5	13.5	20.8	11.8	12.5
JP	16.8	15.0	18.8	18.8	13.5
MH	9.8	10.3	11.3	13.0	9.8
MEAN	11.5	11.8	16.2	16.4	10.7

Of all the results obtained, the sensitivity of purely verbal contingencies to response deprivation was the most surprising and the most challenging. Mischel's cognitive social learning model predicts that this kind of performance should be possible. The subjects' verbal behavior is reporting the accumulated effects of many experiences with contingencies, and the subjective transformation of probabilities and values produces a final result not obviously related to a specific history. Mischel makes no specific claim about the mechanism for this integration of experience, referring generally to research on information processing. It is also possible to formulate a behavioral account of this performance. The only substantive body of operant research in this area is the work on correspondence training discussed earlier. The language community of most people is likely to have shaped correspondence between actual behavior and reports of that behavior. Given that the subjects spent time in the specific setting to which the verbal reports were generalized, it is not in principle surprising that correspondence was quite good. It is less obvious, however, that the language community would have provided differential consequences for verbal reports of behavior under response deprivation conditions, so an account of the origin of self-reports sensitive to variations in deprivation should be considered speculative. A first guess would be that these particular subjects have had recent experience with behavioral contingencies which varied in deprivation, and the discriminative training from the language community generalized from any distribution of behavior to a specialized distribution situation. A second study was undertaken to explore this phenomenon with subjects who did not have a specific experimental history of contingencies based on response deprivation.

RATINGS BY SUBJECTS WITHOUT CONTINGENCY EXPERIENCE

The results of the verbal contingencies were so unexpected that it was necessary to replicate them before seriously considering a full analysis of the limits of subjects' verbal performances. Six additional subjects were trained in the functional measurement scales, and they made ratings of time distribution among a set of activities appropriate to the laboratory setting. These subjects did not actually live in the laboratory, but the living conditions were described and they listed the activities they would choose if they were to live in the laboratory for several weeks. The contingency procedures and response restrictions used in the long-term study were not described. If these subjects' distributions of chips were not sensitive to the deprivation variable, then either some experience with response deprivation contingencies in the laboratory was necessary for correct self-description or the previous results were a random or artifactual finding. If on the other hand these subjects made ratings of contingency performance which were sensitive to deprivation in the schedule parameters, then it would be demonstrated that the earlier finding was not artifactual and that specific previous laboratory experience was not a necessary condition for accurate self-descriptions.

The procedures and instructions were identical to those used in the final phase of the long-term study. Subjects made ratings of a baseline distribution of time, and on the basis of those ratings contingency values were imposed which included three levels of response deprivation. Subjects' performances were very close to those of the subjects in the long-term study; the ratings showed instrumental increases in those conditions with deprivation schedules but there was no increase when the schedules did not produce response deprivation. The data are shown in Table 7-II. The group averages showed very orderly trends and data from individual subjects revealed the same pattern. All six subjects increased ratings of the instrumental activity more when the schedule met the response deprivation condition than when it did not. In four of the six subjects the schedule with greater response deprivation produced a larger instrumental increase. Of the six subjects, four had the same rank order of rated instrumental performance as the averages, and the other two subjects had identical increases for the two higher levels of response deprivation.

Table 7-II

Distribution of time (in percent) on instrumental response in verbal contingencies for replication subjects. Individual ratings shown for each subject (adapted from Bernstein, 1983)

Subject	Baseline 1	No Response Deprivation	Moderate Response Deprivation	Strong Response Deprivation	Baseline 2
MS	14	12	23	33	10
DM	13	14	19	25	13
FF	10	12	17	17	6
CS	3	10	12	15	10
KW	4	7	8	13	5
TS	5	5	7	7	5
MEAN	8.2	10.0	14.3	18.3	8.2

The results of the replication suggest that the phenomenon is a real one and that it does not require a recent or specific behavioral history. Mischel's cognitive model would probably describe this performance as the result of an outcome expectancy developed from lengthy experience with contingencies and various states of deprivation. The mechanism for this extrapolation would likely be derived from contemporary cognitive accounts of information processing (c.f. Mischel, 1981). A behavior analyst would probably describe this performance as an intraverbal response (verbal behavior under the control of verbal discriminative stimuli), and this complex intraverbal class would have been shaped by interaction with the language community. Unfortunately, both accounts leave the most difficult part of the explanation without specific empirical grounding. While there is cognitive research on the formation of predictions and operant work on the conditions necessary for the establishment of verbal responding, neither account can identify a controlled demonstration of the development of a complex and generalized verbal response class with a clear referent in a known history of contingencies. Proper construction of an operant account of these data will require synthesis of a particular contingency history that selectively enhances appropriate verbal contingency performance. This history might include unusual or specific forms of contingencies or it might simply involve looking for increased accuracy with increased exposure to behavioral contingencies. Systematic development of complex verbal discriminative stimuli will be necessary to demonstrate a functioning intraverbal response class.

VERBAL BEHAVIOR AND INDIVIDUAL DIFFERENCES

In a behavioral analysis of performance in a given setting, the contingencies operating play the largest role, with stimulus control from previous contingencies also contributing. Differences between individuals are not typically considered important, and most procedures include strong independent variables so that variation across subjects is obscured by the main effects of the intervention. In fact, standard operant experimental design requires that effects be equivalent in all subjects (Sidman, 1960). While this limits experimental analysis to important, strong variables, it has also precluded a behavioral analysis of situations in which people perform differently under superficially identical circumstances. Informally, behavior analysts might assert that idiosyncratic performance reflects the variable reinforcement histories of different subjects, and the widespread preference for naive subjects is evidence of a general belief in this basic proposition. It would be inappropriate to limit our analysis of individual differences to such conceptual speculation, however, for there are still large gaps in the data we have about human verbal and nonverbal performance.

A more appropriate response from an operant perspective might be to use an individual differences framework to guide research on verbal behavior. Mischel's personality model adopts a behavioral framework to guide the identification of verbal measures that can predict behavior, and verbal assessment will certainly be a desirable and important tool in behavior analysis. Although the model is expressed in mentalistic terms, it is a useful first step in the analysis of the determinants of individual performance. Whenever individual verbal accounts of controlling variables differ from observations of those variables, it will be necessary to analyze the sources of the verbal behavior as a replacement for Mischel's unspecified cognitive transformations.

One approach to this problem would undertake careful measurement and comparison of both objective and subjective elements in a given behavioral context; the comparison can be either functional equivalence or covariation. If the two measures are fundamentally equivalent, then the assertion that perceptual transformations must take place is not universally true. The present research represents such an analysis. When conditions maximize correspondence between verbal and nonverbal measures of reinforcement value, reinforcement operations function as well as or better than subjective perceptions of the same operations. Verbal reports can be an orderly reflection of behavior under most circumstances and need not result from idiosyncratic transformations which qualitatively alter the nature of the controlling event. In addition, verbal behavior without immediate referents in previous behavior or exposure to contingencies allows for predictions which can not be made from available observations of the same variable. To the extent that this finding holds in general, it represents an important tool for analysis of behavior which is difficult to observe directly.

Another valuable approach would undertake a behavioral analysis of the processes of construction and perception. Some verbal behavior reflects a broad and perhaps idiosyncratic concatenation of previous exposure to contingencies, and data from the present research suggests that this complex verbal repertoire has come under the control of verbal discriminative stimuli. Such a phenomenon challenges both behavior analysts and cognitivists to identify the conditions which produce a verbal repertoire which is sensitive to subtle changes in the variables controlling nonverbal performance. If the perception of likely outcomes is in fact different from the contingencies which actually operate, it should be possible to identify a reinforcement history which will produce such verbal behavior. Instead of stating a priori that personal constructs or unspecified reinforcement histories account for the differences in subjects' descriptions of the controlling variables, research would involve analysis and synthesis of such idiosyncratic verbal behavior. That kind of research would be an interesting and useful combination of personality and operant psychology.

REFERENCES

Ajzen, I. & Fishbein, M. Attitude-behavior relations: A theoretical analysis and review of empirical research. *Psychological Bulletin*, 1977, *84*, 888-915.

Anderson, N. H. Functional measurement and psychophysical judgment. *Psychological Review*, 1970, *77*, 153-170.

Bernstein, D. A comparison of cognitive and behavioral assessments of value in human behavior. Unpublished manuscript, 1983.

Bernstein, D. & Ebbesen, E. Reinforcement and substitution in humans: A multiple-response analysis. *Journal of the Experimental Analysis of Behavior*, 1978, *30*, 243-253.

Bernstein, D. & Dearborn, M. The utility of time-based theories of reinforcement. Unpublished manuscript, 1980.

Brodsky, G. The relation between verbal and non-verbal change. *Behavior Research and Therapy*, 1967, *5*, 183-191.

Catania, A. C. Behavior analysis and behavior synthesis in the extrapolation from animal to human behavior. In G.C.L. Davey (Ed.), *Animal models of human behaviour*. Chichester: Wiley, 1983.

Catania, A. C, Matthews, B. A., & Shimoff, E. Instructed versus shaped human verbal behavior: Interactions with nonverbal responding. *Journal of the Experimental Analysis of Behavior*, 1982, *38*, 233-248.

Ciminero, A. R., Calhoun, K. S., & Adams, H. E. (Eds.) *Handbook of behavioral assessment*. New York: Wiley, 1977.

Cone, J. D. & Hawkins, R. P. (Eds.) *Behavioral assessment: New directions in clinical psychology*. New York: Brunner-Mazel, 1977.

Fishbein, M. A theory of reasoned action: Some applications and implications. In M. Page & H. Howe (Eds.) *Nebraska Symposium on Motivation*. Lincoln: University of Nebraska, 1980.

Fishbein, M. & Ajzen, I. Attitudes toward objects as predictors of single and multiple behavioral criteria. *Psychological Review*, 1974, *81*, 59-74.

Goldfried, M. R. Behavioral assessment. In I. B. Weiner (Ed.), *Clinical methods in psychology*. New York: Wiley-Interscience, 1976.

Goldfried, M. R. & Sprafkin, J. M. *Behavioral personality assessment*. Morristown: General Learning Press, 1974.

Goldfried, M. R. & D'Zurilla, T. J. A behavioral-analytic model for assessing competence. In C. D. Spielberger (Ed.), *Current topics in clinical and community psychology*. New York: Academic, 1969.

Israel, A. C. & O'Leary, K. D. Developing correspondence between children's words and deeds. *Child Development*, 1973, *44*, 575-581.

Kelly, G. *The psychology of personal constructs*. New York: Basic Books, 1955.

LaPiere, R. T. Attitudes vs. actions. *Social Forces*, 1934, *13*, 230-237.

Lovaas, O. I. Control of food intake in children by reinforcement of relevant verbal behavior. *Journal of Abnormal and Social Psychology*, 1964, *68*, 672-678.

Lowe, C. F. Determinants of human operant behaviour. In M. D. Zeiler & P. Harzem (Eds.), *Advances in analysis of behavior: Reinforcement and the organization of behavior*. Chichester and New York: Wiley, 1979.

Lowe, C. F. Radical behaviourism and human psychology. IN G.C.L. Davey (Ed.), *Animal models of human behaviour*. Chichester: Wiley, 1983.

Matthews, B. A., Shimoff, E., Cataia, A. C., & Sagvolden, T. Uninstructed human responding: Senstivity to ratio and interval contingencies. *Journal of the Experimental Analysis of Behavior*, 1977, *27*, 453-467.

Mischel, W. *Personality and assessment*. New York: Wiley, 1968.

Mischel, W. Toward a cognitive social learning reconceptualization of personality. *Psychological Review*, 1973, *80*, 252-283.

Mischel, W. A cognitive social learning approach to assessment. In T. V. Merluzzi, C. R. Glass, & M. Genest (Eds.), *Cognitive assessment*. New York: Guilford, 1981.

Nisbett, R. E. & Wilson, T. D. Telling more than we can know: Verbal reports on mental processes. *Psychological Review*, 1977, *84*, 231-259.

Paniagua, F. A. & Baer, D. M. The analysis of correspondence training as a chain reinforceable at any point. *Child Development*, 1982, *53*, 786-798.

Premack, D. Reinforcement theory. In D. Levine (Ed.), *Nebraska Symposium on Motivation*. Lincoln: University of Nebraska, 1965.

Risley, T. R. & Hart, B. Developing correspondence between nonverbal and verbal behavior of preschool children. *Journal of Applied Behavior Analysis*, 1968, *1*, 267-281.

Rotter, J. B. *Social learning and clinical psychology*, Englewood Cliffs,: Prentice-Hall, 1954.

Sidman, M. *Tactics of scientific research*. New York: Basic Books, 1960.

Skinner, B. F. The operational analysis of psychological terms. *Psychological Review*, 1945, *52*, 270-277.

Skinner, B. F. *Verbal behavior*. New York: Appleton-Century-Crofts, 1957.

Smith, E. R. & Miller, F. D. Limits on perception of cognitive processes: A reply to Nisbett and Wilson. *Psychological Review*, 1978, *85*, 355-362.

Vernon, P. E. *Personality assessment: A critical survey*. London: Methuen, 1964.

Commentary

VERBAL INTERACTIONS AND NONVERBAL BEHAVIOR

A. Charles Catania

THE CENTRAL QUESTION addressed in Daniel J. Bernstein's chapter is the relation between verbal and nonverbal behavior and it is this question that deserves commentary. Other points could be examined here. If, for example, we could consider whether the language of *attitudes, objective-subjective,* and so on, is advantageous or disadvantageous in this type of treatment; we could question whether the class of verbal responses called intraverbal is adequate to the tasks performed without the involvement of autoclitic verbal behavior as well; and we could debate the accuracy of statements that individual differences are considered unimportant in behavior analysis and that its experimental designs preclude "a behavioral analysis of situations in which people perform differently under superficially identical circumstances." But it is probably sufficient simply to call attention to those issues. Let us not allow them to deflect us from the main point.

The important contribution of the present data is in demonstrating correspondences between verbal and nonverbal behavior. A critical feature of the demonstration was that ratings of time allocated to an activity and actual time allocated to the activity were similarly affected by constraints imposed on the distribution of time to activities. In particular, for a given activity both the rating and the actual time allocation increased relative to baseline only if engaging in that activity provided an opportunity to engage in a second activity the availability of which had been reduced relative to baseline. These kinds of effects of contingencies are among the criteria for speaking of changes in behavior in terms of reinforcement.

A problem, however, is that the language of reinforcement is inappropriate to the ratings of time allocation. The effect was not upon the rate of rating but rather upon what the particular ratings were. This was verbal behavior presumably under the control of some features of the experimental setting. Some history within that setting was important to the establishment of this verbal behavior, but it is not yet evident what the critical dimensions of that history might have been.

The reason for raising this issue here is not that there was anything unclear about it in the text; the author has provided a sophisticated treatment. Rather, it is to make the point that the origins of these performances have yet to be specified. Are actual time allocations a response to contingencies, with verbal behavior in the form of ratings following from them (or perhaps from their covert derivatives)? Or does the verbal behavior come first, producing ratings and, as a derivative, also producing performances superficially like those under the control of contingencies but in reality instances of rule-governed behavior (Skinner, 1966)? Would the results have been the same if these performances had been obtained by letting the participants discover the contingencies instead of establishing them through instructions?

It seems unlikely that these questions can be answered on the basis of the present data. Although it is correct that rule-governed behavior is relatively insensitive to contingencies (Matthews, Shimoff, Catania & Sagvolden, 1977), the insensitivity need not be complete (e.g., it may be evident in some dimensions of responding but not others), and the present performances are not sufficiently fine-grained to show more than the single dimension of increase or decrease. In recent research, the role of verbal behavior in controlling nonverbal performances in humans has been ubiquitous (e.g., Catania, Matthews & Shimoff, 1982; Lowe, 1979). To the extent that nonverbal behavior is controlled by verbal behavior, correspondence between the two can be expected as a matter of course (though correspondences between different sets of verbal responses should not be taken for granted on these grounds, as is well documented in the present account).

The issue is an open one, ripe for further study, and Daniel Bernstein has given us a good start. Do the present findings mainly demonstrate interactions among different sets of verbal responses, some of which affected actual allocations of time, or can it be shown that at some point contingencies on time allocation affected that allocation directly, and in that way also affected verbal behavior? The issue is important because it will tell us where to look for human contingency-shaped behavior; it has too often been hard to find. It appears that in human behavior the rule is control of nonverbal behavior by verbal behavior rather than by contingencies. How likely is it that the time allocations here were an exception?

REFERENCES

Catania, A. C., Matthews, B. A., & Shimoff, E. (1982). Instructed versus shaped human verbal behavior: Interactions with nonverbal responding. *Journal of the Experimental Analysis of Behavior, 38,* 223-248.

Lowe, C. F. (1979). Determinants of human operant behavior. In M. D. Zeiler & P. Harzem (Eds.), *Reinforcement and the organization of behaviour*. Chichester: Wiley.

Matthews, B. A., Shimoff, E., Catania, A. C., & Sagvolden, T. (1977). Uninstructed human responding: sensitivity to ratio and interval contingencies. *Journal of the Experimental Analysis of Behavior, 27,* 453-467.

Skinner, B. F. (1966). An operant analysis of problem solving. In B. Kleinmuntz (Ed.), *Problem solving: research, method, and theory*. New York: Wiley.

Chapter Eight

A FUNCTIONAL ANALYSIS OF READING

Roy Moxley

A functional analysis of reading is presented in contrast to more traditional mechanistic accounts. Some distinguishing features of the two approaches and their implications for school practices are examined. It is argued that mechanistic accounts of reading are prematurely simplified and restrictive and that a functional approach would lead to a far more natural and extensive acquisition of reading skills.

A FUNCTIONAL ANALYSIS OF READING

WHAT HAPPENS when a child reads? If this question is asked, the answer may be sought by looking at the beginning reader with text in hand who tries to read aloud. The child's voice proceeds haltingly in a linear, step-by-step progression with periodic hesitations and false starts before a word, syllable, or letter. In puzzling over what to say next, the reader often seems confused over what sounds go with what parts of print and how to put the sounds together. It may appear as if the child's task is to transform elements of print into elements of sound, part by part, until the whole meaningful expression is assembled. The task of reading instruction then is to teach the child to transform distinct marks of print into distinct sounds of speech that are properly connected, sound to sound. Behind this question and answer there are a lot of assumptions. In particular there are the assumptions that the answer to the question tells us how to teach reading and that the answer should be in terms of linear, contiguous connections in space and time, leading to a kind of assembly-line model of the reading process. This analysis of reading is mechanistic, and similarly conceived reading instruction is often obtrusively mechanical.

The first part of this chapter will focus on mechanistic explanations as they relate to reading. Such explanations are characteristic of approaches to reading that are identified with S-R psychology, which is often erroneously cited as *the* behavioral position (see Chapter One), and with some forms of mentalism, which may be advanced within a cognitive or structural orientation. While there are some isolated areas of reading where mechanistic explanations may seem appropriate, for example, where the relevant factors of a situation have been highly determined through empirical investigation, safely simplified, and unlikely to change, this presentation will primarily focus on the problems of pursuing an extended, rationally-derived mechanistic account of reading.

The second part of this chapter will focus on a functional analysis of reading from a behavioral perspective based on the three-term contingency of antecedent occasion, behavior, and consequences. Many of the concerns of mechanistic explanations in reading can be adequately addressed within a functional analysis. However, much of what a functional analysis addresses can never be adequately represented within a mechanistic account. In particular, a functional analysis is strong in investigating an area of uncertainty and accounting for change.

As indicated above, one reason for clarifying the mechanistic/functional distinction is that behavioral approaches to reading are identified with mechanistic S-R and subskills approaches (see Otto, 1982). There is a widespread need to disabuse people of any notion that a functional analysis of behavior necessitates a mechanistic explanation. Another reason is that even with the current unpopularity of the term *mechanistic*, mechanistic explanations and practices continue to thrive in reading. Terminology can change according to the educational fashion with little alteration in the patterns of the formulation. Thus, one cannot assume that a rejection of the term *mechanistic* or a rejection of one version of mechanistic analysis means that a non-mechanistic formulation has been put in its place. The features of mechanistic explanation need to be recognized in detail beyond the terminology. Similarly, it is important to see how a functional analysis differs in detail beyond the term *functional*.

Mechanistic Explanation

Mechanistic explanations have been characterized by linear chains of if-then accounts that avoid gaps between parts of the analysis. The details of such an analysis do not get "filled in" so much, in the sense of filling in an existing gap between one part and another part, as they get "added on" to a structure, element by element. A part-to-whole process of composition from paired elements is one of the distinguishing features of mechanistic explanation (Broad, 1925, p. 45). Any gap is regarded as a threat to the entire explanation and avoided from the start. A gap between the parts of the analysis is like a gap between the gears of a machine. The "driving force" cannot be transmitted gear by gear if there is a gap between the gears transmitting the force. Most machines that our culture has long been familiar with require fairly conspicuous, contiguous connections to operate. And it has often been assumed that much of nature must behave like a machine. As a result of this method of analysis, "nature has from time to time been endowed with many weird properties, spirits and essences" (Skinner, 1972a, p. 272) that were considered necessary for avoiding gaps in the explanation. Many cognitive psychologists, for example, seek to eliminate the conceptual gap between an external stimulus and an organism's response. Something must be happening inside the organism between the stimulus and the response, and any explanation would be defective on a priori grounds if a gap were allowed to exist in what was happening "inside."

The mentalist's position expressed by Katz (1964), who is an advocate of that position, illustrates the mechanistic viewpoint in language:

> The mentalist explains the facts about a speaker's and hearer's linguistic performance in terms of a model that reconstructs the process by which a message is transmitted from the speaker to the hearer through the speaker's encoding the message in the form of an utterance and the hearer's decoding that utterance back to the speaker's original message. Such a model explains why an utterance has a certain linguistic property, and what function that property has in the process of communication, by locating the property in the causal chain which links the utterance on one side to the neurophysiological mechanisms that perform the encoding and articulation, on the other side to those that accomplish the perception and decoding. But if . . . we interpret any of the elements of the mentalist's description of the process of communication as merely fictions, rather than references to neurophysiological links in such a causal chain, the whole explanation collapses. For that interpretation would amount to the claim that there are gaps in the causal chain. If there are gaps, we cannot account for the causal antecedents of a linguistic property and of its effects (pp. 135-136).

One of the first things a mentalist who pursues a mechanistic explanation does is to substitute an abstract, tightly connected, if-then model to replace the complexity of the original problem. The assumption that the model and its analysis must be in terms of two-part, if-then accounts of cause and effect is not questioned. Once this assumption and the mentalist's model are in place, the analysis follows with the irresistible conviction of a logical deduction.

In reading, it has often been irresistibly tempting to apply this kind of reasoning to explain what is happening. It seems particularly appropriate to the situation we observe when a text is read aloud. The words in spatial contiguity within the text are uttered in oral contiguity by the reader, one by one. The printed words are transformed into, and duplicated in, the spoken words. From this analysis, reading instruction appears as a task of having children learn the decoding process by which one elementary part is connected to another elementary part in a systematic way. This has often meant that smaller units must be distinguished first and then connected to form larger units in a hierarchical arrangement until the entire mechanism for transforming print into speech has been acquired.

Samuels (1976), who has been an editor of the International Reading Association's *Reading Research Quarterly*, describes the hierarchical piece-by-piece accretion for learning to read in the following way:

> Leaving the psychomotor domain, one can find examples from perception and learning to illustrate the principle that smaller units are mastered prior to mastering the larger units. The model of perception learning developed by LaBerge and Samuels (1974) is a hierachical model and shows the sequence and progression of learning from distinctive features, to letters, to letter clusters, and on to words. In the process of learning to recognize a letter, the student must first identify the features that comprise the letter. For the lower-case letters b, d, p, and q, the features are vertical line and circle in a particular relationship to each other; that is, the circle may be high or low and to the left or right side of the vertical line. Having identified the parts and after an extended series of exposures to the letters, the learner sees it as a unit (p. 170).

In the logic of this model and its analysis, the atomic elements of language are distinctive features. After repeated exposures to seeing these features connected to one another in the various forms of letters, the child is then to see the individual letters as units. Similarly, after repeatedly seeing the letters connected to one another in the various forms of words, the child is then to see individual words as units. And so on, ever upward. In reading, this kind of analysis has been referred to as a bottom-up approach with definite implications for a part-to-part-to-whole method of teaching reading. Much of traditional reading instruction over the centuries appears to be consistent with this kind of analysis. What distinguishes Samuels' approach from that of the ancient Greeks and the *New England Primer* is that he recommends beginning at an elementary level of distinctive features below the letter unit. The child now has a little higher climb to make before acquiring the ability to read. Presumably, once this ability has been acquired, other skills inherent in it will follow automatically.

Much of this analysis would seem plausible if we were designing a machine that could read a text aloud. The problem is: Do we really want to teach a child to read like such a machine might read? Is that really teaching an ability to read? The Kurzweil Reading Machine will read printed words aloud for the blind. Using an optical scanner, the machine can read over 200 different styles of letters aloud. Pronunciation comes from the use of over a thousand linguistic rules that are blended in the computer's memory with some 1,500 exceptions to the rules. If the question were asked, "What does the Kurzweil Reading Machine do when it reads aloud?" we could study the technical manual and talk to the experts. The answer could be traced in a detailed description of its electronic circuitry. If we looked for contiguous connections, we could find them. We could trace the pathway from the machine's contact with the printed page to its pronunciation of the print, step by step. We might well agree we now have a thorough and adequate explanation of what is happening inside the machine when the Kurzweil Reading Machine is reading aloud. We would not, however, expect or look for other ways in which the Kurzweil Reading Machine shows us that it knows how to read. Reading aloud is one thing, answering questions or following directions is another. What then should we expect from a child who can read aloud? If we have taught a child to read aloud by following a tightly-connected model of contiguous connections, have we really taught the child an ability to read? Would it really be worth the effort to assure that children know over a thouand linguistic rules and some 1,500 exceptions to them?

When we build a machine, we build contiguous connections of some kind into it before it will work. Afterwards we can give a mechanistic account for what we deliberately did, even though our behavior in originally inventing the machine was more under the control of diverse contingencies than the narrow rules which we are now able to formulate. With a child, we begin with an organism that has a vast evolutionary background and a significant personal history whose details are largely unknown to us. There are gaps in our knowledge of the child unlike our knowledge of the machine we have made. If we try to preempt those gaps with a machine-like model of contiguous connections, we risk inventing "weird" mentalisms which ignore the rich, if gap-filled, variety of interrelationships involved in reading.

Abstract mechanistic models of reading are extremely simplified substitutes for a complex network of concrete contingencies. As a result, mechanistic explanations of reading are deficient in accounting for how the reader develops responses to the many relationships between the different units of language and their characteristic patterns and contexts. For example, according to a part-to-part-to-whole account like Samuel's, once the printed units can be discriminated and matched up with the oral language system, the child can then "decode" print. By means of this direct decoding, the child can then comprehend text-related relationships just as speech-related relationships are comprehended. The problem in making this assumption is that the temporal relationships between the sounds of speech and its contexts are different in fundamental ways from those that exist in a text. Much of what controls our responses to speech is far different from what controls our responses to text, and our behavior in response to speech is not the same as our behavior in response to a text.

Spoken communication takes place on occasions where there are extensive environmental supports — in the setting and the interaction between speaker and listener — to clarify what is being said. Written communication often has little additional support from the setting in which it takes place or from the interaction between writer and reader. Compared to speech, writing is "on its own" and relies on different and more extensive internal patterns and relationships than speech does. For example, the use of space to separate units in a written text is more systematic and has a different function than the pauses in speech. The increasing length of a space in a text signals whether the separation is between letters, words, sentences, paragraphs, chapters, or books. The increasing length of a pause in speech has little connection with units of organization and is more related to providing an opportunity for the speaker to compose further speech or for the listener to respond. As another example, the different forms of a word in writing like *marine* and *mariner* may have a common similarity in the visible forms to indicate a common similarity in meaning. The pronunciation of speech does not rely so much on this means of communicating meaning, and there is little commonality in the speech sounds of *marine* and *mariner* to suggest their shared meaning. Thus, if our writing were simply a phonemic transcript of speech sounds, it might be easier to spell but harder to understand. These and other differences between writing and speaking are not accounted for when the reading task is seen as a simplified problem of decoding the structural units of a text into the structural units of speech, a task simplified even further by following a tightly connected model of reading.

We might well wonder then why the mechanistic model of reading has been embraced so strongly. It is apparent that many people want to believe that the simplifications of mechanistic explanations are true. They want to assume that an accurate, tightly connected account for reading has been determined. One reason for this would be that, if the simplifications were true, a lot of time would be saved in working to manage the original complexities. Another reason would be that a simple, more tightly connected account lends itself more easily to immediate stimulus control. Like the color-coded lines on hospital floors guiding visitors to one section of the hospital or another, it is an easy way to direct people. It thus offers itself as an easy way for teachers to follow and an easy way for teachers to get students to follow. Mechanistic oral reading models also help to establish a particular form of classroom control. If students are sounding out, they can't be doing other things and can easily be detected if they try. Where teachers and students end up by following such models, of course, is another matter. Understandably, you may want to believe that the easily traveled, straight and narrow path is the right one to follow. You may want to believe it is the path to take even though you have no certain knowledge of where it will take you. In reading, many have chosen to stay on the familiar straight and narrow pathways, wanting to believe that it will only take a little more time until the destination is reached and the students learn how to read. It is easy to explain children who continue to read poorly as those who need more time and help on the road to reading.

Whatever the approach to reading that is used in the classroom, students can always be found who have learned how to read. But that does not mean they have learned to read by following the prescribed route of the classroom reading program in whole, or even in part. Students have other pathways to follow outside the classroom. Many of these alternative ways have produced readers even before they get to school (Durkin, 1966; Price, 1976; Torrey, 1973). One of the striking characteristics of early readers is that they often show an early interest in producing writing. Another is how unlike their early experiences are to those school practices that follow mechanistic models. An examination of how children actually do learn to read, naturally, on their own has played little part in the development of mechanistic accounts of reading.

The recent interest in *how* children learn to read on their own has been accompanied in the reading literature by *process* accounts that are opposed to a *subskills* or S-R analysis (see Barrs, 1983; Goodman, 1972;

Goodman & Burke, 1980; Otto, 1982; Smith, 1978). This opposition, however, has not prevented process approaches from employing many of the characteristics of mechanistic explanations in their accounts. References to the information processing model of computer programming, hypothesis-testing concepts, flow chart diagrams, and an interest in maintaining internal mental contiguity are often conspicuous (see Goodman, 1972; Smith, 1978). Although the particulars of the fairly diverse collection of viewpoints identified with process approaches have nonmechanistic features as well, it is clear that the invention of internal mechanisms is difficult to resist in the field of reading.

Functional Analysis

In a general sense the concept of a function implies some orderly relationship between two or more events. While the mathematical usage of function may indicate a one-to-one correspondence between elements, the biological usage of function implies multiple and diverse relationships in the contribution of a part to its organic whole. In written language we might discuss the function of a word in relationship to another word as well as to an extended context of many other words and to setting events beyond the text. In a more particular sense, the usage of function implies that the critical relationship is to a consequence. We speak of an instrument's function as the end or purpose for which it was made. In written language we can discuss the function of a word in terms of the effects it produces. According to the above distinctions, a functional relationship may be (1) connected in an orderly correspondence, (2) context bound, and (3) consequence-oriented.

When a functional analysis of behavior is based on the contingencies of operant reinforcement, orderly relationships and consequences are both implied. Sometimes the analysis of behavior may emphasize a formal, tightly connected, one-to-one correspondence between a source of control and the behavior as in echoic behavior. At other times the analysis may indicate multiple, diverse sources of control as in much of creative or contingency-shaped behavior in natural settings. Whatever the sources of control, the consequence relationship is essential in an operant analysis.

Note that while the concept of a function does assume some correlation between the events in a functional relationship, there is no necessity for the relationship to be one of contiguous contact in order to be functional (see Baum, 1973; Chase, this text; Lacey & Rachlin, 1978; Meadowcroft

& Moxley, 1980; Rachlin, 1976; Staddon, 1973; Wahler & Fox, 1981). When a chain of conditioned reinforcers in temporal contiguity is worked into a functional analysis of behavior, it is for reasons other than inherent a priori assumptions. The appeal of contiguous contact explanations may have lingered on from the mechanistic sources of early behaviorism in S-R reflex physiology and associationism. Or the circumstances of a particular investigation may happen to favor such an explanation on *a posteriori*, not on *a priori*, grounds.

A functional analysis can move along quite nicely without extending a contiguous chain of contacts. In the operant definition of the functional behaviorist, for example, we begin with emergent behavior rather than an immediate prior stimulus. As Skinner (1974) has pointed out in distinguishing the emitted operant from the elicited reflex, "The principle feature is that there seems to be no necessary prior causal event" (p. 53). Nor does there need to be an explicated chain of contiguous events between the functional consequences of behavior at one time and its occurrence at another time. There is no need to appeal, for example, to the storage and retrieval of "copies" of experiences. Nor does a functional explanation of behavior need to account for what goes on in the gap inside the head of the organism in order to be effective. This is not to say that contiguous connections do not exist or that they will not be found at a later time. It is to say that some gaps can be left unaccounted for in the details of a functional analysis of behavior without risking the collapse of the entire explanation.

In this respect, the functional analysis of behavior shows a tolerance for gaps that the mechanistically-inclined mentalist finds appalling. The functional behaviorist seems quite willing to disregard the most fundamental assumptions that mechanistic reasoning demands for scientific work. As Day (1969) put it, "In attempting to discover functional relationships the radical behaviorist does not accept any *a priori* logical assumptions of a universe that is orderly in a mechanistic sense upon which he must base his scientific work" (p. 318).

In an additional contrast to mechanistic explanations, a functional analysis has different compositional requirements. A functional analysis does not require a particular ordinal sequence in which separate smaller units must first be joined together before larger units can occur. As described by Skinner (1957), smaller units of verbal behavior emerge from larger units: "From responses such as *I have a* . . . and *I want a* . . ., a smaller unit *I* emerges. Such functional units may, of course, be separately learned, particularly through the educational reinforcement supplied by those who teach children to speak, but they also appear to emerge as by-products of the acquisition of larger responses containing identical elements . . ." (p. 120). And larger units result from smaller units in the following manner: "In general, as verbal behavior develops in the individual speaker, larger and larger responses acquire functional unity. . . . It also seems reasonable to suppose that, as a verbal environment undergoes historical development, it reinforces larger and larger units" (p. 336). There is no a priori requirement here for atomistic elements to be joined in some linear connection of paired parts to form a hierarchy of language units.

There are other differences between mechanistic explanations and functional analyses, and there are different kinds of functional analyses just as there are different kinds of mechanistic explanations (cf. Bunge, 1979; Ringen, 1976; Skinner, 1981; Wright, 1976). However, for our purposes in addressing reading, we will be content in having pointed out some of the differences in contiguity requirements and the appearances of new units of behavior. Mechanistic explanations impose restrictions here that are simply not binding for a functional analysis.

In a functional analysis of reading, we attack the problem of teaching reading in a different way from the very beginning. Instead of asking "What happens when a child reads?" we ask "How does a child show that it can read?" This frees us from assumptions of contiguity requirements and mentalistic inventions. Then, instead of indirectly teaching an abstract ability to read, we directly teach the various behaviors that belong to a reading repertoire. Instead of gradually building up a hierarchy of reading skills from atomic elements, we gradually "fill in" an extensive reading repertoire. This frees us from blindly following abstract models that have been prematurely substituted for empirical events.

In perhaps his most perceptive commentary on learning to read, Skinner (1972b) gave the following analysis:

> Traditional characterizations of verbal behavior raise almost insuperable problems for a teacher, and a more rigorous analysis suggests another possibility. We can define terms like "information," "knowledge," and "verbal ability" by reference to the behavior from which we infer their presence. We may then teach the behavior directly. . . . Instead of teaching "an ability to read," we may set up the behavioral repertoire which distinguishes the child who knows how to read from one who does not.
>
> To take the last example, a child reads or "shows that he knows how to read" by exhibiting a behavioral repertoire of great complexity. He finds a letter or word in a list on demand; he reads aloud; he finds or identifies objects described in a text; he rephrases sentences; he obeys written instruc-

tions; he behaves appropriately to described situations; he reacts emotionally to described events; and so on, in a long list. He does none of this before learning to read and all of it afterwards. To bring about such a change is an extensive assignment, and it is tempting to try to circumvent it by teaching something called "an ability to read" from which all these specific behaviors will flow. But this has never actually been done. "Teaching reading" is always directed toward setting up specific items in such a repertoire. . . . In the long run, all parts of the repertoire tend to be filled in, not because the student is rounding out an ability to read, but because all parts are in their several ways useful. They all continue to be reinforced by the world at large after the explicit teaching of reading has ceased (pp. 177-178).

Besides being free of mechanistic restrictions for constructing an "ability to read," Skinner's analysis is distinguished by the comprehensive variety of behaviors that it would include within a reading repertoire. Other approaches to reading might include many of these behaviors, but it is difficult to imagine one that would lead to a list more extensive than the above implies.

Reading behavior can now be defined simply as behavior controlled, at least in part, by a text. As long as we can infer that a response was under the control of a text, reading responses can occur even when there is an extended temporal gap between the reader's exposure to a text and the reader's responses to it. This means that discussions of a text, even though they take place sometime after exposure to it, are still reading responses to the extent that they are under the control of the text. This also means that a reading response is not limited by any restrictions on the topological form of the behavior either. Speaking, writing, and other actions may all be reading behaviors. Whether we refer to these behaviors as reading behaviors or as indicators of reading behavior need make little practical difference as long as we avoid the trap of teaching reading as an ability confined to immediately contiguous contacts with the text. A reading response can also be either overt or covert. For the purposes of instruction, however, it is easier to deal directly with overt behavior.

Sources of Control for Reading

In addition to texts in general as a source of control for reading, there are other distinctions to be made in the sources of control for a functional analysis of reading. There are distinctions that can be made within the text as well as outside the text. A reading response may be under the control of sources other than the text such as the reader's previous experiences with the events described in the text. Skinner has made that point for verbal behavior in general.

In his chapter on multiple causation in *Verbal Behavior* (1957), Skinner said it was "highly probable that any sample of verbal behavior will be a function of many variables operating at the same time" (p. 228). He then went on to identify some of these many, diverse, and simultaneous sources for determining verbal behavior. Sources in a repetitive one-to-one correspondence with the verbal behavior were identified as *formal* sources. Echoic behavior, in which the words heard are simply repeated, illustrates the more restricted sense of the term formal (pp. 68-69, 243). Here, the one-to-one correspondence between the stimulus and the response product can be quite fine-grained if the pitch, stress, rhythm, and other features of the verbal sounds are also imitated. A one-to-one correspondence can still occur, albeit less fine-grained, when the patterns of the stimuli are in one modality and the patterns of the response are in another. Reading a text aloud word by word is one such instance of one-to-one correspondence that crosses modalities. Here, "'formal' contributions" indicate a more general sense of the term formal (p. 243). Following the general concept of one-to-one correspondence, formal sources have their structural patterns duplicated to some degree in a response product. They are a subset of the many, diverse, and simultaneous sources that determine verbal behavior. The other sources of multiple causation may not have a structural similarity with the verbal behavior, but they do have a functional relationship. In contrast to formal sources, they may simply be termed *nonformal* although Skinner used the term *thematic* to contrast with *formal*: "Two responses are thematically related when they are controlled by a common variable with respect to which they lack the point-to-point correspondence seen in echoic and textual behavior" (p. 243).

Since most of the reading behaviors we value have nonformal, functional relationships to a prominent degree, we often wish to distinguish this kind of reading from merely repetitious responses to formal sources. For a convenient reference to this distinction between reading behaviors, we may refer to reading (or writing) behavior in response to multiple, functional sources of control as *compositional* in contrast to *matching* responses that are heavily dependent on one-to-one correspondence. A compositional response depends on functional relationships in the way that the different units of language are arranged with each other and with extended contexts. Letters, words, sentences, paragraphs, themes, immediate setting, personal history, and cultural history all have their various webs of interrelationships. Compositional responses have multiple relationships to a number of different sources of control, whereas matching responses have some kind of one-to-one correspondence with single sources of control.

This distinction in the sources of control for compositional and matching responses is largely one of proportional strength for practical reading behaviors, since a formal source may be one of the many sources of control for compositional responses. We need to make accurate matches between words and events and between our spellings and the dictionary's spellings if we are to produce successful compositional writing. And we need to make accurate identifications of at least some of the language elements in a text if we are to produce a successful compositional reading. Similarly, while matching responses do not need to entail compositional responses in any extended strength, it would be difficult to exclude all nonformal sources of control in typical, everyday settings.

Formal, nonformal, immediate, and remote sources of control can be distinguished in order to classify verbal behaviors. But this does not mean that a particular verbal behavior which meets the definition for one classification is not under other sources of control. Skinner has distinguished and separated "intraverbal" from formal sources of control on the basis of contiguity and the absence of multiple one-to-one correspondences (1957, p. 71). The nonformal intraverbal "I pledge allegiance" immediately evokes "to the flag" in the absence of an immediate formal stimulus. This does not mean, however, that a memorized recitation of the Pledge of Allegiance is not functionally related to and partially determined by other sources of control.

Consider the way a classroom of children might be taught the Pledge of Allegiance. The teacher writes it on the blackboard and the children say the words aloud after the teacher says them. Some children may only echo what the teacher says, but others may respond to both the written and spoken words. The accuracy of a child's subsequent recitation without the presence of the teacher's written or spoken words may be evaluated according to its formal correspondence to the Pledge of Allegiance. Teacher approval may follow accurate matches. Corrections may follow inaccurate matches. There may be other various consequences for those who quickly memorize the Pledge of Allegiance and those who do not. The classroom setting, the teacher, the flag, and the personal history of the student also play a part in determining when, where, and how well a child says the Pledge of Allegiance. For the student who recites the Pledge of Allegiance from memory without help, "I pledge allegiance" may evoke "to the flag." This is a nonformal relationship although there is a direct connection between the one phrase as a unit and the other phrase as a unit. It would be simplistic to say that "to the flag" has been determined solely by "I pledge allegiance." It would be more accurate to say that the student's recitation displays conspicuous matching responses, which have been determined by multiple one-to-one correspondences from formal sources and simple one-to-one connections from intraverbal sources. Yet, as the above illustrates, this still does not exhaust all the sources of control.

LEVELS OF RESPONSE DEMANDS. Different kinds of compositional responses in writing and reading may be distinguished on the basis of different contexts with different response demands. We might refer to compositional responses where a complete text is composed for a particular environmental context; for example, writing a poem. If we extend the specification of the context to include a textual context as well as the rest of the environment, we can consider compositional responses that bear an additional or supplementary relationship to an already completed text. We can consider the compositional relationship, for example, between one person's letter and another's reply to it.

In addition to extra-textual relationships, we can also consider intra-textual relationships such as those where there is a skeleton or frame for the student to fill in. For example, given the brief framework of "I used to . . . but now I . . .," the student completes the expression with the student's own composition. Such textual contexts can be extended to the point where the student is only asked to supply one word. For example, "He went up the _____ to his room." At this level the student has only to select and write one word to complete the text. If the student is provided with a multiple choice of responses to select from, the student only needs to make a token response with a pencil mark. For example, "He went up the _____ to his room. (a) box (b) down (c) stairs (d) tree." As we reduce the freedom in selecting among alternatives, we reduce the demands on context sensitivity. Multiple choice items on standardized reading tests have corresponding limitations in assessing reading skills (Guthrie & Tyler, 1976; Stewart & Green, 1983).

At this point we can see that the distinction between writing and reading is not as great as it has traditionally been made to appear (Moxley, 1984). When a student is producing a text, the student is responding to the text that is being produced as well as to any other texts controlling the production. Writing and editing a text implies that it is being read. Furthermore, the point at which a student is not producing a text but only reading it is not all that clear. Do we wish to consider a close exercise like the above where the student must write in the word as a writing task because the student makes a handwritten construction? How is that importantly different from completing the task with preformed symbols like those on a typewriter, or a word card, or a multiple choice item? At what point are we no longer dealing with a writing type of response? When we can observe no conspicuous overt behavior for determining a text? Instead of struggling with a writing/reading distinction, it may be more useful to think in terms of different textual contexts and different responses to those contexts.

Another level of context-related responses may be considered in the covert responses to a text by which a reader "makes sense" out of what is being read. These are responses in which the reader privately "sees" the text and parts of the text as context related. Readers may even "see" relationships and make a relationship response without matching the word form that is actually there. It may not be possible to directly observe what the reader "sees" but we can infer it from other responses. One revealing source for these inferences comes from oral reading miscues when the reader substitutes one word for another in the text. This provides evidence not only for what the reader "sees" but also for the sources of control that the reader is responding to. Oral miscues that preserve meaning illustrate the strength of compositional responding. Given the sentence in writing, "She stopped to pick a *flower*," we would regard the child who said "She stopped to pick a *daisy*" as a more experienced and successful reader than the child who said "She stopped to pick a *flower*" (Taylor, 1977, pp. 68-69).

The "seeing" of a text is a behavior in and of itself and a behavior that is under a substantial amount of formal control. This formal control is particularly conspicuous when we read a text aloud. In reading aloud, the formal sources may be strong enough to exclude nonformal sources of control. Many readers have had the experience that when they intently concentrated on reading a text aloud they could not comprehend what they had read. It is as if they were deliberately brought under the control of formal sources to the exclusion of other, functional sources of control. Another way that nonformal, functional sources are impaired is when a text is read aloud very, very slowly. If the individual words are read slowly enough, even a concentrating listener will be unable to comprehend what is being read although the formal sources of control will still be effective.

While some ingredient of formal control is necessarily included among the multiple sources of causation for reading, formal sources by themselves are inadequate for explaining most reading behaviors of interest. If we are concerned with reading comprehension and responses to a text as a composed text rather than a list of words, then we are necessarily concerned with nonformal, functional sources of control. This has not, however, prevented some reading theories and practices from giving the impression that it is those behaviors controlled by formal sources which hold the "key" to "decoding" a text (see Smith, 1973). This viewpoint belongs with reductionistic, mechanistic explanations that favor contiguity and one-to-one correspondences. And it belongs to that group of mechanistic explanations which owe more to their appealing simplicity of implementation than to their successful resolution of the problem at hand.

DESCRIPTIONS AND DIRECTIONS. Another distinction in the sources of control for reading can be made in terms of the different sources for consequences. In *Verbal Behavior* (1957), Skinner distinguished the "tact" and its "mnemonic suggestion of behavior which 'makes contact with' the physical world" (p. 81) from the "mand" and its "mnemonic value derived from 'command,' 'demand,' and 'countermand'" (p. 35). These terms are similar to, although more precisely defined than, the traditional uses of "descriptions" and "commands." Skinner's primary definitions of the tact and mand are in terms of the speaker: "A tact may be defined as a verbal operant in which a response of given form is evoked (or at least strengthened) by a particular object or event or property of an object or event. We account for the strength by showing that in presence of the object or event a response of that form is characteristically reinforced in a given verbal community" (pp. 81-82). In contrast, a mand "may be defined as a verbal operant in which the response is reinforced by a characteristic consequence and is therefore under the functional control of relevant conditions of deprivation or aversive stimulation. . . . In particular, and in contrast with other types of verbal operants . . . the response has no specified relation to a prior stimulus" (pp. 35-36).

With tacts or descriptive statements, the significant sources of controlling consequences for the listener are not under the direct control of the speaker. Instead, descriptive statements have a value to the listener as discriminative stimuli for reinforcing occasions. You may, for example, describe an experience to me, and I may then seek or avoid an experience like that in the future. With mands or command-type requests and directives, a significant source of controlling consequences is the speaker who provides reinforcing consequences for those who comply.

In reading, we might say in the cases of written tacts that the child is reading a description. In the cases of written mands, we might say the child is reading a direction. While the traditional terms of *descriptions* and *directions* do not capture all that Skinner wants to say, they do indicate a distinction in reading behavior under the control of different sources of consequences.

In addition to consequences, there are other differences for the reader in the stimulus controls for descriptions and directions. Many descriptions refer to remote events in space and time which are not directly accessible to the reader. In school, children are typically introduced to reading complete expressions in the form of stories which are a descriptive narration of events. In the context of these stories, children are helped to "make contact" with physical reality not so much by the presence of physical objects as by the presence of illustrations for physical objects in the book. We might wonder what advantages there would be if children were to read expository descriptions of objects that were actually present, such as might occur in scientific accounts of objects that could be found in or brought into the classroom. We might even wonder about the advantages of reading graphs that classify and record events that physically occur in the classroom. Although science-like activities are not usually planned with early reading in mind, there is evidence that reading benefits from such activities (Barufaldi & Swift, 1977).

The advantages of having the physical events, including consequences, actually present for early readers are brought home more clearly in following directions. When children are reading directions they are to follow, present concrete events and immediate consequences can occur quite easily. The child's overt responses in following directions can be observed, and the child may be exposed to conspicuous consequences for each step of the directions. These consequences may be arranged and augmented by the teacher who wrote the directions, say for learning stations (see Davidson & Steely, 1978), but they are also naturally inherent in following many written directions. In following a cooking recipe or the directions for a scientific experiment, there are immediate consequences, often self-correcting, that "show" the child how well the directions were understood.

Implications for Reading Instruction

In considering the overall sources of control for reading, we would have the following implications for a functional analysis of reading based on the three-term contingencies of antecedent occasions, behaviors, and consequences. (1) We can increase reading behaviors by expanding the variety of behaviors that are directly addressed in the reading curriculum and by making it easy for children to perform them. This means including tasks like self-generated questions and actions in response to a text as an integral part of the reading curriculum rather than a frill-like enrichment if time permits. We would then expect that a reading curriculum would properly consist of a much more representative sampling of the vast domain of behaviors controlled by a text than reading aloud letter, word, and text units and perhaps answering some questions on factual recall. We would also expect a much more representative sampling of reading behaviors under multiple, diverse, and simultaneous sources of control.

(2) We can increase the frequency of these reading behaviors by assuring and arranging reinforcing consequences for them. If we increase the consequences, and if the consequences are reinforcing, then we will be increasing the frequency of the reading behaviors. This means using extended sequences of consequences for diverse reading behaviors, including records of performance. When a child composes a story, for example, it can be read and reread at different levels of response demands, displayed on the wall, acted out, collected in a booklet, and indicators of progress can be recorded. Many of these consequences, and records, can be arranged, and kept, by the students themselves.

And (3) we can increase the occasions for reading by extending opportunities for reading behavior to occur across the curriculum, particularly in science activities, rather than confining reading instruction to a reading period. When the domain of reading and its consequences wraps around the entire school curriculum, we make it easy for children to learn to read naturally, as they learned to listen, with a lot of consequences and a lot of opportunities for a variety of behaviors.

One particular implication of the above is that reading instruction should include instruction in writing, since writing is evidence for a variety of the reading behaviors produced under the control of a text. This is particularly apparent when we consider the repertoire of reading behaviors that come into play when editing a text. For the most part, the inferences for relationships between writing and reading are much stronger than the inferences for relationships between speaking and reading. This would seem to be an obvious truism, but when we consider how little attention many reading programs give to writing, in contrast to speaking, it seems there is still a need to make this point. In fact, to the extent that writing is a response product under the control of previously produced text, we can regard writing behavior as one type of reading behavior. We read what we write like we hear what we say.

We can increase writing behavior much in the way that we can increase any reading behavior, by making it easy to be produced and reinforced. For example, children can produce a text more easily by dictation as illustrated in language experience approaches to reading. Children can spell a word more easily by using a typewriter or by using a phonemic transcript like i.t.a. or their own invented spelling. Children can edit a text more easily by using a word processing program on a microcomputer. The children who went to school in early Greece may have had little choice but to laboriously construct their own texts by hand, but we have many easier alternatives today. Even handwriting can be made easier by using approaches such as D'Nealian handwriting to bridge the transition from manuscript to cursive writing. When we arrange many opportunities and consequences for a variety of writing behaviors, we are making learning to write as natural as learning to speak (see Moxley, 1982b).

We can further address the various levels of behaviors and their sources of control in writing and reading by making them more conspicuous within an overall organization. Figures 8-1 and 8-2 illustrate an outline sketch of the three-term contingency for writing and reading at the levels of texts, words, and letters. This outline does not assume there is any necessity for postulating linear chains of connections for avoiding gaps. It does assume that writing and reading behaviors exist under multiple stimulus controls, including those in the evolutionary and personal history of the individual, which are not represented in this outline sketch. It would be fairly easy, however, to indicate these and other levels of relationships in diagrams for three-term contingencies (see Moxley, 1982a).

In designing instruction for filling in the multiple levels of reading behaviors, some questions and priorities should be kept in mind. (1) What is the highest level of reading behaviors that the child can make progress in? The more important level is the higher, more inclusive level. It is more important for the child to understand a complete text than to understand which isolated sound goes with which isolated letter. (2) What is the most productive instruction? All things equal, priority should be given to instruction that results in the most effective and efficient learning. This means that a lower level of instruction may be preferred when the child can make large gains in that level but not in a higher level. For example, progress in matching sounds to isolated letters may be pursued when this results in subsequent high level reading that would not otherwise have occurred as quickly. (3) What is the easiest way to have children learn a particular level? Priority should be given for any savings in time and effort on the part of the students and teacher. For example, all other things equal, if it is easier for children to record and monitor their own progress, then they should do so.

The answers to these questions are given by the performances of chil-

```
         A₁  texts  B₁
            ─C₁─
         A₂  words  B₂
            ─C₂─
         A₃ letters B₃
            ─C₃─
```

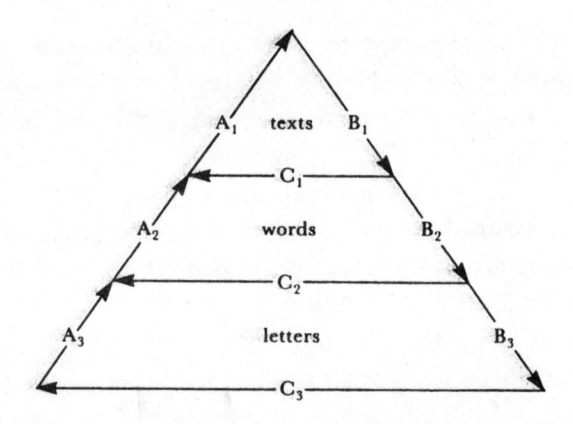

	Antecedents	Behaviors	Consequences
[1]texts	Given a purpose for writing after a field experience, creative play, listening to a story, or looking at a picture; given a pattern or outline in actions, objects, pictures, or words; given access to a variety of resources.	Dictate; type — using microcomputer, word processing program or typewriter; use preformed picture cards, word cards, letter tiles, or handwritten letters to produce a complete text.	Display, discuss, illustrate, act out; collect tokens for level of difficulty; chart number of words or stories written.
[2]words	Given a text and helping references; given resource people and materials like a dictionary and a typewriter; given a slot to be filled in a sentence.	Spell or edit for spelling by lookiong up work; invent spelling; use a phonemic transcript; select an appropriate word for the context from word cards or by assembling the component letters.	Display and discuss edited text; collect words spelled correctly, tokens for level of difficulty; chart number and rate of corrections.
[3]letters	Given an occasion to produce texts, words, or letters; given a variety of writing instruments and writing surfaces, some that are easily erasable and some with a line to cue the left-hand margin.	Produce handwritten forms of letters; assembe parts of letters; produce legible writing.	Display best work; collect tokens for level of difficulty; chart number and rate of legible letters or words in a text.

Figure 8-1. Whole-to-parts-to-whole Differentiation of Writing Tasks.

dren. Records over time provide the answers over time. The initial entry and follow-up into the multiple levels of reading (e.g. letters, words, or complete texts) will vary according to the background of the teacher and students and the setting. If we keep in mind that we are dealing with cyclical, whole-to-part-to-whole relationships over an extended time pe-

A Functional Analysis of Reading

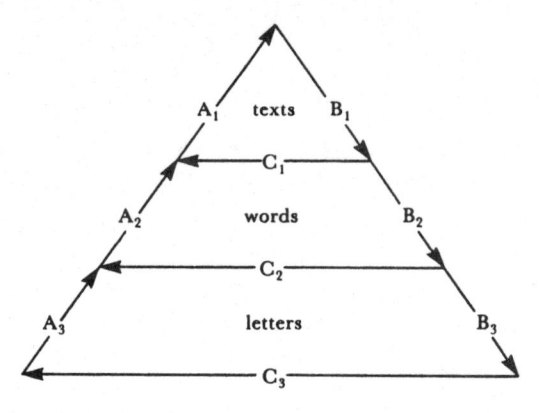

```
            texts
       A₁ ↗       ↘ B₁
          ← C₁ ←
       A₂ ↗  words ↘ B₂
          ← C₂ ←
       A₃ ↗ letters ↘ B₃
          ← C₃ ←
```

	Antecedents	Behaviors	Consequences
[1]texts	Given a text of descriptions and/or directions; given stimulus support by having the text read aloud while viewing it in the reader's lap or at a listening post; given predictable contexts of familiar pictures, phrases and words.	Display behavior controlled by the text; generate and/or find the answer to a question; follow directions; discuss; write a response.	Display results of following directions; act out stories; collect tokens for level of difficulty of questions answered; discuss results and answers; chart number and rate of questions answered.
[2]words	Given a sentence with unknown or nonsense words as in "Jabberwocky."	Produce an equivalent or partial paraphrase; suggest another word that would also make sense.	Collect cards for new words, tokens for level of difficulty; chart number and rate of understanding new words.
[3]letters	Given flash cards, letter wheels, or a word with missing or alternative letters; given a mnemonic image of a letter shape and its sound.	Given the sound of the word, point to or say the name of the letter indicated; shown the word, say the sound of the letter within its natural context of sounds or alone.	Collect letters known, tokens for the level of difficulty; chart number and rate of words identified.

Figure 8-2. Whole-to-parts-to-whole Differentiation of Reading Tasks.

riod, the specific initial entry point is not all that critical. What is important are the changes over time and the values that determine those changes. Much of what is missing in any individual child's repertoire of reading and writing behaviors can be filled in, in different ways for different children.

The above analysis may be regarded as favoring a relatively holistic or molar approach in that it addresses large classes of events and presents an immediate, comprehensive approach to reading instruction without any a priori requirement that a more detailed and focused analysis must first be in place before proceeding. It should be clear that such a view does not preclude instruction based on a more fine-grained behavioral analysis of reading, for example, in terms of a "type-to-read" program (Flanders, 1973), a programmed instruction approach to comprehension with reading "mazes" and latent images (Vargas, 1981), the development of print and sound relationships that occurs in SRA's Distar Reading Program, or reading instruction that might result from some particularly close matching-to-sample analysis (Sidman, Cresson & Willson-Morris, 1974). When a detailed analysis of some type of reading behavior leads to effective instruction for the acquisition of that behavior, then such instruction is appropriately included in the overall classroom reading program if it is cost-effective in terms of overall advantages and disadvantages.

Conversely, an instructional program in reading based on a detailed, fine-grained analysis does not preclude a comprehensive examination of the reading repertoire. A particular method of focused instruction may improve one type of reading behavior but not another. The only way to determine what a specific behavioral reading program can and cannot do is to examine, or at least representatively sample, the full range of reading responses. And if some important reading response is not being acquired that too will need to be addressed somehow by any complete reading program based on a functional analysis of behavior.

Note that the above approach to a functional analysis of reading in no way implies that the task is to translate mechanistic theories and practices into behavioral terms. It does not mean simply adding reinforcers to traditional practices. A functional analysis is an alternative to mechanistic explanations from the very inception in which the problem is addressed. Just as reading is not simply decoding print into speech, a functional analysis is not simply decoding traditional mechanistic accounts and extending them on the basis of the new code.

Conclusion

Over time, we would expect the details of a functional analysis of reading to be filled in, somewhat as we would expect a reading repertoire to be filled in. But, unlike the mechanistic mentalist, we do not need to demand a gapless model of reading before we have confidence we are heading in the right direction. We begin, without preconceived contiguity requirements, and fill in what we subsequently discover to be the case. A gap in our knowledge is not a threat to our analysis or an insurmountable obstacle to further progress. We simply circumvent intractable gaps, return and fill them in after we have moved forward in other areas. When we return to them, we may find that these gaps appear much less intractable. We may even find they seem to have disappeared.

Someday all the gaps in our knowledge about reading may be eliminated, and we may even be able to indicate contiguous connections wherever we are asked to look. Until that day, however, we do not need to construct a mechanistic model of reading which has contiguous connections between its parts but is based on little evidence. We do not need such models to find our way. They are more likely to mislead us. Nor do we need to act as if children need to acquire certain, particular rules before they can learn to read. Neat, tightly-connected, streamlined models and rules of reading are for the end of the story, after we have learned to teach reading more effectively and after we have learned more than we now know. When that day arrives, we may well have lost interest in such models because we will have resolved the problem of teaching reading in another way.

REFERENCES

Barrs, M. The new orthodoxy about writing: Confusing process and pedagogy. *Language Arts*, 1983, *60*, 829-840.

Barufaldi, J. P., & Swift, J. W. Children learning to read should experience science. *The Reading Teacher*, 1977, *30*, 388-393.

Baum, W. L. The correlation-based law of effect. *Journal of the Experimental Analysis of Behavior*, 1973, *20*, 137-153.

Broad, C. D. *The mind and its place in nature.* N.Y.: Harcourt, Brace, 1925.

Bunge, M. *Causality and modern science* (3rd ed.). N.Y.: Harcourt, Brace, 1925.

Davidson, T., & Steely, J. *Using learning centers with not-yet readers.* Santa Monica, Calif.: Goodyear, 1978.

Day, W. F. Radical behaviorism in reconciliation with phenomenology. *Journal of the Experimental Analysis of Behavior*, 1969, *12*, 315-328.

Durkin, D. *Children who read early.* N.Y.: Teachers College Press, 1966.

Flanders, R. G. *Type to read with the new dico system.* Eltham, London: Dico Education International, 1973.

Goodman, K. S. Reading: A psycholinguistic guessing game. In L. A. Harris & C. G. Smith (Eds.), *Individualizing reading instruction.* N.Y.: Holt, Rinehart and Winston, 1972.

Goodman, Y., & Burke, C. *Reading strategies: Focus on comprehension.* N.Y.: Holt, Rinehart and Winston, 1980.

Guthrie, J. T., & Tyler, J. Operational definitions of reading. In T. A. Brigham, R. Hawkins, J. W. Scott, & T. F. McLaughlin (Eds.), *Behavioral analysis in education: Self-control and reading.* Dubuque, Iowa: Kendall/Hunt, 1976.

Katz, J. J. Mentalism in linguistics. *Language*, 1964, *40*, 124-137.

Lacey, H. H., & Rachlin, H. Behavior, cognition and theories of choice. *Behaviorism*, 1978, *6*, 166-202.

Meadowcroft, P. M., & Moxley, R. A. Naturalistic observation in the classroom: A radical behavioral view. *Educational Psychologist*, 1980, *15*, 23-34.

Moxley, R. A. Graphics for three-term contingencies. *The Behavior Analyst*, 1982, *5*, 45-51. (a)

Moxley, R. A. *Writing and reading in early childhood: A functional approach.* Englewood Cliffs, N.J.: Educational Technology, 1982. (b)

Moxley, R. A. The compositional approach to reading in practice and theory. *Journal of Reading*, 1984, *27*, 636-643.

Otto, J. The new debate in reading. *The Reading Teacher*, 1982, *36*, 14-18.

Price, E. H. How thirty-seven gifted children learned to read. *The Reading Teacher*, 1976, *30*, 44-48.

Rachlin, H. *Behavior and learning.* San Francisco: Freeman, 1976.

Ringen, J. D. Explanation, teleology, and operant behaviorism: A study of the experimental analysis of purposive behavior. *Philosophy of Science*, 1976, *43*, 223-253.

Samuels, S. J. Hierarchical subskills in the reading acquisition process. In J. T. Guthrie (Ed.), *Aspects of reading acquisition.* Baltimore: The Johns Hopkins University Press, 1976.

Sidman, M., Cresson, O., & Willson-Morris, M. Acquisition of Matching-to-sample via mediated transfer. *Journal of the Experimental Analysis of Behavior*, 1974, *22*, 261-273.

Skinner, B. F. *Verbal behavior.* N.Y.: Appleton-Century-Crofts, 1957.

Skinner, B. F. What is psychotic behavior? In his *Cumulative record* (3rd ed.). N.Y.: Appleton-Century-Crofts, 1972. (a)

Skinner, B. F. Why we need teaching machines. In his *Cumulative record* (3rd ed.). N.Y.: Appleton-Century-Crofts, 1972. (b)

Skinner, B. F. *About behaviorism.* N.Y.: Knopf, 1974.

Skinner, B. F. Selection by consequences. *Science*, 1981, *213*, 501-504.

Smith, F. "Decoding: The Great Fallacy." In F. Smith (Ed.), *Psycholinguistics and reading.* N.Y.: Holt, Rinehart and Winston, 1973.

Smith, F. *Understanding reading* (2nd ed.). N.Y.: Holt, Rinehart and Winston, 1978.

Staddon, J. E. R. On the notion of cause, with applications to behaviorism. *Behaviorism*, 1973, *1*, 25-63.

Stewart, O., & Green, D. S. Test-taking skills for standardized tests of reading. *The Reading Teacher*, 1983, *36*, 634-638.

Taylor, J. Making sense: The basic skill in reading. *Language Arts*, 1977, *54*, 668-672.

Torrey, J. W. Learning to read without a teacher: A case study. In F. Smith (Ed.), *Psycholinguistics and reading.* N.Y.: Holt, Rinehart and Winston, 1973.

Vargas, J. S. *Something to think about.* Piscataway, N.J.: New Century, 1981.

Wahler, R. G., & Fox, J. J. Setting events in applied behavior analysis: Toward a conceptual and methodological expansion. *Journal of Applied Behavior Analysis*, 1981, *14*, 327-328.

Wright, L. *Teleological explanations: An etiological analysis of goals and functions.* Berkeley: U. of California Press, 1976.

Commentary

A BEHAVIORAL ANALYSIS OF MOXLEY'S *FUNCTIONAL ANALYSIS OF READING*

Kent R. Johnson

ROY MOXLEY has written a very provocative account of current reading models and practices, their deficiencies, and a radical behavioral alternative. The paper has 3 main sections. In the first Moxley presents and compares mechanistic and functional definition of reading behavior. In the second part Moxley describes the vast variety of variables that may control the behavior of a reader. These include sources both within and apart from textual stimuli, the classes of reading responses that may be required, and the different consequences that control reading behavior. In addition, through a description of different consequences for textual behavior, Moxley relates his analysis to *Verbal Behavior* (Skinner, 1957). In the third section, Moxley provides a global framework for reading and writing curriculum design based upon implications of a radical functional analysis of the two skills. Each section is stimulating in its own way. Moxley's paper helped me to integrate my strategies for designing reading instruction. I owe a debt for that, as well as his contributions to my further work. I will discuss each section, in turn.

MECHANISTIC VS. FUNCTIONALISTIC EXPLANATION

Moxley clearly outlines at least three distinctions between mechanistic and functionalistic explanation. All three have important implications for reading. First, a functional analysis does not require a contiguous chain of events that occurs between the environment and the behavior it controls. Second, a functional analysis does not require larger units of behavior to emerge from the synthesis of smaller units. Third, the major functional strategy for teaching reading is derived from an analysis of *how* children show that they can read, *not what happens* when a child reads. Thus emerges the general requirement of a functional analysis — to directly teach the various behaviors that belong to a reading repertoire instead of indirectly "teaching" an abstract ability to read. Moxley's comparison of the two explanatory approaches is right on the mark.

Moxley's comparison culminates in a definition of reading that incorporates textual, intraverbal, and tact control. The definition is useful, not so much as a classification schema for the behaviors we observe during learning, but for the design of broadly-based, integrative language arts instruction. Yes, indeed, as Moxley emphasizes, decoding training is not enough.[1]

All well and good for the definitions of functional analysis and reading. This section of the paper, however, has one major flaw. Moxley begins his paper with a look at a beginning reader trying to decode textual stimuli. From observing the child learning this first prerequisite or tool skill in reading, Moxley cautions that we not conclude that reading should be taught as:

> ... linear, contiguous connections in space and time, leading to a kind of assembly-line model of the reading process. This analysis of reading is mechanistic, and similarly conceived reading instruction is often obtrusively mechanical.

Throughout the paper, and in this section in particular, Moxley appears to devalue *all* fine-grained procedures, thereby deemphasizing important fine-grained *functional* procedures. By fine-grained functional procedures I mean those that teach decoding as a linear chain of behaviors, with correlated discriminative stimuli and conditioned reinforcers, from the child's initial contact with a text to her vocal emission of sound. Such procedures are also rule-oriented, and produce rule-governed behaviors. Moxley seems to equate such functional *procedures* with "mechanistic analysis" and thereby dismisses the *procedures* as rival, incorrect alternatives to functional *analysis*.

However, we should put decoding skills in their proper place in the analysis of reading. Without decoding there is no chance for other more

---

[1] For those of you who are unfamiliar with the jargon of reading, decoding is the skill of correctly pronouncing textual stimuli. This "sounding out" skill is different from the larger class of "reading comprehension" skills that are dependent upon "correctly seeing" what a writer wrote.

complex and important reading behaviors to occur. If you don't believe this, try commenting upon, writing about, or otherwise reacting to a simple text written in an unfamiliar foreign language.

Many children actually learn to decode "on their own" as a kind of transfer from other analytic observing behaviors and intraverbals mastered earlier in their histories. For these children, fine-grained functional procedures for teaching reading are dangerously boring and unnecessary. For many children,[2] however, Skinner's (1968) dictum that the environment is a lousy teacher is very accurate. Sometimes their decoding is controlled by some but not all of the critical features of textual stimuli, resulting in saying "relevation" for "revolution," or "bad" for "dad," for example. Other times their decoding is controlled more by intraverbal history than current textual stimuli, resulting in word substitutions or additions, such as, "Let her play with the collar," for "let her pay one dollar," in a story about a pet shop; or "She did look well." Such decoding errors often preclude the learning of other complex behaviors that "shows that he knows how to read" (Skinner, 1972), such as rephrasing and predicting the outcome of text. For these students, so-called "mechanistic" teaching procedures are a necessity, and a tragic error occurs when teachers think otherwise. Illiteracy is too high a price to pay for permitting teachers to rigidly adhere to global functional or natural humanistic models in which repertoires are "filled out."

The frequent necessity for "mechanistic procedures," must not be confused with the uselessness of a mechanistic *explanation* of the reading process. The author presents an excellent description of mechanistic explanation and quite rightly criticizes the metaphors inherent in such models as inadequately and erroneously depicting reading behavior and human nature in general. I heartily agree that mechanistic explanation is worthless. But while a fine-grained analysis of decoding may not be necessary for all children, we need to adjust our functional analyses to the entering repertoire of the child, which often makes functional, molecular analyses essential.

SOURCES OF CONTROL FOR READING

In the second section Moxley presents an excellent radical behavioral description of reading, including a large variety of behaviors not typ-

---

[2] Estimates vary between 15% and 30% of a school district's population.

ically correlated with the term, reading. The context for Moxley's description is a continuum of reading responses, from formal to nonformal. Reading behaviors under formal sources of control, for example textual stimuli, are called matching responses. Reading behaviors under nonformal (thematic) sources of control — writing a summary or relating of text events to personal history, for example — are called compositional responses. In this context, Moxley radically clarifies the definition of reading to show the variety of compositional responses partially controlled by other sources.

Although he continues to downplay the importance of matching responses like decoding and copying, they are not implicated so heavily in this section as being mechanistic and not functional. Moxley also gives more credit to the influence of formal control, but the credit is a two-edged sword, since the examples emphasize the tension between formal and informal sources and how formal control can disrupt compositional behavior.

Moxley ends section two with reading behaviors that set the occasions for further behavior. Descriptions (textual tacts, I'll call them) provide discriminative stimuli for later environmental contact or avoidance. Directions (textual mands) provide discriminative stimuli for behaviors largely reinforced by the writer or those who provide the text to the student.

Accompanying his discussion of descriptive and directive reading behavior are two suggestions for teaching them:

> We might wonder what advantages there would be if children were to read expository descriptions of objects *that were actually present* (italics mine). . . .
> When children are reading directions they are to follow, *present events and immediate consequences can both occur* . . . *that "show" the child how well the directions are understood* (italics mine).

Although such suggestions do not describe procedural contingencies for the teacher, they do provide verbal behavior that could control the design of procedures.

IMPLICATIONS FOR READING INSTRUCTIONS

In section three, Moxley presents implications of a functional analysis of reading, based on the three-term contingency. For antecedents, Moxley suggests extending reading occasions into other areas of the curriculum. For behaviors, he recommends greatly expanding the variety required by the reading curriculum. As a corrolary, he promotes the teaching of writing as part of reading instruction. For consequences, he calls for diversifying and multiplying the natural and arbitrary reinforcers currently used in reading instruction.

These are all excellent recommendations, but like the two suggestions at the end of section two, they are all too general and not particularly prescriptive. None of the general illustrations under each recommendation are likely to teach teachers to avoid potential but not necessarily obvious pitfalls that define the difference between tight and loose contingency control over learning to read. For example, Moxley proposes a loose and incomplete task analysis of reading/writing, devoid of systematic sequencing and programming. Such a curriculum may be fine for learners with extensive and easily rearrangeable repertoires, such as gifted students, but many misrules, errors, and frustrations will be the end result for the vast majority of learners. From my experience, other recommendations, such as student self-recording and language experience methods, are total failures unless the teacher uses molecular functional analysis to define foolproof contingencies. Moxley is simply too ambivalent about the importance of both foundations and student entering behaviors, which may not be important in and of themselves but make possible the more practical behaviors that he stresses. The few references to Vargas, Sidman, and Engelmann which do specify tight contingencies do not balance his discussion.

Two aspects of Moxley's analysis of implications deserve mention for their importance in understanding and designing a reading curriculum. First,

> relationships between writing and reading are much stronger than . . . relationships between speaking and reading . . . we read what we write like we hear what we say.

Too much curriculum does not recognize that writing and reading are dialectical products of each other, while speaking is important for instructional purposes only — to monitor reading until decoding and comprehension are accurate enough to set the dialectical process between reading and writing in motion.

Second, Moxley states that fine-grained analysis should not preclude a comprehensive examination of reading.:

> The only way to determine what a specific behavioral reading program can and cannot do is to . . . sample the full range of reading responses. And if some important reading response is not being acquired, that too will need to be addressed somehow by any complete reading program based on a func-

tional analysis of behavior.

Fine-grained programs need to be designed in the context of behaviors a program is preparing the student to learn, as well as the behaviors a learner brings to the program. Too few fine-grained analyses start from such comprehensive assessment, and are thus barren at the complex and practical level.

In sum, Moxley provides a stimulating global analysis of the instructional design of reading and writing. Unique and important aspects include an expanded definition of reading and a continuum of responses, from matching to compositional, that define a context for reading instruction. He also fairly critiques the shortcomings of mechanistic analysis and the advantages of functional analysis. Problems with his treatment include an underestimation of the importance of fine-grained functional procedures, and the match between student entering skills and instruction. His recommendations for reading instruction also fall short of sound procedures that can be implemented in the classroom and thus remain theoretical. I hope that Moxley and various readers of his paper translate his broad strokes into solutions to the problem of teaching reading. His radical analysis is ripe for technological innovation.

REFERENCES

Skinner, B. F. *Verbal Behavior*. Englewood Cliffs, New Jersey: Prentice-Hall, Inc., 1957.

Skinner, B. F. *Technology of Teaching*. Englewood Cliffs, New Jersey: Prentice-Hall, Inc., 1957.

Skinner, B. F. "Why We Need Teaching Machines." In his *Cumulative Record* (3rd ed.). New York: Appleton-Century-Crofts, 1972.

AUTHOR INDEX

A

Adams, H. E., 189, 204
Ajzen, I., 188, 204
Allinson, J., 193, 197, 198, 205
Anderson, J. r., 14, 17, 40
Anderson, N. H., 193, 195, 204
Anrep, G. v., 178
Atkinson, R. C., 39
Austin, J. L., 171, 177
Azrin, N. H., 159, 172, 173, 177, 178

B

Baddeley, A. D., 39
Baer, D. M., 24, 83, 84, 86, 189, 205
Baltes, M. M., 84
Barrs, M., 215, 231
Barufaldi, J. P., 225
Baum, W. L., 216, 231
Bergmann, G., 84
Bernstein, D. J., 187, 192, 195, 199, 201, 204
Bickel, W. K., 14
Bijou, S. W., 24, 83, 84, 103, 117
Bransford, J. D., 25
Brigham, T. A., 231
Broad, C. O., 211, 231
Brodsky, G., 189, 204
Bunge, M., 218, 231
Burke, C., 216, 231
Butterfield, E. C., 38

C

Calhoun, K. S., 189, 204
Campbell, D. T., 37
Catania, A. C., 125, 126, 187, 189, 204,
205, 206, 207, 208
Chase, P. N., 31, 39, 41, 42, 64, 128, 216
Chomsky, N., 8, 15, 39, 44, 45, 46, 47, 48,
49, 50, 51, 52, 53, 54, 55, 56, 57, 58,
59, 61, 62, 128, 161, 177
Ciminero, A. R., 189, 204
Claxton, G., 10, 25
Cone, J. D., 189, 204
Contrad, R., 39
Cornford, F. M., 80
Craile, F. I., 39
Cresson, O., 230, 232
Crowley, M. A., 19, 40
Crowder, R., G., 39
Cruttendon, A., 103, 117

D

Davey, G. C. L., 204, 205
Davidson, T., 225, 231
Day, W. F., 85, 217, 231
Dearborn, M., 192, 204
Denver, P. R., 32
Descartes, R., 67, 68, 69
deVilliers, P., 25
Donahoe, J. W., 19, 40, 44
Durkin, D., 215, 231
D'Zurilla, T. J., 189, 204

E

Ebbesen, E., 192, 204
Ellis, H., 7
Estes, W. K., 39
Etzel, B. C., 86

F

Feldman, R. S., 7, 18

Ferster, 23, 163, 177
Fishbein, M., 188, 204
Flanders, R. G., 230, 231
Fodor, J. A., 13, 15
Fox, J. J., 20, 23, 24, 217, 232
Fraley, L., 128

G

Gabain, M., 178
Gagné, R. M., 10
Genest, M., 205
Glass, C. R., 205
Goldfried, M. R., 189, 204
Goldiamond, I., 25, 26, 125, 126
Goodman, K. S., 215, 216, 231
Green, D. S., 222, 232
Guthrie, J. T., 222, 231

H

Hake, D. F., 159, 173, 177
Hare, R. M., 157, 178
Haring, N. G., 31
Harris, L. A., 231
Hart, B., 187, 189, 190, 205
Harzem, P., 86, 163, 178, 204, 208
Hawkins, R. P. 189, 204, 231
Hayes, S. C., 125, 127
Hearst, E., 6
Hefferline, R., 128
Herrnstein, R. S., 25, 42
Higgins, S. T., 14
Hineline, P. N., 123
Hinson, J., 42
Holland, A., 153
Holland, J. G., 153
Howe, H., 204
Humphrey, J., 128
Hutchinson, R. R., 159, 173, 177

I

Israel, A. C., 187, 189, 204

J

James, W., 85
Jenkins, J., 39
Johnson, J. M., 15, 20, 30
Johnson, K. R., 64, 233

Julia, P., 44

K

Kantor, J. R., 23, 24, 76, 93, 97, 100, 103,
    104, 105, 107, 112, 117, 123
Katz, J. J., 211, 231
Kelly, G., 191, 204
Kleinmuntz, B., 208
Kosslyn, S. M., 16
Kram, R., 42
Krantz, P. J., 24
Krapfl, J. E., 83
Kuhn, T. S., 68, 81

L

Lacey, H. H., 216, 232
Lachman, J. L., 38
Lachman, R., 38
Lakatos, I., 81
LaPiere, R. T., 188, 204
Lattal, K. A., 86
Le Blanc, J. M., 86
Levine, D., 205
Lockart, R. S., 39
London, J., 140
Loudan, L., 81, 84
Lovaas, O. I., 189, 204
Lowe, C. F., 187, 204, 205, 207, 208

M

Mac Corquodale, K., 8
Mandelstam, S., 42
Mapel, B. M., 85
Marshall, R. C., 178
Matthews, B. A., 187, 189, 204, 205, 207,
    208
Matthews, J., 153
Mayr, E., 37
McCarrell, N. S., 25
McLaughlin, T. F., 231
Meadowcroft, P. M., 216, 232
Merluzzi, T. V., 205
Mervis, C., 18
Michael, J. L., 24, 132, 134, 138, 165, 178
Miles, T. R., 163, 178
Millard, W. J., 19, 40
Miller, F. D., 188, 205
Miller, G. A., 57

Author Index

Mischel, W., 188, 189, 190, 191, 201, 205
Morris, E. K., 14, 15
Moxley, R. A., 139, 209, 217, 222, 227, 232
Murdock, B. B., Jr., 39

N

Neisser, J., 38, 39
Newell, A., 39
Nisbett, R. E., 188, 205

O

Ogden, C. K., 178
O'Leary, K. D., 187, 189, 204
Osgood, C. E., 6, 7, 8, 13
Otto, J., 210, 216, 232
Overton, W. F., 81

P

Page, M., 204
Palmer, D., 15, 61, 62, 63
Paniagua, F. A., 189, 205
Parrott, L. J., 86, 91, 98, 114, 115, 117
Pavlov, I. P., 80, 162, 178
Payne, T. R., 80
Pear, J. L., 31
Pennypacker, H. S., 15, 20, 30
Pepper, S. C., 81, 82, 85
Peterson, L. R., 39
Peterson, M. J., 39
Peterson, N., 138
Piaget, J., 82, 176, 178
Place, U. T., 156, 161, 166, 167, 173, 178
Premack, D., 190, 193, 198, 205
Price, E. H., 215, 232

R

Rachlin, H., 25, 216, 217, 232
Reese, H. W., 81, 84, 86
Rescorla, R. A., 42
Ribes, E., 65, 66, 76, 80, 82
Richards, I. A., 178
Rickard, J. P., 32
Ringen, J. D., 218, 232
Risley, T. R., 24, 187, 189, 190, 205
Rosch, E., 18
Rotter, J. B., 191, 205
Royer, J. M., 7, 8, 10, 18

Rudel, R. G., 9
Russell, B, 39, 166, 178
Ryle, G., 16

S

Sagnolden, T., 187, 205, 207, 208
Sallery, R. D., 159, 177
Samuels, S. J., 212, 232
Schnaitter, R., 179
Schoenfeld, W. N., 71
Scott, J. W., 231
Searle, J. R., 166, 171, 178
Sechenov, I., 68
Shakespeare, W., 145
Shaw, G. B., 80
Shiffrin, R. M., 39
Shimoff, E., 187, 189, 204, 205, 207, 208
Shimp, C., 68
Shwartz, S. P., 16
Sidman, M., 25, 202, 205, 230, 232
Simon, H. A., 12
Skinner, B. F., 13, 19, 21, 23, 39, 40, 41, 53,
    55, 56, 57, 59, 63, 64, 66, 68, 69, 70,
    71, 72, 73, 74, 75, 76, 77, 81, 83, 84,
    85, 93, 95, 97, 100, 102, 103, 105, 106,
    107, 117, 118, 119, 120, 122, 125, 126,
    127, 128, 129, 130, 131, 132, 133, 134,
    135, 136, 137, 138, 139, 140, 141, 142,
    143, 146, 147, 148, 152, 153, 154, 155,
    161, 162, 163, 164, 165, 166, 167, 177,
    178, 183, 187, 189, 196, 205, 207, 208,
    211, 217, 218, 220, 221, 224, 232, 233
    235, 238
Smith, C. G., 231
Smith, E. R., 188, 205
Smith, F., 216, 224, 232
Spielberger, C. D., 204
Sprafkind, J. M., 189, 204
Staddon, J. E. R., 42, 217, 232
Steely, J., 225, 231
Stevenson, C. L., 157, 178
Stewart, O., 222, 232
Stickney, K. A., 19, 40
Sulzer—Azaroff, B., 64
Sundberg, M. L., 138
Swift, J. W., 225, 231

T

Tailby, W., 25

Taylor, J., 223, 232
Thorndike, E. L., 7, 9
Timberlake, W., 193, 197, 198, 205
Tolman, E. C., 82, 85
Torrey, J. W., 215, 232
Tulving, E., 39
Twain, M., 148
Tyler, J., 222, 231

U

Ulrich, R. E., 173, 178

V

Vargas, E. A., 64, 132, 152, 154, 155
Vargas, J. S., 128, 141, 230, 232
von Bechterew, W. K., 68
Vaughan, M., 128
Vernon, P. E., 188, 205

W

Wagner, A. R., 42

Wahler, R. G., 20, 23, 24, 217, 232
Weiner, I. B., 204
Wessels, M. G., 13, 16, 40
White, O. R., 31
White, R. T., 10
White, S. H., 84
Wicksteed, P. H., 80
Williams, B. A., 24
Willson—Morris, M., 230-232
Wilson, T. D., 188, 205
Winograd, T., 46
Wittgenstein, L., 166, 178
Woodsworth, R. S., 7, 9
Wouk, H., 144
Wright, L., 218, 232

Y

Yourgran, W., 42

Z

Zeiler, M. D., 204, 208
Zettle, R. D., 125, 127

SUBJECT INDEX

A

Active organism model, 84
Adjustments
  direct, 111, 112
  indirect, 111, 115
  mediate, 112, 113
  referential, 113
  nonreferential, 115
Analogies, 8, 9
Antecedent stimuli, 6, 21, 83, 131, 132
Approval, 15, 159, 176
Arbitrariness of form, 115
  interverals, 155
  structures, 53
Association, 165
Associationism, 37, 38, 69, 70, 217
  assumption, 12
  bonds, 6
  learning theory, 7, 8, 9, 10, 11
  model, 6, 13, 20, 21, 22, 32
  rules, and principles of, 7
Astronomy, 36
Atomistic elements, 212, 218
Atomistic, R definition, 75
Attitudes, 206
Audience, 130, 170
Autoclitic, 130, 131, 150, 152, 206
Autoverbal, 130
Aversive control, 177
  event, 160
  stimulus, 130

B

Behavior change procedures, 189
Behavior modification, 156, 161, 171, 180, 182

Behavior segment, 76
Behavioral contingency semantics, 166
Behavioral unit, 57
Behaviorism, 40-42
Biology, 37
Bistimulation, 113, 115, 116, 119, 120, 122, 124, 125
  behavior segments, 110
  event, 111
Blame, 172-177, 181, 182
Braille, 138

C

Cartesian mechanics, 66-69, 70, 72, 80, 82, 84
Categorical imperative, 168, 169
Causal interpretation of
  functionally, 93, 94
Causal relationship, 163
Causality, 69, 70, 94
Chaining, 71, 154
Choice, 25
Codic, 134, 138, 141, 147, 149, 150, 155
Cognitions, 192
Cognitivism, 38, 39, 40
  assessment strategy, 191
  assumptions, 12
  model, 12, 13, 15, 16-19, 22, 32, 196
  social learning model, 199
  transformations, 203
Collateral behavior, 144
Collateral effects, 139, 140
Communicative language, 107
Competence, 58
Complex relations, 8, 9
Complex verbal relations, 5
Complexity, 36, 37, 39, 40, 41, 42, 147, 148

Compositional behavior, 220, 221, 222, 236
Comprehension, 223
Concrete contingencies, 214
Conditional discriminations, 119
  conditioned response, 162
  conditioned stimulus, 162
Consequences, 21, 30, 33, 197, 108, 158, 179, 180, 216, 224, 225, 226, 233, 237
Context, 25, 29, 222, 223
Contexual factors, 75
Contextualism, 82
Contiguity, 69, 218, 221, 224
  chain, 217, 233
  connections, 213, 231
  contact, 216, 217, 219
  usage, 145
Contingencies, 55, 106, 162, 163, 164, 165, 166, 170, 180, 208
  of correspondance, 196
  of disinforcement, 163
  history, 202
Contingency-shaped behavior, 163, 207
Contingency-specifying stimulus, 181
Contingency ratio, 193, 194, 195, 196, 197
Continuous repertoire, 152, 153, 155
Control of behavior, 64, 85, 86, 92, 94
Controlling variables, 51, 130
Control, 140
Conventional behavior, 103, 107
Conventionality of response forms, 108, 109, 117
Conventions, 173
Conversational behavior, 120
Copy theory, 16
Copying, 236
Correspondence, 133, 134, 188, 189, 190, 192, 193, 194, 195, 196, 197, 199, 203, 206, 207
Correspondence training, 187, 189, 190, 192
Cosmology, 81, 82, 83, 84, 85
Covariations, 203, 199
Culture, 183

D

Decoding, 17, 18, 212, 214, 234, 235, 236
Deductive logic, 13
Definition, 126
Deprivation, 83
Determinism, 174
Dictation, 138, 139

Direct effects, 122
Direct function, 125
Directions, 225
Directness of effect, 120
Disapproval, 157
Discrete repertoire, 155
Discriminative functions of stimuli, 165, 168
Discriminative stimulus, 132, 134, 141, 152, 154, 162, 163, 164, 165, 166, 180, 224
Distal consequences, 23
Distal control, 24, 25, 30, 33, 41, 42
Distal environmental relations, 118j
Dualism, 69
  philosophy, 76
  world view, 77
Duplic, 134, 135, 141, 142, 147, 149, 150, 155

E

Echoic, 132, 134, 136, 142, 149, 152, 153, 154, 155, 220
Emotional states, 146
Encoding, 17, 18
Environmentalism, model 19, 20
  perspectives, 6
  supports, 214
Episodic interactions, 76
Equivalences, 25
Essentialist approach, 37, 38, 39
Establishing operations, 24, 132
Establishing stimulus, 132
Ethics, 156, 179, 182, 183
Event fields, 92, 93, 106, 110
Evolutionary background, 213
Experimental analysis of behavior, 156, 161
Experimentally induced attack behavior, 160
Explicit conditioning, 102, 103, 104, 107, 108, 116
Expressive language, 107
Extratextual context, 222
Extraverbal, 130, 147

F

Factorial design, 194
Family resemblance, 18, 19
Far transfer, 8, 9
Five-grained analysis, 237
Fine-grained functional procedures, 234, 235, 237, 238

Formal, 221
  analysis, 59, 234
  control, 223, 236
  definition of sentence, 61
  levels of similarity, 9
  similarity in associative learning, 7, 8, 9, 10, 12
  sources, 220, 222, 224
  unit, 56
Freedom, 174
Frustration, 159, 160
Functional, analysis, 59, 190, 210, 216, 217, 218, 219, 230, 235, 236, 238
  approach, 209
  control, 154, 223, 224
  definitions, 92
  explanation, 233
  equivalence, 196, 203
  independence, 154
  relations, 90, 93, 100, 220

G

Generalization, 8, 9, 10, 12
Generalized reinforcement, 141
Genetic capacities, 47, 49
Grammar, 44, 58, 59
  analysis, 55
  conventions, 52
  definition of sentence, 56, 57
Graphic stimulus, 137

H

Heisenberg's principle of indeterminacy, 82
Histories, 140
Histories (individual), 27, 29, 30, 31, 51, 72
Histories of practice, 9, 10, 12
History, 83, 201, 207
Homunculus, 51

I

Idealism, 13
Identical elements theory, 8, 9, 11
Identification, 170
Identigraphic, 135, 149, 155
Identity of matter, 9
Identity of procedures, 9
Idiosyncratic assessment, 192, 198
Idiosyncratic perceptions, 191
Idiosyncratic transformations, 203
Imitation, 152
Imperative mood, 167
Indicative mood, 167
Individual differences, 9, 10, 19, 38, 187, 188, 202
Indirect effects on the environment, 120, 122
Indirect function, 125
Inechoic interactions, 202
Inescapable aversive stimulation, 173, 175
Infinite regression, 16
Information processing, 199, 201, 216
Innate behavior, 55, 56
  capacities, 52, 54
  mechanicsm, 45, 51
Instructed verbal behavior, 189
Instructions, 187, 207
Instrumental
  activity, 198
  performance, 197, 201
  requirement, 193
Internal biological events, 77
Internal mechanisms, 216
Internal validity, 194
Interpersonal adjustments, 97
Interpersonal origins, 98
Intraverbal, 120, 130-135, 141, 142, 149, 150, 152, 154, 155, 201, 206, 221, 235
  context, 222
  control, 234
  disjunctive, 155
  intuition, 51
  simple, 155
  sources, 222

L

Language acquisition devices, 56
Language community, 199, 201
Learning hierarchies, 10, 12
Litters as units, 212
Libertarian, 175
Linear analysis, 26, 69
Linear chains, 210
Linear unidirectional relations, 73, 74
Listener, 161, 162, 164, 166, 167, 168, 170
Lying, 182

M

Mands, 130, 152, 166, 167, 168, 169, 224

Manipulation of variables, 30, 94
Matching responses, 220, 221
Meaning, 105-108, 126, 214
Mechanism, 82, 83, 84, 85
  explanations, 209, 210, 211, 213, 216, 217, 218, 224, 230, 233, 234, 235
  abstract model, 214
  model, 215, 231
  procedures, 235
Mediation, 112
Medium, 133-135, 138, 142, 155
Memory, 12, 17
Mentalism, 210, 213
  activity, 12, 13, 16, 17
  events, 6, 76
Mentalistic explanations, 224
  mechanisms, 70
  position, 211
Metaphors, 8, 9, 25
Methodological criteria, 81
Methodology, 84
Mimetic, 138, 142, 149, 155
Minimal duplic unit, 137
Minimal repertoire, 153, 154
Mischel's cognitive model, 201
Modality, 138, 220
Models of learning, 6
Molar account of learning, 25
Molar aggregates as controlling variables, 42
Molar analysis, 33
Molar approach, 229
Molecular functional analysis, 237
Molecular variables, 42
Moral
  blame, 157, 159, 160, 171
  education, 161, 169, 171
  criticism, 172, 173
  imperative, 169
  judgment, 156, 157, 158, 168, 169, 171, 172, 173, 176, 177, 180, 182
  praise, 157, 171, 172
  principle, 171, 176
Morals, 179
Motivation conditions, 24, 119
  functions of stimuli, 165, 168
  relations, 132
Multiple causation, 220, 223
Multiple conditioning, 149
Multiple control, 130, 145, 150, 226, 227

N

Nativism, 44
Natural selection, 52, 53
Naturalism, 179
Nomothetic, 198
  assumptions, 191
  derived measures, 197
Nonformal control, 221, 223, 224, 236
Nonlinear analysis, 26, 27
Nonsocial environment, 115
Nonsocial stimuli, 115
Nonverbal
  adjustments, 113
  behavior, 111, 112, 115, 118, 121, 125, 206, 208
  stimuli, 114
Neuropsychology, 40, 41
Newtonian mechanics, 84

O

Objective, 206
Objective psychology, 68
Observation, 96, 192
Observations of behavior, 196
Observed behavior, 197
Operant, 50, 51, 74
  approach, 189
  behavior, 71
  conditioning principles, 80, 82, 84, 86
  conditioning theory, 66, 68
  definition of verbal units, 63
  level, 75
  methodologies, 30, 33
  model, 6, 19, 20-27, 29, 30, 31, 32, 33
  psychology, 203
  theory, 70

P

Paradoxical effects, 73
Part-to-whole account, 214
Pattern analysis, 93, 94, 106, 110, 125
Personal mediation of consequences, 108
Personal history, 213
Personality psychology, 189
Phoneme, 153, 154
Phylogenetic mechanism, 72
Physical violence, 173

Point-to-point correspondence, 134, 135, 138, 142, 147, 149, 154, 220
Postcedent stimuli, 131, 132
Practical effects, 144
Pragmatic function, 167
Pragmatics, 152
Pragmatism, 85
Praise, 181, 182
Prediction
  of behavior, 29, 85, 86, 92, 94, 188, 190, 191, 192, 196
  of verbal behavior, 64
Private events, 76, 77, 78
Probability differential rule, 190, 198
Problem solving behavior, 164
Process accounts, 215, 216
Process analysis, 93, 94
Prospective moral judgment, 169, 180, 181
Proximal
  consequences, 22, 23
  control, 33
  relations, 118
Psychological adjustment, 111
Psychological determination, 175
Psychology, 36
Punctuate events, 71
Punishment, 138
Puns, 140
Purposivism, 83

R

Radical behaviorism, 161
Reactions to absent events, 113
Reactive organism model, 84
Reading, 129, 139, 140, 141, 209, 212, 213, 215, 218, 219, 220, 222-238
  instruction of, 226, 227, 229, 230, 237, 238
Realism, 13
Recent behavioral history, 196
Reciprocal
  exchanges, 76, 90
  interpersonal adjustments, 101
  social relations, 100
Reductionism, 69, 224
Reference, 115, 116, 121
Referential character of verbal behavior, 122
Referential function, 78, 117, 119
Reflex, 73
Reflex paradigm, 68, 69, 70, 72, 74, 76
Reflexes, 71

Reflexive fighting, 172
Reinforcement, 92, 134, 138, 143, 147, 152, 157, 158, 206, 207
  automatic, 153, 154
  history, 192, 203
  theory, 19
  value, 193, 194, 203
Reinforcing stimulus, 198
Relativity of verbal relations, 18
Representations, 12, 18
  in memory
  process, 17
  variability, 18, 19
Respondent behavior, 71, 83
Response
  classes, 21
  deprivation, 193, 194, 197, 198-201
  functions, 111, 116, 125
  product, 134, 135, 149
  similarity, 21
  variability, 32
Response-stimulus relations, 73
Retrieval, 12
Retrospective moral judgments, 157, 169, 171, 180
Reversibility of reinforcement relation, 198
Rule-governed behavior, 123, 163, 164, 181, 207, 234

S

Scapegoat, 159, 160
Scientific
  knowledge, 81
  analysis of behavior, 179
  method, 81
Search process, 17
Selection from random variation, 36
Selectionist approach, 37, 38, 41, 48
Self-corrective process, 39, 40
Self-reports, 188, 190-193, 196, 199
Semantics, 152, 165
Semantic level, 167
Sentence, 58-61, 162, 164, 165, 167, 168, 170
  as a unit, 62, 63, 65, 161
Sequeled verbal relations, 142-147, 149
Sequelic, 134, 141, 142, 149, 150, 155
Sequelic subcategories, 147
Seriality, 134
Setting factors, 23, 24, 92, 110, 111, 216

Shaped verbal responses, 189
Shaping, 154
Sign language, 138
Similarity, 11, 12, 17, 19
  cognition accounts of, 17
  definition, 9, 10
  variability of, 9, 10
Social
  adjustments, 116
  behavior, 91, 96, 97, 98, 100, 101, 102-109, 110, 112, 116, 117, 118, 119-122, 124-126, 171
  context, 145
  contingencies, 147, 182
  control, 105, 156, 177
  definition of, 123, 124
  effects of verbal behavior, 63
  environment, 21, 22, 29, 116
  events, 63, 95
  group, 160, 169, 175, 176
  learning analysis, 190, 191
  mediation of consequences, 109, 117
  psychology, 188, 189
  reinforcer, 172
  rejection, 176
Sources of control, 219, 233
Space, 72, 73
Speaker, 161, 162, 163, 164, 167, 168, 169, 170
Special history, 146, 147
Speech episode, 150
Specificity, 148, 149
Spontaneous unpredictability, 100
Stimulational functions, 90, 101
Stimulus control, 54, 55, 225
  immediate control, 24, 215
  irrelevant control, 141
Stimulus events, 92
Stimulus fields, 155
Stimulus function, 97, 111, 116, 125
Stimulus objects, 97
Stimulus-response psychology, 210
Stimulus-response reflex physiology, 217
Style, 146
Subjective representations, 191, 206
Subskills analysis, 215
Substitute stimulus, 109, 115, 116
Superordinate category, 124
Surface structure, 49

T

Tact, 130, 152, 166-168, 181
  control, 234
Temporal gaps, 217, 219
Temporal relations, 23
Terminology, 46, 47, 210
Text, 219
Textual, 132, 134, 138-141, 153
  behavior, 129, 220
  control, 234
  mands, 236
  stimulus, 139, 223, 234, 235
  tacts, 236
Thematic source, 220
Three-term contingency, 20, 27, 73, 75, 83, 131, 132, 141, 163, 166, 168, 181, 225, 227, 236
Time allocation, 207-208
Total verbal episode, 74
Traits, 188
Transcriptive, 134
Transgraphic, 142
Truth telling, 182

U

Underlying processes, 39, 40
Unidirectional metaphors, 10, 11, 27, 29
Unistimulational, 119, 120, 124, 125
  behavior segments, 110
  events, 111
Unit of analysis, 56, 58, 61
Unit of behavior, 50, 51, 59, 70, 71, 153, 218
Unit of behavior-environment relations, 64
Unit of grammar, 50
Unit of verbal behavior, 217
Universal grammar, 45-49, 52, 53, 62

V

Validity, 195
Valley Girl Talk, 146
Values, 181
Variability, 53, 56
Variability of behavior, 57, 58, 90, 98, 100, 102, 109, 116, 121, 148
Variable reinforcement histories, 202

Verbal adjustments, 112, 116
Verbal assessment, 192
Verbal behavior, 91, 96-98, 101-110, 113-116, 118-122, 124-130, 132-136, 138, 141-142, 145-146, 149-150, 152, 154, 161, 181, 187-188, 202, 206-208, 219, 221
  acquiring functions of other stimuli, 114, 122
  definition, 123, 124
  episode, 100, 111, 131, 134
  forms of, 132
  gestural, 132
  spoken, 132
  written, 132
  under the control of verbal stimuli, 130, 131-134
Verbal community, 134, 136, 138, 141-150, 161-162, 164, 166, 224
Verbal constructions, 96
Verbal contingencies, 199, 200
Verbal event fields, 95
Verbal events (speaking, writing, gesturing), 63
Verbal history, 147
Verbal learning, 12
Verbal motivator, 166, 168, 181
Verbal operant, 58, 59, 64, 153, 167, 168, 170, 224
  as a unit, 65
Verbal punisher, 159
Verbal relations, 133, 134, 135, 137
Verbal reports, 196, 203
Verbal stimulus, 114, 134, 135, 136, 138, 142-147, 149-152, 154
Vernacular definition, 125
Vernacular usage, 124

W

Words, 167
Words as units, 212
Writing, 215, 223, 226, 227, 229, 233, 237
  instruction of, 238